LISTEN TO SOUL!

**Recent Titles in
Exploring Musical Genres**

Listen to New Wave Rock! Exploring a Musical Genre
James E. Perone

Listen to Pop! Exploring a Musical Genre
James E. Perone

Listen to the Blues! Exploring a Musical Genre
James E. Perone

Listen to Rap! Exploring a Musical Genre
Anthony J. Fonseca

Listen to Classic Rock! Exploring a Musical Genre
Melissa Ursula Dawn Goldsmith

Listen to Movie Musicals! Exploring a Musical Genre
James E. Perone

Listen to Psychedelic Rock! Exploring a Musical Genre
Christian Matijas-Mecca

LISTEN TO SOUL!

Exploring a Musical Genre

JAMES E. PERONE

Exploring Musical Genres
James E. Perone, Series Editor

BLOOMSBURY ACADEMIC
NEW YORK · LONDON · OXFORD · NEW DELHI · SYDNEY

BLOOMSBURY ACADEMIC
Bloomsbury Publishing Inc
1385 Broadway, New York, NY 10018, USA
50 Bedford Square, London, WC1B 3DP, UK
29 Earlsfort Terrace, Dublin 2, Ireland

BLOOMSBURY, BLOOMSBURY ACADEMIC and the Diana logo
are trademarks of Bloomsbury Publishing Plc

First published in the United States of America by ABC-CLIO 2021
Paperback edition published by Bloomsbury Academic 2025

Copyright © Bloomsbury Publishing Inc, 2025

For legal purposes the Acknowledgments on p. xvii constitute
an extension of this copyright page.

Cover photo: Aretha Franklin performing at the Austin City Limits Live at the
Moody Theater in Austin, Texas. (WENN Rights Ltd/Alamy Stock Photo)

All rights reserved. No part of this publication may be reproduced or
transmitted in any form or by any means, electronic or mechanical, including
photocopying, recording, or any information storage or retrieval system,
without prior permission in writing from the publishers.

Bloomsbury Publishing Inc does not have any control over, or responsibility for,
any third-party websites referred to or in this book. All internet addresses given
in this book were correct at the time of going to press. The author and publisher
regret any inconvenience caused if addresses have changed or sites have
ceased to exist, but can accept no responsibility for any such changes.

Library of Congress Cataloging-in-Publication Data
Names: Perone, James E., author.
Title: Listen to soul! : exploring a musical genre / James E. Perone.
Description: [First edition.] | Santa Barbara : Greenwood, 2021. |
Series: Exploring musical genres | Includes bibliographical
references and index.
Identifiers: LCCN 2020035091 (print) | LCCN 2020035092 (ebook) |
ISBN 9781440875250 (hardcover) | ISBN 9781440875267 (ebook)
Subjects: LCSH: Soul music—History and criticism.
Classification: LCC ML3537 .P47 2021 (print) | LCC ML3537 (ebook) |
DDC 781.64409—dc23
LC record available at https://lccn.loc.gov/2020035091
LC ebook record available at https://lccn.loc.gov/2020035092

ISBN: HB: 978-1-4408-7525-0
PB: 979-8-2162-1948-4
ePDF: 978-1-4408-7526-7
eBook: 979-8-2161-1201-3

Series: Exploring Musical Genres

To find out more about our authors and books visit www.bloomsbury.com
and sign up for our newsletters.

Contents

Series Foreword	ix
Preface	xiii
Acknowledgments	xvii
1 Background	1
2 Must-Hear Music	15
"Ain't No Mountain High Enough": From Marvin Gaye and Tammi Terrell to Diana Ross	15
Beyoncé	18
Blue-Eyed Soul: The Men	20
Blue-Eyed Soul: The Women	25
Boyz II Men	29
James Brown: Live at the Apollo	32
James Brown: Two Mid-60s Hits: "I Got You (I Feel Good)" and "Papa's Got a Brand New Bag"	35
Mariah Carey	39
Ray Charles: "I Got a Woman"	42
Ray Charles: "What'd I Say"	44
The Commodores and Lionel Richie	45
Sam Cooke: Ain't That Good News	48

Contents

D'Angelo: Brown Sugar	52
The Drifters	56
Aretha Franklin: I Never Loved a Man the Way I Love You	59
Aretha Franklin: "Think"	63
Marvin Gaye: Let's Get It On	65
Marvin Gaye: What's Going On	68
Al Green: Greatest Hits	73
Isaac Hayes: Hot Buttered Soul	75
Lauryn Hill: The Miseducation of Lauryn Hill	79
Whitney Houston	83
The Impressions: "People Get Ready"	86
The Isley Brothers: The Heat Is On	88
Michael Jackson and the Jackson 5	92
Etta James	96
Alicia Keys	98
Ben E. King: "Stand by Me"	102
Gladys Knight and the Pips	104
John Legend	107
Curtis Mayfield: Super Fly	111
Wilson Pickett: Land of 1000 Dances: The Complete Atlantic Singles, Vol. 1	114
Elvis Presley	117
Otis Redding: Otis Blue/Otis Redding Sings Soul	119
"Respect": From Otis Redding to Aretha Franklin	123
Minnie Riperton: Perfect Angel	126
Smokey Robinson and the Miracles	129
Sam & Dave	133
Nina Simone: Feeling Good: The Very Best of Nina Simone	136

Percy Sledge: "When a Man Loves a Woman"	141
Dusty Springfield: Dusty in Memphis	143
The Staple Singers: Be Altitude: Respect Yourself	147
The Supremes	150
The Temptations	153
Sister Rosetta Tharpe	156
Jackie Wilson	158
Bill Withers	161
Stevie Wonder in the 1960s	164
Stevie Wonder: Songs in the Key of Life	167
"(You Make Me Feel Like a) Natural Woman": Aretha Franklin and Carole King	171
3 Impact on Popular Culture	175
4 Legacy	187
Bibliography	197
Index	209

Series Foreword

Ask some music fans and they will tell you that genre labels are rubbish and that imposing them on artists and pieces of music diminish the diversity of the work of performers, songwriters, instrumental composers, and so on. Still, in the record stores of old, in descriptions of radio-station formats (on-air and Internet), and at various streaming audio and download sites today, we have seen and continue to see music categorized by genre. Some genre boundaries are at least somewhat artificial, and it is true that some artists and some pieces of music transcend boundaries. But categorizing music by genre is a convenient way of keeping track of the thousands upon thousands of musical works available for listeners' enjoyment; it's analogous to the difference between having all your documents on your computer's home screen versus organizing them into folders. So Greenwood's Exploring Musical Genres series is a genre- and performance-group-based collection of books and e-books. The publications in this series will provide listeners with background information on the genre; critical analysis of important examples of musical pieces, artists, and events from the genre; discussion of must-hear music from the genre; analysis of the genre's impact on the popular culture of its time and on later popular culture trends; and analysis of the enduring legacy of the genre today and its impact on later musicians and their songs, instrumental works, and recordings. Each volume will also contain a bibliography of references for further reading.

We view the volumes in the Exploring Musical Genres series as a go-to resource for serious music fans, the more casual listener, and everyone in between. The authors in the series are scholars who probe into the details of the genre and its practitioners: the singers, instrumentalists, composers, and lyricists of the pieces of music that we love. Although the authors' scholarship brings a high degree of insight and perceptive analysis to the reader's understanding of the various musical genres, the authors approach their subjects with the idea of appealing to the lay reader, the music nonspecialist. As a result, the authors may provide critical analysis using some high-level scholarly tools; however, they avoid any unnecessary and unexplained jargon or technical terms or concepts. These are scholarly volumes written for the enjoyment of virtually any music fan.

Every volume has its length parameters, and an author cannot include every piece of music from within a particular genre. Part of the challenge, but also part of the fun, is that readers might agree with some of the choices of "must-hear music" and disagree with others. So while your favorite example of, say, grunge music might not be included, the author's choices might help you to open up your ears to new, exciting, and ultimately intriguing possibilities.

By and large, these studies focus on music from the sound-recording era: roughly the 20th century through the present. American guitarist, composer, and singer-songwriter Frank Zappa once wrote:

> On a record, the overall timbre of the piece (determined by equalization of individual parts and their proportions in the mix) tells you, in a subtle way, WHAT the song is about. The orchestration provides *important information* about what the composition IS and, in some instances, assumes a greater importance than *the composition itself* [Italics and capitalizations from the original]. (Zappa with Occhiogrosso 1989, 188)

The gist of Zappa's argument is that *everything* that the listener experiences (to use Zappa's system of emphasizing words)—including the arrangement, recording mix and balance, lyrics, melodies, harmonies, instrumentation, and so on—makes up a musical composition. To put it another way, during the sound-recording era, and especially after the middle of the 20th century, we have tended to understand the idea of a piece of music—particularly in the realm of popular music—as being the same as the most definitive recording of that piece of music. And this is where Zappa's emphasis on the arrangement and recording's production comes into play. As a result, a writer delving into, say, new-wave rock will examine and analyze the B-52s' version of "Rock Lobster" and not just the words, melodies, and chords that any band could sing and play and still label the result "Rock Lobster." To use Zappa's graphic way of highlighting particular words, the B-52s' recording *IS* the piece.

Although they have expressed it in other ways, other writers, such as Theodore Gracyk (1996, 18) and Albin Zak III (2001) concur with Zappa's equating of the piece with the studio recording of the piece.

In the case of musical genres not as susceptible to being tied to a particular recording—generally because of the fact that they are genres often experienced live, such as classical music or Broadway musicals—the authors will still make recommendations of particular recordings (we don't all have ready access to a live performance of Wolfgang Amadeus Mozart's *Symphony No. 40* any time we'd like to experience the piece), but they will focus their analyses on the more general, the notes-on-the-page, the expected general aural experience that one is likely to find in any good performance or recorded version.

Maybe you think that all you really want to do is just listen to the music. Won't reading about a genre decrease your enjoyment of it? My hope is that you'll find that reading this book will open up new possibilities for understanding your favorite musical genre, and that by knowing a little more about it, you'll be able to listen with proverbial new ears and gain even more pleasure from your listening experience. Yes, the authors in the series will bring you biographical detail, the history of the genres, and critical analysis on various musical works that they consider to be the best, the most representative, and the most influential pieces in the genre. However, ultimately the goal is to enhance the listening experience. That, by the way, is why these volumes have an exclamation mark in their titles. So please enjoy both reading and listening!

—*James E. Perone, Series Editor*

REFERENCES

Gracyk, Theodore. 1996. *Rhythm and Noise: An Aesthetics of Rock*. Durham, NC: Duke University Press.

Zak, Albin, III. 2001. *The Poetics of Rock: Cutting Tracks, Making Records*. Berkeley: University of California Press.

Zappa, Frank, with Peter Occhiogrosso. 1989. *The Real Frank Zappa Book*. New York: Poseidon Press.

Preface

Defined perhaps most simply as the fusion of African American gospel music and its performance practice with African American R&B music, soul is often thought of as a musical genre that revolved around such artists as Ray Charles, Aretha Franklin, and James Brown. The roots of soul music, however, extend back beyond the important work of Ray Charles in fitting secular lyrics to music that was originally associated with sacred music in black churches and the subsequent iconic recordings and performances by artists such as Brown and Franklin. The history of soul music continues to the present, although the genre continues to evolve and perhaps move away from some of its gospel-inspired roots.

This volume traces the history of soul music back to spirituals and gospel and the 1920s crossover of Thomas A. Dorsey from blues to gospel, to the 1930s and 1940s and the pioneering work of Sister Rosetta Tharpe, a singer-guitarist who straddled the lines between gospel, blues, and jazz. In performing in these media, Tharpe broke down the barriers between the sacred and the secular—between gospel and blues—in a way that set the stage for Ray Charles and others, who helped give this composite genre its name in the 1950s and 1960s.

Like most of the other volumes in this series that focus on musicians, albums, iconic concert events, and songs, the chapter "Must-Hear Music" of *Listen to Soul!* focuses entirely on 50 popular and/or significant examples of the many faces of soul music and musicians. Many of these are among the most iconic performers, albums, and songs from the 1930s to the present; however, I have included a few that the reader might not have expected. These somewhat-left-field examples, though, tell us something important about either the development of the genre or what was going on in the world of the popular culture of the musicians' or musical examples' times. The chapter "Must-Hear Music" is arranged alphabetically, in the manner of encyclopedic entries.

Because I treat the 50 major entries in the chapter "Must-Hear Music" as stand-alone entries in an encyclopedic work, the reader will find some duplication of information. For example, I include discussion of the importance of Aretha Franklin's recording of the Otis Redding composition "Respect" in the chapter "Background," discuss the song in detail in its entry in the chapter "Must-Hear Music," and provide some references to Franklin's recording of the song in the chapters "Impact on Popular Culture" and "Legacy."

In the major entries in the chapter "Must-Hear Music," I discuss the overall importance of the music and/or artist, its/their reception by the public, some of the major songs that were featured on albums, and the wider social ramifications of some of the music. In addition to the discussion of the lyrics of various songs, the chapter carries a discussion of the music itself, including melodies, harmonic usage, instrumental and vocal arrangements, and so on. I have made every attempt to limit the use of specialized terms in these discussions to make them as accessible as possible to the lay reader.

One of the challenges of separating the discussion of the impact on popular culture and the legacy of soul—or any genre—into different chapters is that there can be a degree of overlap. In the chapter "Impact on Popular Culture," I focus on uses of classic soul songs out of context (e.g., advertising agency Luckie & Co.'s use of the song "My Girl," originally a hit for the Temptations, in its 2003 and 2005 campaign for McKee Foods' Little Debbie snack products) and on film and television references to classic soul that only function in their entirety if the viewer is at least familiar with the original musical styles, performers, and/or types of vocal ensembles associated with soul from various eras. Some of the television and film references to soul music and/or performers is reverential; however, even the humorous parody-oriented references are predicated on familiarity with the genre, its sound, and some of its stars.

The chapter "Legacy" focuses on the continuing relevance, popularity, and/or notoriety of the various musicians, songs, and albums that defined soul through the music of today. Although for some of the longtime popular and iconic songs, albums, and artists there is some degree of overlap between the basic themes of the chapters "Impact on Popular Culture" and "Legacy," I have attempted to minimize redundancy. In this chapter, I have included discussion of some of the biopics of soul musicians (e.g., the 2004 Taylor Hackford biopic, *Ray*, about Ray Charles), films about important soul record labels (e.g., the 2008 Darnell Martin film *Cadillac Records*), as well as 21st-century tribute albums to particular record labels or collections of soul songs (e.g., Rod Stewart's 2009 album *Soulbook*, and Michael McDonald's several soul-oriented projects of the first decade of the 21st century). Films and theatrical works based on the soul music of the past continue to further the genre's legacy, right up to the time of this writing, with the 2019 Broadway musical *Ain't Too Proud to Beg: The Life and Times of the Temptations*, and a biopic about Aretha Franklin that is scheduled for release in fall 2020.

The book concludes with its bibliography that includes the works that I cited in the narrative, sources I used to research soul and its impact, and other sources that might be of interest to readers who seek more information on various aspects of soul and related genres that I have not detailed. For some of the bibliographical entries, I have provided annotations, particularly for works that are somewhat on the periphery of providing a primary focus on soul or where the title alone does not provide a great deal of information about its subject.

Throughout the book, I have provided URLs for YouTube and other internet sources for audio recordings and—especially—for live and television performances that are either difficult or nearly impossible to find elsewhere. I attempted to cite official videos and those that appear to be the most reputable. For questions of fair use, please consult the policies of these websites.

Acknowledgments

I wish to thank the entire staff at ABC-CLIO, as well as the copyeditors and others with whom they subcontract for their help in getting this volume from the concept to the published stage. I wish to thank my wife and best friend, Karen Perone, for all the support she continues to give me on all my writing projects. I also thank the staff of Rodman Public Library in Alliance, Ohio, for helping me with my numerous requests for CDs and DVDs through SearchOhio and OhioLINK.

CHAPTER 1

Background

One of the challenges in tracing the history of any musical genre is deciding where to start. In the case of soul music, let us begin by considering the African American spirituals of the 19th century. These songs, born out of the institution of slavery, expressed the sorrow of the slaves, offered hope for freedom, and—in some cases—contained coded messages that used either Old Testament biblical stories as metaphors for the situations the African Americans found themselves in or non-biblical, coded calls for escape or some other form of deliverance from slavery.

Some of the 19th-century spirituals were written down, arranged for solo voice or choir, and became part of the concert repertoire late in the century and into the 20th century. Of particular importance was the work of composer-arranger Henry Thacker Burleigh, who wrote and published arrangements of spirituals that might otherwise have been forgotten; because of their association with the bad old days of slavery, some of these spirituals were falling into disuse. Perhaps the most famous group to take published choral arrangements of spirituals across the United States as well as to Europe, Fisk University's Jubilee Singers originally were organized to raise funds for the university in the early 1870s. However, by keeping the earlier 19th-century spirituals alive at a time when they might otherwise have been forgotten, the group's significance in the history of African American music far exceeded its original purpose.

By the early 20th century, African American sacred music was evolving from the spirituals and breaking free of the published arrangements composed by Burleigh and others. Sanctified Church gospel recordings from the late 1920s by Elder J. E. Burch's Cheraw, South Carolina, church, show the direction in which at least one strand of gospel music was heading. These include songs such as "My Heart Keeps Singing," which is highlighted in episode two of the PBS television series *American Epic*, directed by Bernard MacMahon. At the time of this writing, a recording of the 1920s' performance of the song is also available on YouTube (see, for example, https://www.youtube.com/watch?v=sNbNldA0W_s, accessed January 28, 2020). This and the other Victor recordings that Burch and members of his congregation made reflect many of the musical elements that eventually connected gospel music and soul music, including call-and-response form, virtuosic solo singing, the lead singer assuming the role of a preacher, syncopation, and blue notes, as well as a focus on inspirational lyrical themes.

As gospel music developed, it maintained ties to both the spirituals of the previous century and to the blues. In fact, Thomas A. Dorsey, sometimes referred to as the father of gospel music (e.g., "Peace in the Valley" and "Take My Hand, Precious Lord"), was a blues-based pianist in the early part of his musical career, using the name Georgia Tom. Georgia Tom worked only in secular music; not in sacred. Some of the recordings he made with artists such as Tampa Red were ribald in character (e.g., "It's Tight Like That"). Although Dorsey turned away from this type of material when he began to focus on sacred music, this mixing of the sacred and the secular played a central role in the development and early definition of soul music.

Singer and guitarist Sister Rosetta Tharpe also freely mixed sacred and secular music throughout her career, from the 1930s through the 1960s. Although most of Tharpe's work predates what is usually considered soul music, her mix of gospel, folk, jazz, and blues material demonstrated that it was possible for an artist to cross over between genres. Tharpe's 1956 album, *Gospel Train*, focused on sacred-themed music but included her blues-oriented electric guitar fills, bridging the gap between gospel and electric blues. On the more purely sacred side of the proverbial fence, Mahalia Jackson was a major influence, both on gospel singers who stayed in the sacred realm and on the female gospel singers who later turned to secular music, including Aretha Franklin, Mavis Staples, and others.

Even some songwriters and performers more commonly considered R&B musicians than soul musicians acknowledged the connection between their professional work and their earlier experience singing gospel music in church. Roy Brown is best known for his enduring 1947 song, "Good Rocking Tonight," a hit single for both Brown and Wynonie Harris that was later covered by numerous singers, including Elvis

Presley. He stated, "The same style I'm using singing the blues, I did when I was singing spirituals" (Hildebrand 1994, 28). In fact, other popular jump blues recordings of the late 1940s included elements of gospel music, including handclapping, generally on beats two and four of quadruple-meter songs, and call-and-response form.

The work of the vocal groups that became popular in the 1940s and 1950s also contributed to the integration of the musical style of sacred gospel music and secular lyrics. As Jon Hartley Fox wrote in his history of King Records, "The bird groups [groups named after birds, such as the Ravens, the Orioles, the Flamingos, and so on] sounded gospel but were sold as R&B and (with luck) pop" (Fox 2009, 94). Fox continues by quoting Charlie Gillett's early 1970s' study of the development of rock and roll, "Indirectly and directly, gospel styles and conventions were introduced into rhythm and blues—and constituted the first significant trend away from the blues as such in black popular music" (Gillett, quoted in Fox 2009, 94–95).

Fox describes some of the music that came out of King Records that exhibited the musical connections to gospel but contained highly secular lyrics with unmistakable sexual connotations and double meanings, such as Billy Ward and his Dominoes' 1951 song "Sixty Minute Man" and the Midnighters' 1954 hit "Work with Me, Annie." These singles were highly successful on the R&B charts and caught the attention of white teens. As Fox and other authors point out, their crossover nature —helped define what would be called "rock and roll," when Cleveland disc jockey Alan Freed began using that term—which had been a blues euphemism for sex—for commercial crossover R&B songs. Despite helping establish gospel music as one of the components of rock and roll, they were probably too sexually charged to be considered the direct ancestors of what came to be known as soul music by the late 1950s. They, and other black vocal group recordings from the late 1940s and early 1950s, were important, however, in bringing at least some of the musical components of gospel into the world of secular popular music that impacted an increasingly large audience demographic.

One important aspect of the development of soul was the familial and neighborhood connections that helped artists to grow, sometimes as collaborators and sometimes as friendly—and sometimes not so friendly—competitors. To cite just a few examples of the family ties, the Jackson 5 and the Isley Brothers were brother acts; Gladys Knight and the Pips consisted of siblings and cousins; the Staple Singers consisted of Pops Staples and his children; Carolyn and Erma Franklin were frequent backing vocalists on their sister, Aretha's, recordings; and so on.

4   Listen to Soul!

In the early 1950s, the southside Chicago neighborhood known as the "Dirty Thirties" in the Bronzeville area, future soul stars such as Lou Rawls, Roebuck "Pops" Staples, Sam Cooke, and others sang in church on Sundays and during the week "were jumbling the sacred with the secular—so long as the grown-ups weren't listening" (Kot 2014, 25). Other cities, including Memphis, Atlanta, Detroit, to name just three, had similar scenes where gospel and secular music mixed, and musicians who would play significant roles in the history of soul music knew each other's work, learned from each other, and engaged in competition, all while honing their skills as performers. In her autobiography, Gladys Knight recounts the importance of amateur nights and competitions in her native Atlanta (Knight 1997, 54–55). As Knight describes it, young rising musicians saw these competitions as their tickets to gigs in well-established, well-respected ballrooms and another step on their possible rise to stardom.

Although the vocal groups of the 1950s might have represented a move away from the direct impact of the blues on African American popular music, the connections between blues and soul remained into the 1960s, the heyday of soul. To put it another way, blues never entirely left the mix. To name just a few of these connections, Otis Redding's 1965 album *Otis Blue* included B. B. King's "Rock Me Baby." Blues guitarist-singer-songwriter B. B. King himself recorded several songs during his career that actually ventured closer to issues-based and inspirational soul music than electric blues, including "Help the Poor." A generation later, guitarist-singer-songwriter Robert Cray took King's occasional blending of blues, jazz, and soul a step further and built a following with his blend of electric blues and soul. Although Cray's straddling the line between blues and more commercial styles did not sit well with some music critics, *All Music Guide* biographer and critic Bill Dahl responded by writing, "Tin-eared critics have frequently damned him as a yuppie blues wannabe whose slickly soulful offerings bear scant resemblances to the real down-home item. In reality, Robert Cray is one of a precious few young blues-based artists with the talent and vision to successfully usher the idiom into the 21st century without resorting either to slavish imitation or simply playing rock while passing it off as blues" (Dahl n.d.).

The emergence of Ray Charles as a force to be reckoned with when he moved to Atlantic Records in 1952 seems to have played perhaps the most widely recognized role in the public's definition of soul as the merger of gospel and secular R&B. Charles's songs, such as the 1954 R&B chart-topping song "I Got a Woman"; the 1955 No. 9 R&B chart hit, "This Little Girl of Mine"; and the 1956 No. 5 R&B chart hit, "Hallelujah,

I Love Her So" played major roles in defining soul as a genre. This is not to imply that Charles's work represented the first soul music, as we have seen above. The sheer popularity and influence of songs such as these, which freely mixed musical and lyrical references from the sacred and secular worlds, were rhythmically appealing, and resonated with the young fans of the new rock and roll genre both established Charles as the leading exponent of soul music of the mid-1950s and established the early definition of the genre in the minds of the public.

Beginning roughly around the same time and extending into the 1960s, instrumental jazz began incorporating aspects of gospel music, including melodic, rhythmic, and harmonic cues. Hard bop jazz, particularly that associated with Blue Note Records and artists such as Art Blakey, Cannonball Adderley, and Horace Silver, is particularly notable in its connection to the gospel tradition. Jazz pianist and scholar Ted Gioia describes the commercial appeal and continuing importance of soulful hard bop pieces such as Herbie Hancock's "Watermelon Man," Lee Morgan's "The Sidewinder," and Joe Zawinul's "Mercy, Mercy, Mercy" (originally recorded by saxophonist Cannonball Adderley), writing that "this crossover appeal continues in the current day, when hard bop licks and beats from back in the day are sampled and recycled by hip-hoppers and DJs" (Gioia 2016, 132).

Decades before Lil Nas X's 2018 hit "Old Town Road" raised a multitude of questions about musical genres, race, and musical identity, there were connections between African American musical forms and genres and what has traditionally been thought of as white country music. For example, both A. P. Carter of the original Carter Family and Hank Williams Sr. were known to have learned from African American musicians, undoubtedly an influence on their compositions in the country genre.

In the world of soul music, too, there were several interesting intersections with country music. Perhaps one of the most persistent hit songs of the late 20th century and early 21st century was country singer-songwriter Dolly Parton's "I Will Always Love You." Although Parton's versions charted multiple times—for example, the original single release from 1974 and a re-release when it appeared as part of the soundtrack of the 1982 film *The Best Little Whorehouse in Texas*—the song became a soul classic in 1992 when Whitney Houston recorded it for the soundtrack of *The Bodyguard*. It became a signature piece for both singers, and Houston's recording re-entered the record charts in 2012 after her untimely death.

An even more unusual connection between country and soul music was made in 1969 by keyboardist, songwriter, producer, and singer Isaac

Hayes in the form of his 14-minute-long version of "By the Time I Get to Phoenix," originally a so-called countrypolitan hit for singer Glen Campbell. Hayes's deconstruction, or perhaps better put, his dismantling and reconstruction, of the Jimmy Webb composition was not only one of the most unusual recordings in the soul repertoire, it also demonstrated the importance of the producer and arranger in the genre. This emphasis on both large-scale musical shaping and the minute details of production anticipated the importance of producers in the digital hip-hop age.

Back in the early 1960s, the demographics of soul music had broadened with the development of what came to be called blue-eyed soul—in other words, soul music performed by white singers. The Righteous Brothers were the first acknowledged blue-eyed soul singers; however, subsequent artists, such as Dusty Springfield, Boz Scaggs, Hall & Oates, Michael Bolton, Amy Winehouse, Adele, and others have been associated with the subgenre. And well before the Righteous Brothers seemed to define blue-eyed soul in the early 1960s, singer Johnnie Ray's 1952 hit "Cry" exuded soulfulness. In fact, Gladys Knight described Ray as "a white guy with the sound of a black woman" who "sang soul" (Knight 1997, 65). The fact that several of them, such as Johnnie Ray, crossed over from the pop charts to the R&B charts of their day confirms the validity of their work of as soul music.

Interestingly, although performers such as the Righteous Brothers were highly visible examples of the connection of white performers to soul music in the 1960s, several of the studio instrumentalists associated with various soul labels, such as Stax and Atlantic, were white. In fact, Booker T. & the M.G.'s, which functioned as a group of studio musicians when they were not recording and touring as one of the leading instrumental acts of the era, was a racially integrated group. In addition, the Muscle Shoals, Alabama, studio musicians known informally as the Swampers, was an all-white group of studio musicians who backed up both country singers and Aretha Franklin and other soul giants. What might be even more surprising is the backing singers for Al Green's hits on Hi Records, Sandra Rhodes, Charles Chalmers, and Donna Rhodes, were a white vocal group that came out of the country and white gospel tradition.

In addition to illustrating the perhaps surprising racial integration in soul and R&B in the 1960s and 1970s (in the studio, but infrequently in live performances as the touring groups tended not to be as commonly integrated), all the studio musicians of the heyday of soul—instrumentalists and singers—deserve careful consideration for their role in defining the music. In addition to the members of Booker T. & the M.G.'s and the others mentioned above, the Bar-Kays backed up numerous musicians on the Stax label, including Otis Redding. Like Booker T. & the M.G.'s, the Bar-Kays also enjoyed some chart success as a standalone instrumental unit. One of the most commercially successful, most frequently heard on the radio, and most successful corporation on the pop and R&B charts in the 1960s was Berry Gordy Jr.'s Motown, with its Tamla, Gordy, Soul, and Motown labels. Although the singers might have been different from recording session to recording session and from hit to hit, the Motown sound was, in part, defined by a group of studio musicians known informally as the Funk Brothers.

Although the percussionists, keyboardists, guitarists, and so on, that performed on numerous Motown hits all helped define the recordings credited to the Supremes, the Four Tops, the Temptations, Stevie Wonder, the Miracles, and the other Motown acts of the era, perhaps the most famous member of the Funk Brothers was electric bassist James Jamerson. Although rarely credited by name on any Motown releases, Jamerson is generally acknowledged as one of the most influential bass players of all time. His bass lines have been transcribed and analyzed (see, for example, Dr. Licks 1989), and several current YouTube channels include tutorials on playing both Jamerson's lines and in Jamerson's style (see, for example, Jake Hawrylak's Reverb tutorial on learning Jamerson's approach to fast (16th) notes and syncopation, https://www.youtube.com/watch?v=-1LyepqoOiI, accessed January 17, 2020). The number of these tutorials available on the internet provide testimony to not only his importance but also to the significance of the cadre of studio musicians of which he was a part.

In addition to the instrumentalists, sometimes unheralded backing vocalists helped define the sound of soul recordings of the 1960s and 1970s. Perhaps the most heavily recorded were Jackie Hicks, Marlene Barrow, and Louvain Demps, known collectively as the Andantes. In addition to singing backup on recordings by Marvin Gaye and Tammi Terrell, the Four Tops, the Temptations, and others, the group also contributed to recordings that were credited to all-female vocal groups, including the Supremes and Martha and the Vandellas.

To the earlier consideration of the crossing of genre, racial, and other boundaries in the continuum that is labeled soul, we must also add the complexity of defining the genre in its relationship to record-chart designations. For example, at various times, what one might call soul music has appeared on the soul, R&B, adult R&B, black singles, or R&B/hip-hop charts in trade magazines such as *Cash Box* and *Billboard*. To make matters perhaps even more complex, virtually all singles by black artists marketed to black listeners that made the charts, say, in 1967 were on *Billboard* magazine's R&B charts. In 1970, when the magazine dropped the R&B designation (1969–1982), had those same songs been on the charts, they would have been on the soul charts.

Many of the soul classics from the mid-1950s through the present crossed over between the R&B, soul, black singles, and so on charts and the pop charts. This suggests the widespread appeal that many of the classics have had to a record-buying and radio-listening public outside of the African American community. Rarer were other kinds of chart crossovers (e.g., R&B to country, or R&B to adult contemporary); however, some of the hits of groups such as the 5th Dimension and the Commodores, as well as the Commodores' one-time lead singer and songwriter Lionel Richie, released singles that not only made it to the upper reaches of the pop and R&B (or soul) charts, they also topped or placed high on the adult contemporary charts. This suggested an appeal for this strand of soul music that transcended generations. Some of these singles were in rotation with middle-of-the-road songs by older artists on adult contemporary format radio stations, as well as on pop and R&B stations.

As the history of soul music progressed into the 1970s, soul shouters remained. However, a new understated approach helped broaden the genre. Singer-songwriters such as Bill Withers and Al Green used a vocal approach that seemed to be tailor-made for the microphone, as opposed to an approach that was meant to resonate through a church. Understated soul singers had been part of the genre's story before Withers, Green, and similar artists appeared on the scene; however, the male singers who took an understated approach often sang in falsetto, either as leads in vocal groups or as solo artists—for example, in Curtis Mayfield's work with the Impressions and his subsequent solo recordings.

The work of artists such as Withers, particularly on his well-known hit "Ain't No Sunshine," and Green, particularly on his well-known hit "Let's Stay Together," aligned with the introspective singer-songwriter style that was also sweeping the pop music world in the form of largely white artists such as Joni Mitchell, James Taylor, Jackson Browne, Gordon Lightfoot, and others, in the early 1970s. The importance of this more laid-back approach within the soul genre was recognized by the well-established singer Gladys Knight, who said of the style of her recording of "Midnight Train to Georgia," "I listened to Cissy's [Cissy Houston] version and loved it—but I knew I wanted something different. I wanted an Al Green thing going, you know?" (Myers 2016, 219).

One of the most difficult-to-categorize musicians of the 1980s into the 21st century, Prince helped shape soul, particularly in perhaps his best-known song, "Purple Rain." The song includes touches of gospel, particularly in the backing vocal arrangement and the anthemic structure and inspirational and religious imagery of the lyrics. In this and in his other soul ballads, Prince brought his virtuosic searing electric guitar work into the genre. Reminiscent of both Jimi Hendrix and Carlos Santana, Prince's guitar work brought a solid rock/blues-rock element into soul music, an element that had been in some previous soul recordings, but that Prince ratcheted up a level or two.

Even as soul gave way to a harder-hitting funk style, ties to gospel music could be felt in some songs. For example, the musical style of James Brown's "Say It Loud—I'm Black and I'm Proud" might be several steps away from the gospel music of his youth. However, in the song, Brown turns the title of the spiritual "I Been 'Buked and I Been Scorned," sung perhaps most famously by Mahalia Jackson during the 1963 March on Washington, where Rev. Dr. Martin Luther King Jr. delivered his "I Have a Dream" speech, into a more direct and pointed political message. Brown transforms the title line of the old spiritual into the phrase "we've been 'buked and we've been scorned" to describe the subjugation blacks have endured.

The focus of some soul musicians on social and political issues continued well beyond Brown's "Say It Loud—I'm Black and I'm Proud." Some of the work of issues-based musicians has also creatively integrated what might have been, at one time, considered disparate styles. For example, poet, songwriter, and singer Gil Scott-Heron combined spoken-word poetry, soul singing, and jazz in the work of perhaps his most influential period of the 1970s and 1980s. As rap and hip-hop took hold in the 1980s and 1990s, artists integrated rap and rhythms of hip-hop in music that also took on social issues. Lauryn Hill's 1998 debut solo album, *The Miseducation of Lauryn Hill*, a must-hear album, did so to critical acclaim.

In the 21st century, one of the most critically acclaimed soul singer-songwriters of the past two decades, Alicia Keys, also integrated the rhythms, sampling, and production techniques of hip-hop with soul. Trained as a classical pianist, Keys also integrates classical influences, making her issues-based songs connect not only to her contemporaries such as Lauryn Hill, but also back to the soul-jazz-classical mix of Nina Simone, one of the most musically unique issues-based soul musicians of the 1960s.

At the same time that artists such as Hill, Keys, and others brought soul, hip-hop, and rap together, other 21st century artists, including Beyoncé Knowles-Carter (hereafter referred to by her professional name, Beyoncé), Jennifer Hudson, and John Legend have maintained more obvious ties to the classic soul tradition of the 1960s and 1970s. This has especially been the case with the performances of Beyoncé, Hudson, Legend, and artists such as Queen Latifah in films that reflect on the classic soul of the past (e.g., *Dreamgirls, Cadillac Records, Hairspray*, and so on).

More recently, young artists such as Khalid have added additional dimensions to what is understood to be soul. Khalid's principal contributions to date include the ballad "Location" in 2016; his highly acclaimed debut album, *American Teen*, in 2017; and the follow-up, *Free Spirit*, in 2019. Khalid's connections to the soul tradition might be best summed up by critic Andy Kellman who wrote, "The album [*Free Spirit*] works through emotional struggles of early adulthood" (Kellman n.d.-b). While time and style separate their music, these kinds of emotional struggles could be found in Stevie Wonder's coming-of-age recordings of the early 1970s.

Although her career goes back several years and includes work as a backing vocalist with Prince, as well as solo releases going back to 2013, the soul singer-songwriter, rapper, and flutist Lizzo (Melissa Jefferson) moved into the mainstream in 2019. Lizzo's singles "Good as Hell" and "Truth Hurts" topped the R&B charts, with "Truth Hurts" also topping the pop charts. *TIME* magazine named Lizzo its Entertainer of the Year for 2019, not only for her commercial and critical achievements, but also for her positive messages, including those concerning body image issues (Irby 2019). *The Associated Press* also named Lizzo its Entertainer of the Year (*The Associated Press* 2019). Lizzo's major label debut album, *Cuz I Love You*, an Atlantic release, was her first to chart, reaching No. 4; the album received eight Grammy Award nominations. Lizzo's combination of influences brings yet another dimension to the ongoing evolution of soul music.

The spirit of 1950s' and 1960s' soul has remained part of general American popular culture by virtue of the continuing popularity of the original songs and original recordings, which can still be heard on oldies radio, in movie soundtracks, and in soundtracks for television programs. Some of these original songs were reinvigorated in public consciousness by virtue of historically based films such as *Cadillac Records* (the story of the Leonard and Phil Chess and their Chicago-based company, Chess Records) and *Ray* (a biopic about the life and music of Ray Charles). This trend should continue with a biopic about Aretha Franklin, scheduled for release in fall 2020 and starring Jennifer Hudson.

In the late 20th and early 21st centuries, the style of 1960s' soul (albeit not the original songs) has also returned to general American popular culture in musicals and films such as *Hairspray*, *Little Shop of Horrors*, *Dreamgirls*, and others. In *Hairspray*, for example, rapper and singer-actress Queen Latifah provided Aretha Franklin-inspired vocals as the character Maybelle "Motormouth" Stubbs, and in the film version of *Little Shop of Horrors*, former lead singer of the Four Tops, Levi Stubbs, sang one of the musical's more-memorable songs as the voice of the show's killer plant.

In discussing the development and history of soul music, in addition to noteworthy performers it is important to consider record labels such as Motown, Chess, Stax, Volt, and Atlantic, the leading labels of the classic soul era, and their contributions to the genre.

Motown billed itself "The Sound of Young America," which can be taken as a suggestion of owner Berry Gordy Jr.'s aim to create a type of soul music that would resonate across racial boundaries. However, part of the success of Motown's brand of soul is that it also included aspects that cut across generational boundaries. For example, the sequined evening gowns worn by the Supremes and the tuxedos worn by the Temptations seem like the kind of stage costumes that might appeal to the groups' older listeners. Motown hired vocal coaches, such as Maurice King, and choreographers, such as Cholly Atkins, after they successfully helped mold other, non-Motown soul artists, including Gladys Knight and the Pips in the early 1960s (before Knight and the Pips moved to Motown). The record charts of the 1960s and 1970s suggest that Gordy was successful in building a musical empire that broke down barriers. Interestingly, some Motown artists' singles performed notably better on the pop charts than on the R&B and soul charts of their time. This suggests that this music might have resonated more with non-black audiences than with black audiences.

Chicago's Chess Records also played a prominent role in defining soul music, in bringing to the world some of the first music that clearly blended R&B and gospel music. This was the label of Etta James, whose recordings included soul, jazz, and R&B material, and the label of artists such as the Dells, Fontella Bass, Little Milton, and others. In addition to its direct connections to soul, Chess also produced recordings in the 1950s by blues artists such as Willie Dixon, Jimmy Reed, and John Lee Hooker, and rock-and-roll artists such as Chuck Berry.

Especially interesting in the history of the record labels associated with some of the giants of classic soul is the story of Stax Records and its subsidiary Volt. This Memphis-based label produced the hits of Otis Redding and the early hits of Sam & Dave, among others. The label also boasted a particularly strong contingent of studio musicians, including

Booker T. & the M.G.'s, as mentioned early. The story of the company became especially interesting when the distribution agreement that Stax/Volt had with Atlantic Records ended. Incidentally, it was also at about this time that the great Otis Redding perished in an airplane crash. As a result of the ending of the distribution agreement and the associated entanglements between the companies, Stax and Volt lost some of their stars and the rights to their earlier music to Atlantic. Although Stax attempted to rebuild, the label never achieved the heights it had enjoyed before the end of the distribution agreement.

Atlantic was unquestionably one of the major players in classic soul. Ahmet Ertegün and Herb Abramson founded the company in the late 1940s and concentrated, at first, on jazz recordings. By the early 1950s, the label had moved squarely into the R&B and soul realms. Ray Charles's first R&B chart hits, including the songs in which he famously fitted secular lyrics to sacred music, which some interpreted as the start of soul music. Aretha Franklin, Ruth Brown, Sam & Dave, Wilson Pickett, the Coasters, and Big Joe Turner, were some of the major soul and R&B stars who recorded on the label during its heyday.

Although there is not sufficient space available to delve into all the great cities that developed unique approaches to soul and the labels in those locations, let us also consider Philadelphia and its important Philadelphia International Records. The songwriting and production team of Kenny Gamble and Leon Huff were important in establishing the sound of Philadelphia soul and Philadelphia International Records and its associated labels. Other writers and producers, including Linda Creed and Thom Bell, also helped establish the style. Philadelphia soul differentiated itself from the styles coming out of Detroit, Memphis, and other centers for the genre in the string scoring and the way in which it can be heard as a precursor of the disco music that swept the United States in the 1970s. The Philadelphia soul scene included hits by artists such as the O'Jays, Billy Paul, Patti LaBelle, Lou Rawls, the Stylistics, and others, with Billy Paul's "Me and Mrs. Jones" and the O'Jays' "Back Stabbers" being just two of the subgenre's most memorable songs. The Philadelphia soul style also played a significant role in the blue-eyed soul recordings of artists such as Hall & Oates and David Bowie.

As was the case with Detroit, Memphis, and other soul centers during the 1960s and 1970s, Philadelphia had its core group of studio musicians who contributed to countless recordings by the various solo singers and singing groups. This group of musicians, known collectively as MFSB (for Mother, Father, Sister, Brother) also enjoyed one hugely successful and iconic hit, "TSOP (The Sound of Philadelphia)," which included vocals by the Three Degrees. Although the piece was most closely associated with the African American-oriented television music program *Soul Train*, "TSOP" was also a pop and R&B chart-topping 1974 single. One of the interesting features of this Gamble and Huff composition and production is the high degree to which it represents the way that soul music was heading at the start of the disco era.

I mentioned earlier the production and arranging on Isaac Hayes's massive recording of "By the Time I Get to Phoenix." In addition to Hayes, the soul genre had several diverse producers and arrangers who helped define the sound of recordings that featured prominent, chart-topping singers. Producers such as Hayes, Jerry Wexler, Al Bell, Norman Whitfield, Smokey Robinson, Phil Spector, Richard Rudolph, Arif Mardin, David Porter, the Philadelphia soul producers mentioned earlier and numerous others, the orchestrators and arrangers who composed string and horn section arrangements, and the talented producers of the hip-hop era all helped shape the evolution of the genre. Throughout the "Must-Hear Music" chapter, I mention some of the producers and arrangers and their specific contributions; however, the contributions of these sometimes unsung and under-sung heroes of the recording industry cannot be overestimated in shaping the development of soul music from the 1950s to the present.

CHAPTER 2

Must-Hear Music

"AIN'T NO MOUNTAIN HIGH ENOUGH": FROM MARVIN GAYE AND TAMMI TERRELL TO DIANA ROSS

"Ain't No Mountain High Enough" was one of the more persistent hits of the classic soul era, becoming well known through hit recordings by the duo of Marvin Gaye and Tammi Terrell in 1967, and by Diana Ross in 1970. The Diana Ross recording topped both the pop and the R&B singles charts. In addition, the song was recorded in 1968 as an album cut by the combined Supremes and Temptations, and it came back into public consciousness in 2003 with former Doobie Brothers' member Michael McDonald's recording on his tribute to the Motown sound, an album appropriately titled *Motown*. The McDonald album made it into the Top 20 of both the pop and R&B/Soul album charts. Movie and television soundtracks continue to incorporate "Ain't No Mountain High Enough," and it remains a defining hit for both the Gaye-Terrell duet team and for Diana Ross. The team of Nickolas Ashford and Valerie Simpson, who also produced the Diana Ross recording, wrote this expression of complete devotion even after a romantic love faded.

Although both enjoyed solo careers, Motown artists Marvin Gaye and Tammi Terrell experienced several duet hits in 1967 and 1968. Although "Ain't Nothing Like the Real Thing," "You're All I Need to Get By," and "Your Precious Love" performed better on both the pop and the R&B charts than Ashford and Simpson's "Ain't No Mountain High Enough," the latter was one of the more exuberant male-female soul duets of the mid-1960s. In light of what would transpire over the next three years, "Ain't No Mountain High Enough" is also perhaps the most optimistic way to experience the work of a duo that might have continued to produce successful hits had it not been for Tammi Terrell's struggles with brain tumors that led to multiple surgeries, her retirement from live performances, and her untimely death at age 24.

The song itself possesses a memorable and easily identifiable melodic hook in the chorus, the section that opens with the title phrase. In the first verse, Marvin Gaye and Tammi Terrell trade lines, assuring each other that, no matter what the obstacles, each will always be there for the other. The melody in the verses—the lines that Gaye and Terrell toss back and forth—uses a narrow pitch range, and each short phrase has a similar contour. The full duet harmony texture suddenly emerges in the chorus, which has longer phrases and a noticeably higher pitch range. To put it another way, listeners might hear the verses as being pretty much matter-of-fact statements that are then affirmed by a soaring chorus melody.

Even more than the Marvin Gaye and Tammi Terrell recording of the song, the Diana Ross recording takes advantage of the easy accessibility of this hook by using it as the basis of the introduction, with the backing singers singing the "ain't no mountain high enough…" musical phrases on a neutral syllable. The contrast in the Ross recording is between this chorus-based introduction and her spoken rendition of the verse, followed by a repetition of the soaring chorus, this time with the lyrics.

One of the hallmarks of some of the classics of 1960s' soul are the close ties lyrics maintained with the gospel music tradition. Although "Ain't No Mountain High Enough" seems to be a song about a formerly romantic relationship that ended, but the two characters retained close personal ties of friendship, the imagery of the seemingly impassable mountain and valley also appear to have biblical ties. For example, in passages such as those found in Isaiah 49:11 and Micah 1:4, God levels the mountain and raises the valley to maintain a bond with the people. So, in the Marvin Gaye and Tammi Terrell recording, one could interpret the tie between the singers' characters as a sort of spiritual bond, particularly if one is familiar with the scriptural ties.

The lyrics, too, anticipated the generally platonic—almost agape-like—songs of friendship and support that took on an air of spirituality in songs such as Simon and Garfunkel's 1970 hit "Bridge over Troubled Water," Carole King's 1971 composition "You've Got a Friend," Bill Withers's 1972 hit "Lean on Me," and others. In this respect, the 1967 Gaye and Terrell recording stands out as being somewhat unusual for its time and anticipatory of a trend in American popular music that came to fruition three to four years later. Although Ashford and Simpson penned

"Ain't No Mountain High Enough" before this lyrical theme became a popular trend, their exploration of enduring friendship after a romance ends sounded completely in touch with the times when the solo release by Diana Ross was issued and topped both the pop and R&B singles charts.

The 1970 version of the song that Ashford and Simpson produced and that Paul Riser arranged for Diana Ross exhibits even stronger musical ties to the black gospel tradition than did the version produced by Harvey Fuqua and Johnny Bristol for Marvin Gaye and Tammi Terrell. It also exhibited stronger ties to the gospel tradition than did a 1968 version recorded by the combined Diana Ross and the Supremes and the Temptations. The Supremes and Temptations version—an album cut, as opposed to a single—is similar in structure to the earlier Gaye-Terrell version. The Ross solo recording features an all-star backing vocal group that included the Andantes, coproducers Ashford and Simpson, members of the Undisputed Truth, and others. The backing singers' performance style and size and scope are reminiscent of what one might hear from a large gospel choir backing up a vocal soloist.

Various references, including Valerie Simpson herself (see Kot 2011) have stated that Motown boss Berry Gordy Jr. did not want to release the Diana Ross recording of "Ain't No Mountain High Enough" as a single because the album arrangement was so massive, clocking in at over six minutes, and because Gordy apparently did not like spoken introductions to songs. Some disc jockeys disagreed and programmed the song as it had been released on the album. The interest of the DJs resulted in Gordy finally giving the go-ahead for the release of a truncated single version of the song. Both the album and the single version of the Diana Ross recording are must-hear examples of early-1970s' soul, although some listeners may prefer the shorter, punchier single version.

As the first of four Diana Ross post-Supremes singles that topped both the pop and R&B charts, "Ain't No Mountain High Enough" is considered one of her signature songs. As a career-defining recording by Marvin Gaye and Tammi Terrell, their 1967 single release was selected for the Grammy Hall of Fame in 1999 (The Recording Academy n.d.). In the February 14, 2019 episode of the Amazon Prime program *The Grand Tour*, Jeremy Clarkson introduced his commentary on the present state of the building of highways in China by saying, "There ain't no mountain high enough, and ain't no valley low enough," providing evidence of the extent to which this exuberant song remained etched in popular culture over 50 years after its initial release.

18 Listen to Soul!

BEYONCÉ

From the late 1990s until the group broke up in 2006, Beyoncé Knowles (later Beyoncé Knowles-Carter) was known primarily as part of the commercially successful group Destiny's Child. Destiny's Child recorded chart-topping albums, as well as well-known singles such as "Bills, Bills, Bills" and "Say My Name." Even with the commercial success of Destiny's Child, a worthy successor to the great ensembles of the 1960s' so-called "girl group" tradition (e.g., the Shirelles, the Supremes, Martha and the Vandellas, the Cookies, and so on), Beyoncé began a solo career in the early 2000s. Her debut solo album, *Dangerously in Love*, was as popular as her work with Destiny's Child and spawned the hit singles "Crazy in Love" and "Baby Boy." Even her earliest work in films (e.g., *Austin Powers in Goldmember*) suggested that Beyoncé would be a force to be reckoned with, well beyond the confines of the music industry.

Arguably, Beyoncé's connections to the soul music tradition can best be experienced in her ballads. Perhaps one of the best of her successful soul ballads was "Irreplaceable," a 2006, No. 1 hit. This recording illustrates how traditional soul integrated with hip-hop, a trend not just in Beyoncé's early 21st-century work, but also in the work of other soul artists of the hip-hop age. In the song's arrangement, energetic hip-hop rhythms counterpoint Beyoncé's more lyrical vocal work. In this and other ballads, Beyoncé displays a melismatic vocal technique that calls to mind predecessors such as Aretha Franklin and others of the classic soul and R&B traditions. However, "Irreplaceable" is perhaps one of the best representatives of this aspect of Beyoncé's work.

Another unusual track in which Beyoncé's vocal technique stands out is "Perfect Duet," an adaptation of British singer-sonwriter Ed Sheeran's song "Perfect," recorded and released by Beyoncé and Sheeran in 2017. The song itself is clearly more aligned with Sheeran's style—he wrote and recorded the first version of "Perfect." However, Beyoncé's vocal melismas provide the singer-songwriter-style ballad with a connection to soul that makes "Perfect Duet" fundamentally different in feel to Sheeran's original song. Despite the disparate styles of the two artists, the duet effectively counterpoints the voices of Sheeran and Beyoncé.

One of Beyoncé's more intriguing duet recordings is the 2013 song "Drunk in Love," which features her husband, rapper Jay-Z. The sexually charged song and music video shows Beyoncé's solid place in the world of hip-hop aesthetics. The song takes the implications of, to cite just one example, the sexually suggestive moans of Ray Charles's "What'd I Say" and makes them significantly more explicit. At the time of this writing, the

Vevo video for the song on YouTube had well over 536 million views (see https://www.youtube.com/watch?v=p1JPKLa-Ofc, accessed January 29, 2020), suggesting the popularity of the harder-edged side of Beyoncé's work. The video also makes effective use of Beyoncé's abilities as an actor.

Beyoncé's significance in the soul genre, however, goes well beyond her commercially successful work with Destiny's Child, as a solo recording and concert artist, as a duet partner, and in straddling the lines between classic soul singing and more rap-oriented hip-hop. Some of her fans are likely more familiar with Beyoncé as a movie star than as a chart-topping singer. Beyoncé first came to the attention of movie fans in the 2002 film *Austin Powers in Goldmember*, a spoof of the James Bond films of the 1960s, her work in music-related movies such as *Dreamgirls* and *Cadillac Records* was a significant contribution to the legacy of soul and R&B music.

The 2006 Bill Condon film *Dreamgirls* was an adaptation of the 1981 stage musical of the same name. In this movie, Beyoncé portrays Deena Jones, a member of the Dreamettes and the Dreams, female vocal groups of the 1960s based on Motown's great hitmakers, the Supremes. Jones, who becomes the lead singer of the Dreams, is closely modeled on Diana Ross. Jennifer Hudson, in her movie debut as Effie White, the lead singer of the Dreamettes who was replaced in the lead vocal role by Jones, is arguably the most impressive singing star of the movie. She has the musical's most emotionally charged and most technically challenging songs, and Hudson gave a stellar, Academy Award–winning performance. However, Beyoncé convincingly recreates the more laid-back approach to soul of Diana Ross and some of the other Motown stars of the era.

Instead of portraying a thinly veiled fictional version of Diana Ross, in the 2008 Darnell Martin film *Cadillac Records*, Beyoncé portrayed the real-life soul–blues–rock and roll singer Etta James. The film served as a reminder of James's significance in the early days of Chess Records. For some audiences, *Cadillac Records* helped flesh out a singer who, by the early part of the 21st century was primarily—if not entirely—defined by her 1960 recording of the early 1940s' ballad "At Last."

In the 1940s, the song had been associated with the Glenn Miller Orchestra and its singer, Ray Eberle, and, in the 1950s, with former Miller trumpet player and singer Ray Anthony. James and the Chess Records' arrangers and producers were responsible for turning the song into a soul classic. "At Last" had been a hit for Etta James on the R&B charts in the early 1960s, but it enjoyed resurgences of popularity as a favorite for wedding disc jockeys and, perhaps most significantly, through its inclusion in the soundtracks of the 1988 film *Rain Man*, the 1995 blockbuster movie *Father of the Bride II*, and several television programs in the 1990s, including *Northern Exposure*. As might be expected, Beyoncé performs "At Last" in *Cadillac Records*, and the arrangement and performance captures much of the style of the 1960 James recording. For Beyoncé, "At Last," a song she continues to perform in the earlier soul ballad style associated with James, became something of a signature piece. For one thing, as was the case with Etta James, the song practically invites improvisatory melismas that suggest soul music's connections with the gospel tradition. As such, "At Last" stands in sharp contrast to the hip-hop-oriented material that marks much of Beyoncé's work as a recording artist. The intricate improvisational lines that Beyoncé incorporates in her film and subsequent live performances of "At Last" prove, however, that the song is not entirely an outlier within Beyoncé's output; she goes beyond simply imitating Etta James and demonstrates that she can add her personal touch to 1960s' style soul.

Beyoncé's portrayal of Etta James in *Cadillac Records* and the subsequent resurgence of popularity of "At Last"—in particular, Beyoncé's film and concert renditions of the song—did not go unnoticed by James, and not in a generally favorable way. After Beyoncé performed "At Last" for Barack and Michelle Obama's first dance at one of the 2009 presidential inaugural balls, James was quoted as saying at a live appearance, "You guys know your president, right? You know, the one with the big ears? Wait a minute, he might be yours; he ain't my president. But I tell you that woman he had singing for him, singing my song—she's going to get her ass whupped" (Michaels 2009).

For an artist who is as adept as Beyoncé is at portraying other singers in movies, perhaps it is natural that she has recorded under the moniker of an alter-ego: Sasha Fierce. Her adoption of this alter ego allowed Beyoncé to develop a balance in her music between hard-hitting hip-hop and more melodically based music that more obviously demonstrates a direct connection to the classic soul traditions of the 1960s and 1970s.

BLUE-EYED SOUL: THE MEN

Although soul music came out of the black gospel and R&B traditions, non-black songwriters, producers, singers, and instrumentalists have been drawn to and have worked in the genre. When white singers made some of their first inroads in the soul genre in the early 1960s, the term "blue-eyed soul" was used to identify them. Although not an exhaustive list, some of the principal male blue-eyed soul artists include Johnnie Ray, the Righteous Brothers, the Rascals, Lonnie Mack, Hall & Oates,

David Bowie, Boz Scaggs, and Michael Bolton. Consideration of these artists provides a snapshot into the male side of this subgenre.

Although his popularity predates that of most of the artists usually associated with the blue-eyed soul genre, Johnnie Ray's commanding stage presence and musical style were shaped in venues such as Detroit's Flame Show Bar, a haven for black jazz, R&B, and soul musicians. In her autobiography, Gladys Knight, whose early professional career included stints at the venue, described Ray as "a white guy with the sound of a black woman" who "sang soul" (Knight 1997, 65). Ray's first two singles, "Cry" and "The Little White Cloud That Cried," both dating from 1952, were highly successful on the pop and R&B charts, and "Cry" and Ray's performing style are considered important influences on the development of rock and roll later in the decade.

Although not the most commercially successful male duo in history, the group that defined early blue-eyed soul back in the 1960s was the Righteous Brothers. The duo's biggest singles, "You've Lost that Lovin' Feeling" and "Unchained Melody" remain two of the most iconic singles of the 1960s. Several accounts confirm the duo's ties to soul music. One of the leading Brill Building songwriters and one of the cowriters of "You've Lost That Lovin' Feeling," Barry Mann, said of the Righteous Brothers, "They were white but sounded remarkably like the group Sam & Dave" (Myers 2016, 56). The duo's connection to soul music was responsible for Bill Medley and Bobby Hatfield calling themselves the Righteous Brothers in the first place. As Medley recalled in his autobiography, he and Hatfield regularly performed at military bases in their pre-fame days. At one such base, a black soldier responded to their soulful singing by shouting, "That was righteous, brothers" (Medley and Marino 2014, 12–13). This affirmation was the genesis of the duo's name.

Among the Righteous Brothers' most highly must-hear recordings are "You've Lost that Lovin' Feeling," "Soul and Inspiration," and Bobby Hatfield's solo feature, "Unchained Melody." Bill Medley also produced some of the Righteous Brothers' recordings, most notably "Soul and Inspiration" and "Unchained Melody." In Medley's production work, he took inspiration from Phil Spector's famous "wall of sound" style. For his part, Spector's famous production approach is perhaps best exemplified by his work on the Righteous Brothers' recording of "You've Lost that Lovin' Feeling."

The Righteous Brothers' recording of "You've Lost that Lovin' Feeling" is not only widely acknowledged as perhaps the most complete example of Phil Spector's "wall of sound" approach to record production, but the song was a huge commercial success, topping the pop charts and coming within one spot of topping the R&B charts. As evidence of the impact on popular culture of this Righteous Brothers recording, the music licensing agency BMI named "You've Lost that Lovin' Feeling" the most-performed recording of the 20th century on radio and television (BMI 1999). In 2015, the National Recording Preservation Board of the Library of Congress added "You've Lost that Lovin' Feeling" to the National Recording Registry (National Recording Preservation Board of the Library of Congress n.d.), and, in 2011, *Rolling Stone* ranked the Righteous Brothers' recording of "You've Lost that Lovin' Feeling" at No. 34 in the magazine's "500 Greatest Songs of All Time" (*Rolling Stone* 2011).

The Rascals (known as the Young Rascals during the early part of their career) enjoyed several hits during the mid-1960s, but are best-remembered for "Good Lovin'" and "Groovin'." Notably, the band recorded on the well-known soul label, Atlantic, and recorded some of the same songs that became hits for major soul singers. For example, the Rascals recorded both "Mustang Sally" and "Land of 1000 Dances" around the same time as their Atlantic labelmate Wilson Pickett recorded his hit versions of the songs. Although Pickett's single release of "Mustang Sally" became iconic, the Rascals' recording received a significant amount of exposure as the B-side of the band's hit single "Good Lovin'." Band members Eddie Brigati and Felix Cavaliere wrote "People Got to Be Free," which deals with racism in a similar manner as some of the soul songs of the 1960s associated with black artists (e.g., Sam Cooke's "A Change Is Gonna Come"). The band's most successful blue-eyed soul hit, however, was "Groovin'," which hit No. 1 on the pop charts and No. 3 on the R&B charts in 1967. At the time, it was rare for a white rock band to be this successful on the R&B/black music charts. The song, also written by Cavaliere and Brigati, remains a staple of oldies radio in the 21st century and, in 1999, was elected to the Grammy Hall of Fame by the Recording Academy (The Recording Academy n.d.). The album on which the band's most iconic song appeared, also titled *Groovin'*, made it solidly into the top ten of both the pop and R&B album charts in 1967—again, a rare occurrence for the work of a white rock band.

Listening to some of the soul recordings from Memphis, Tennessee; Muscle Shoals, Alabama; and other Southern cities and realizing that some of the studio musicians in the famous studios in those cities were white supports the notions that soul was a sort of musical melting pop and that at least one of the significant features of a major branch of soul was that it was a Southern music that, at times, straddled the line between R&B and country. The blue-eyed soul singer who might best demonstrate this is Lonnie Mack. Mack was a major influence on American blues rock in the 1960s and 1970s as an electric guitarist. His influence and his standing among musicians far exceeded his success as a solo recording artist. In addition to playing guitar, however, Mack was successful in blending influences from country, electric blues, and R&B as a blue-eyed soul vocalist. Even to a greater extent than is the case with his guitar work, Lonnie Mack's soul singing was not hugely commercial successful, nor is it as easy to come by today as the work of numerous other soul singers. Fortunately, platforms such as YouTube make one of Mack's greatest vocals, "Why," accessible, even though the track cannot be found in some popular download platforms and his original vinyl recordings can be hard to come by (see, for example, https://www.youtube.com/watch?v=GJgoZV0qiLE, accessed January 29, 2020).

The duo Daryl Hall and John Oates were perhaps the best representatives of male blue-eyed soul in the 1970s. However, they blurred genre boundary lines, and some of the duo's biggest hits featured solely Daryl Hall on lead vocals. Some of these hits, too, are not necessarily the most soul-influenced recordings that Hall & Oates made. Arguably, one of the most characteristically soul-like hits that Hall & Oates enjoyed was "She's Gone," a song that is significant in how it focuses on the contrasting tone colors of Hall and Oates's shared lead vocals. As was the case with the contrasting tone colors and ranges of the Righteous Brothers' voices a decade before, the depth and force of John Oates's singing in "She's Gone" counterpoints the lightness of Daryl Hall's voice. This is particularly noticeable in live performances of the song that are available at the time of this writing on YouTube, in which the viewer can clearly see which member sings the individual lead vocal lines (see, for example, https://www.youtube.com/watch?v=bnVXIUyshng, accessed January 29, 2020). The duo's ties to the influence of the Righteous Brothers are best heard in Hall & Oates's cover of "You've Lost That Lovin' Feeling," from their album *Voices*.

David Bowie, a performer whose stylistic range included glam rock, acoustic folk, jazz, new wave rock, disco, and grunge, also recorded a body of work in the blue-eyed soul genre. In particular, Bowie's 1975 album, *Young Americans*, incorporated at least some aspects of the Philadelphia soul style that was popular at the time. Bowie's 1976 album *Station to Station* also touched on blue-eyed soul, particularly in the hit song "Golden Years" and in Bowie's cover of Dimitri Tiomkin and Ned Washington's "Wild Is the Wind." Interestingly, although the latter song was first widely associated with Johnny Mathis—a decidedly middle-of-the-road singer—soul pioneer Nina Simone also recorded it back in the 1950s, and Simone's version seems to have been the inspiration for Bowie's recording (Pegg 2011, 278). Bowie's ties to soul and the racially integrated nature of some of his work of the mid-1970s is clearly visible in a live television performance of "Young Americans," available at the time of this writing on YouTube (see, https://www.youtube.com/watch?v=ydLcs4VrjZQ, accessed January 29, 2020). A black, gospel-like chorus and an integrated instrumental ensemble back up Bowie in this Philadelphia soul–inspired piece.

David Bowie was not the only multigenre white male singer to enjoy success as a blue-eyed soul singer in the mid-1970s. Perhaps one of the most memorable such songs of the era was Boz Scaggs's "Lowdown," originally a track on his 1976 album, *Silk Degrees*, and subsequently a single that placed high on both the pop and soul charts. A Grammy Award for Best R&B Song confirmed the song's soul credibility. Although not as commercially successful, Boz Scaggs's earlier 1969 self-titled album mixed country, blues, and blue-eyed soul, with an over-12-minute-long soul-influenced version of Fenton Robinson's blues classic "Loan Me a Dime" being one of the highlights. Scaggs's 1972 album, *My Time*, included a cover of Allen Toussaint's civil rights anthem, "Freedom for the Stallion," another Scaggs recording that demonstrates his ties to the blue-eyed soul genre.

A singer-songwriter who worked with both Steely Dan and the Doobie Brothers, Michael McDonald is also connected to the blue-eyed soul genre. McDonald cowrote the mid-1980s song "Yah Mo B There" with James Ingram, Rod Temperton, and Quincy Jones, all of whom have solid soul credentials. McDonald and Ingram's recording of the song won a Grammy for Best R&B Performance by a Duo or Group with Vocals. McDonald's 2003 album, *Motown*, and his 2004 album, *Motown Two*, both contained iconic songs from Berry Gordy Jr.'s labels, including "I Heard It through the Grapevine," "Signed, Sealed, Delivered I'm Yours," "Ain't Nothing Like the Real Thing," "How Sweet It Is (to Be Loved by You," "Ain't No Mountain High Enough," "I Was Made to Love Her," "Reach Out, I'll Be There," "The Tracks of My Tears," "What's Going On," and others. McDonald's 2008 album, *Soul Speak*, included a much broader repertoire that was not limited to Motown material but still exhibited McDonald's soul-influenced vocal style. McDonald followed these projects up with the 2009 Joe Thomas-directed concert film, *A Tribute to Motown*, which included songs from *Motown* and *Motown Two* and included guest artists such as Toni Braxton, India.Arie, Take 6, and Billy Preston.

British rock singer Rod Stewart has been associated with rock, blues, and mid-20th-century American pop music. Stewart's 2009 album *Soulbook* focused on soul classics, including "It's the Same Old Song," "(Your Love Keeps Lifting Me) Higher and Higher," "The Tracks of My Tears," "Rainy Night in Georgia," "You've Really Got a Hold on Me," and others. Stewart's foray into blue-eyed soul included collaborative contributions from soul artists such as Stevie Wonder, Mary J. Blige, Jennifer Hudson, and Smokey Robinson.

After starting a professional singing career in heavy metal and hard rock, Michael Bolton turned in the direction of pop and R&B covers and enjoyed considerable success doing so in the late 1980s and early 1990s. In addition to new material, Bolton recorded a cover of Otis Redding and Steve Cropper's "(Sittin' on the) Dock of the Bay" in 1987 and a cover of Percy Sledge's "When a Man Loves a Woman" in 1991. Arguably, Bolton's covers demonstrate his work as a soul singer perhaps better than some of his other recordings, and his cover of "When a Man Loves a Woman" was a Grammy winner for Best Male Pop Vocal Performance. Bolton's work resonated particularly well with pop and adult contemporary audiences. However, his 1995 single "Can I Touch You . . . There?" made it onto the adult R&B charts and is another of Bolton's soul must-hear recordings. Michael Bolton's work has not been without controversy. The Isley Brothers sued Bolton over the song "Love Is a Wonderful Thing," claiming that Bolton's song plagiarized the Isley Brothers' song of the same title. After years of litigation, the Isley Brothers won a multimillion-dollar settlement. Despite the damage to Michael Bolton's reputation, his work remains some of the most popular blue-eyed soul of the late 20th century.

BLUE-EYED SOUL: THE WOMEN

The so-called girl groups of the early 1960s played an important role in the soul genre. African American groups such as the Cookies, the Supremes, the Crystals, the Shirelles, Martha and the Vandellas, and others enjoyed considerable chart success and left a legacy of songs that are still heard over a half century after they were first recorded. Perhaps the white female vocal group most closely associated with soul was the Shangri-Las, although it enjoyed only a limited period of commercial success. The group's main hits were "Leader of the Pack," one of the most iconic examples of the so-called "death rock" of the day; "Give Him a Big Kiss"; and "Remember (Walking in the Sand)." The success of these 1964 releases led to the Shangri-Las participating in tours, both with the new British Invasion sensations (e.g., the Beatles) and with established soul artists (e.g., James Brown). After an interview with the Shangri-Las'

Mary Weiss, the *New York Post*'s Larry Getlen wrote, "At a Texas concert venue in the mid-1960s, as James Brown was preparing to headline an all-black soul revue—complete with segregated audience seating—he doubled over laughing when one of his supporting acts showed up." The supporting act was the Shangri-Las, whom Brown had assumed were black based on their sound (Getlen 2014), thus confirming the blue-eyed soul credential their hits gave them. The group's style, the songs of despair that writers provided to them, and even the instrumental and vocal arrangements of songs such as "Remember (Walking in the Sand)" and "I Can Never Go Home Anymore" impacted later generations of female blue-eyed soul artists, particularly Amy Winehouse in songs such as "Back to Black," which is discussed later in this entry.

During the 1960s, the solo singer who perhaps best personified female blue-eyed soul was Dusty Springfield. Because this chapter includes a detailed look at Springfield's 1969 album *Dusty in Memphis*—the best demonstration of her talents as a blue-eyed soul singer—here we will examine several other non-black female vocalists who also carved out niches in the world of soul music.

Technically, Yvonne Elliman might not entirely fit the blue-eyed soul category, as her parents were of Japanese and Irish ancestry; however, Elliman's work in musical theater, film, and as a recording artist exhibit ties to soul. Elliman first came to public attention through her portrayal of Mary Magdalene on Andrew Lloyd Webber and Tim Rice's 1970 concept album *Jesus Christ Superstar*. Elliman then joined the cast of the stage rock-opera version of the show, eventually reprising the role in the 1973 film version. Elliman lent a soulful vocal approach to songs such as "Everything's Alright" and "I Don't Know How to Love Him." Elliman's greatest commercial success, however, came several years later in the disco era, with her recording of the Bee Gees–penned No. 1 pop hit "If I Can't Have You," a song with some stylistic ties to soul because of Elliman's vocal approach.

Elements of blue-eyed soul can be found in the work of Carole King in her late-1960s' band the City and in her solo work of the early 1970s. King's musical connections to soul go back to the early 1960s, when she and her then-husband Gerry Goffin wrote songs for recording artists such as the Cookies, Little Eva, and the Shirelles. When King formed the City, she recorded primarily rock songs; however, the City did record Goffin and King's "That Old Sweet Roll (Hi-De-Ho)," with King on lead vocals. Although the song later became a popular hit for the jazz-rock group Blood, Sweat & Tears, King's singing and piano playing on the City's recording exhibit particularly strong ties to the gospel and soul traditions.

King's best-known contributions to the blue-eyed soul subgenre came from her 1971 album *Tapestry*, which includes her version of "(You Make Me Feel Like) A Natural Woman," a song that King cowrote with Gerry Goffin and Jerry Wexler for Aretha Franklin several years earlier. You can also hear King's gospel-inspired piano playing and singing to good effect on *Tapestry* tracks such as "I Feel the Earth Move," "It's Too Late," and "Way Over Yonder."

Similarly, singer-songwriter Laura Nyro exhibited ties to blue-eyed soul in her recordings of the late 1960s and early 1970s. However, the Nyro compositions that exhibited the strongest connections to the soul tradition and that were the most iconic were significantly more commercially successful in the hands of artists such as the 5th Dimension (e.g., "Wedding Bell Blues," "Save the Country," and "Stoned Soul Picnic"), Three Dog Night (e.g., "Eli's Coming"), and Blood, Sweat & Tears (e.g., "And When I Die"). Despite this, Nyro's 1968 album *Eli and the Thirteenth Confession* is a must-hear collection that includes her solo versions of "Eli's Coming" and "Stoned Soul Picnic."

One of the most tragic figures in 21st-century popular music, British singer-songwriter Amy Winehouse made her musical reputation on two albums that were released during her lifetime: her 2003 debut, *Frank*, and her stellar 2006, multi-Grammy Award-winning album, the 2006 collection, *Back to Black*. Particularly throughout *Back to Black*, as a singer-songwriter, Winehouse successfully integrated elements of hip-hop with that of the African American so-called "girl groups" that were associated with Brill Building producers and songwriters such as Phil Spector, Gerry Goffin, Carole King, and so on, including the Chiffons, the Cookies, and others. In fact, Winehouse's song "Back to Black" is a close musical descendant of Shadow Morton's "Remember (Walking in the Sand)," a song popularized by the blue-eyed soul group the Shangri-Las in 1964.

Like several girl-group songs of the 1960s, not to mention songs in the more standard soul repertoire, "Back to Black" deals with a dysfunctional relationship. Part of what made Amy Winehouse remarkable in her brief career was her ability to connect with the past, with a decidedly edgier hip-hop era lyrical sensibility. For example, in describing her ex-lover's cheating on her, Winehouse says he "kept his d*** wet," and she is also fully upfront in enumerating her and her former lover's drugs of choice.

Arguably, the best-known track on *Back to Black* was "Rehab." Structurally, melodically, and harmonically, "Rehab" suggests a cross between 1960s' soul and British Invasion rock and roll. The connection to British Invasion music comes in the form of the drum rhythm, which includes the snare drum playing on beat two, between beats two and three (the "and" of two), and on four. This pattern can be heard in a fair number of songs in the 1962 to 1965 period, particularly in recordings by Liverpool groups, including the Beatles, Gerry and the Pacemakers, and the Searchers. Also reminiscent of British Invasion rock and roll is Winehouse's harmonic shift and her use of an A-flat major chord in a context that favors E-minor and A-minor harmonies. Songs by groups as diverse as the Beatles, the Kinks, and the Who also feature unusual key changes and the use of chords from outside the prevailing key.

What tends to separate "Rehab" from many earlier songs about addiction in other genres (e.g., Merle Haggard's country songs "Swinging Doors" and "The Bottle Let Me Down") is that Winehouse's character sounds defiant in her rejection of rehab. Another notable feature of "Rehab" is that she somewhat obliquely name checks Ray Charles and Donny Hathaway. These figures and their songs bring meaning to her character's life; therefore, she sees more value in staying at home listening to Charles and "Mr. Hathaway" than in submitting to the medical help she needs. Tragically, the song proved to be autobiographical; Winehouse's addictions led to her death at the age of 27.

Inspired by jazz, soul, and R&B vocalists such as Ella Fitzgerald, Etta James, and Aretha Franklin, the British singer-songwriter Adele Laurie Blue Adkins—known professionally simply as Adele—received early training at the BRIT School for Performing Arts and Technology. Adele first came to the attention of audiences around the world with the 2008 release of her album *19*, her age at the time. Along with Amy Winehouse's 2006 *Back to Black*, these releases represented a rekindling of British blue-eyed soul from female vocalists—a rekindling that, critically and commercially, quickly eclipsed the work of the 1960s' generation of female blue-eyed soul British singers, led by Dusty Springfield.

With subsequent albums including *21* and *25*, as well as non-numerically named collections topping the charts in several countries around the world, Adele is one of the strongest commercial forces in early 21st-century popular music. In addition to her albums, Adele's recording of "Skyfall," a song she coauthored with producer Paul Epworth, served as the theme song for the 2012 James Bond movie of the same name. Writing in *Rolling Stone*, David Ehrlich (2015) ranked Adele's recording of "Skyfall" at No. 4 in his list of the best Bond themes; the Adele song was bested only by Nancy Sinatra's recording of "You Only Live Twice," Paul McCartney and Wings' recording of "Live and Let Die," and Shirley Bassey's recording of "Goldfinger."

Adele's connections to blue-eyed soul abound but might best be experienced through "Skyfall," which brings back the grandeur of the soulful

1960s' and 1970s' Bond theme recordings of Shirley Bassey, and "Hello," "Someone Like You," and "Rolling in the Deep." These songs represent a variety of styles. "Someone Like You" is a relatively quiet ballad with minimalistic piano arpeggios at its core, while "Rolling in the Deep" instantly calls to mind some of the big production soul music of earlier decades. The instrumental arrangement, the backing vocals, Adele's singing style, and elements of the track's production make "Rolling in the Deep" sound almost like an updated version of a cross between classic late-1960s' Aretha Franklin and Stevie Wonder's "I Was Made to Love Her." However, "Rolling in the Deep" does not sound derivative, despite its stylistic references to the style of 1960s' soul.

BOYZ II MEN

Although Boyz II Men continues to record and concertize at the time of this writing, this male vocal group enjoyed its primary period of commercial success in the 1990s. Although the group underwent several personnel changes prior to becoming famous—as well as several more recently—the most iconic lineup was the 1990s-era quartet of Michael McCary, Nathan Morris, Wanya Morris, and Shawn Stockman.

Boyz II Men is notable for several performance practices. During their heyday of the 1990s, they enjoyed considerable pop and R&B chart success with ballads that combined hip-hop rhythms with accompanied harmony and a cappella singing. Their a cappella work connected Boyz II Men to the vocal quartets of the doo-wop era of the 1950s, as well as to the gospel tradition.

Where Boyz II Men differed fundamentally from many of their contemporaries, as well as from many classic pop, soul, and R&B vocal ensembles of the past, was in the emphasis their vocal arrangements gave to shared lead vocal lines. Before Boyz II Men, vocal ensembles such as Temptations (in their most memorable work up to approximately 1968), the Supremes, the Four Seasons, the Cookies, Martha and the Vandellas, the Four Tops, and so on, typically featured single lead singers with the other members backing them up. In contrast, in a typical Boyz II Men performance, one member might sing a line of the verse, with another member singing the next line. In some cases, one member might be the primary lead focus of the verse, with another member singing lead in the chorus or bridge section. The group's official music videos are perhaps the best way to experience this, as the viewer can clearly see who sings lead for what sections of the songs. The 1992 ballad "End of the Road" which not only topped the charts but also broke a record for the longest stay at No. 1, is one particularly good example of both the passing around of lead vocal lines and of the soulful appeal of the group's love songs. (For the official music video see, for example, https://www.youtube.com/watch?v=zDKO6XYXioc, accessed January 29, 2020.) The 1995 single "Water Runs Dry," although not as commercially successful as "End of the Road," also demonstrates the group's smooth style on ballads, as well as the shared lead vocals (for the official music video see, for example, https://www.youtube.com/watch?v=9N9opF-PK5k, accessed January 29, 2020).

One might think of the passing back and forth of lead vocal lines as an extension of the call-and-response structure that soul inherited from gospel and spirituals. In commercial popular soul, however, the arrangements are an expansion of the work of 1960s' artists such as Sam & Dave and the Righteous Brothers, as well as 1970s blue-eyed soul stars Hall & Oates on songs such as "She's Gone." Interplay between the vocalists was common in the work of these duos. The work of the Temptations after approximately 1968 also anticipated the extensive sharing of lead lines that defined Boyz II Men in the 1990s. Although the heavy sharing of lead vocals in large part helped to define the Boyz II Men sound, it became a general part of the boy-band style of the 1990s and early 2000s. By the time of the Backstreet Boys' 1999 hit "I Want It That Way," the Boyz II Men approach had been expanded in other groups to even more equally share lead vocals. The approach had become a standard paradigm for male vocal ensembles.

The approach to vocal arrangements that Boyz II Men popularized was especially important during the late-1990s and early-2000s' heyday of the boy bands that Boyz II Men influenced, because giving more individual exposure to each member could better satisfy fans who might be drawn to one particular singer over the others. To put it another way, the extensive sharing of lead vocals gives prominence to all the singers, as opposed to just a single lead vocalist. This may help to explain the popularity of groups such as NSYNC and the Backstreet Boys among young female fans, the most important fan base for the boy bands that followed the lead of Boyz II Men, as well as why multiple members of these groups were featured on the covers of magazines aimed at teen girls.

In considering the work of Boyz II Men. it is also important to note the contributions of Kenneth Brian Edmonds, professionally known as Babyface. Babyface not only produced some of Boyz II Men's most iconic recordings of the 1990s, he also wrote the hits "Water Runs Dry," "End of the Road," and "I'll Make Love to You," possibly Boyz II Men's most iconic ballads. Arguably, the best-remembered songs Boyz II Men recorded have been romantic ballads, about budding loves, relationships that the singers' characters hope can be mended, and so on. The group did move beyond ballads and recorded material by songwriters other than Babyface; however, the large degree of success of the 1990s ballads essentially defined the group. Apart from a collaboration with Mariah Carey to be discussed shortly, the group's principle contribution are those smooth soulful ballads from the early part of their career.

In addition to the Babyface-penned and produced hits, another must-hear selection for Boyz II Men is the group's 1995 collaboration with Mariah Carey, "One Sweet Day." The single release of this track, which concerns the death of a loved one and the hope of being reunited in heaven, broke the record for most weeks at No. 1 on the charts. Ironically, this record had previously been held by Boyz II Men. Despite beginning life as a solo Mariah Carey project, the recorded arrangement uses the Boyz II Men paradigm of sharing lead vocals, such that the recording really is a collaboration among the five singers. In addition to being a hugely commercially successful recording and a must-hear track for Mariah Carey and Boyz II Men fans, "One Sweet Day" was sung at Princess Diana's memorial service and continued to be part of Carey's repertoire. Arguably, the song works best in the collaborative work represented by the original single release and in concert performances where Carey and Boyz II Men appeared together.

Because of the wide crossover appeal of Boyz II Men, the group redefined what music fans thought of when they heard the name "Motown." In the hands of Boyz II Men, and particularly in the Babyface-penned and -produced material of the 1990s, Motown became a label that was more ballad heavy than it had been in the 1960s to 1980s. Boyz II Men left Motown's owners, Universal, at the start of the 21st century and, to date, have not recaptured the popularity they enjoyed in the early to mid-1990s. However, Boyz II Men returned to Universal in 2007, and their 2007 album of Motown covers, *Motown: A Journey Through Hitsville USA*, provided tuneful takes on old hits by the Temptations, Smokey Robinson and the Miracles, Marvin Gaye, and others. In contrast to their previous albums of the 21st century, *Motown: A Journey Through Hitsville USA* was critically and commercially successful and demonstrated the group's ability to adapt earlier material to their vocal arrangement and performance style.

Boyz II Men reemerged into the spotlight in January 2020 when the group joined host Alicia Keys at the Grammy Awards ceremony to perform "It's So Hard to Say Goodbye to Yesterday" as a tribute to Kobe Bryant, Bryant's daughter Gianna, and seven others who perished in a helicopter crash just prior to the ceremony. The song, originally a minor hit for Motown singer G. C. Cameron back in 1975, topped the R&B charts for Boyz II Men in 1991 when they recorded their version of the song. *Entertainment Tonight* covered the performance and broadcast a report on how the collaborative effort between Keys and the group came together so quickly on the same day as the helicopter crash. The program's report is available on its official YouTube channel at the time of this writing (see https://www.youtube.com/watch?v=ad_FGzNnC0U, accessed January 27, 2020).

Boyz II Men made their mark in the 1990s as a group that focused on romanticism, both in the lyrics of the songs that they recorded and in their performance style. Although the group incorporated some musical materials that clearly identify Boyz II Men as part of the hip-hop age, their smooth harmonies and lyrical themes stood in sharp contrast to the rap-based hip-hop music—particularly the gangsta rap—of the era. The emotions that their 2020 Grammy Awards performance expressed and captured prove that their smooth approach to soul remained effective decades after their first chart successes.

JAMES BROWN: *LIVE AT THE APOLLO*[1]

It is common knowledge that audiences at Harlem's Apollo Theater were among the toughest music critics in the United States. If a performance was not emotionally and musically top-notch, audience members would let the performers know. James Brown was convinced that his live show needed to be captured on record. The Apollo was a natural venue because, as Brown said, "You had to do a good job at the Apollo . . . I knew I needed everything to be perfect. We practiced for weeks every time we went in there" (Leeds 2004). Because the head of King Records, Syd Nathan, initially refused to honor Brown's request for a live album, Brown funded the recording of an October 24, 1962, appearance at the famed theater. As Jon Hartley Fox writes in his history of the record label, "When Nathan realized that Brown was actually going ahead with the idea at his own expense, he committed King to the project" (Fox 2009, 167). In 1963, King Records issued the recording, which eventually reached No. 2 on the pop charts and surprisingly—for a live album—generated significant radio airplay. More recent digital reissues have used the original unmixed master tapes (long thought to have been lost) as source material. This is important in considering *Live at the Apollo*, because Syd Nathan added overdubbed audience reactions to the masters for the original 1963 vinyl release.

After emcee and organist Lucas "Fats" Gonder introduces Brown, and Brown's band, the Famous Flames, the ensemble launches into a truncated version of Brown's composition "The Scratch." The brief instrumental hints at the excitement of the show to come and demonstrates just how rhythmically tight the band was. Producer Brown and location engineer Tom Nolo used close microphone placement on the horns and achieved a relatively dry sound overall. This meant that any ensemble flaws were not masked by room reverberation or with electronic reverberation; however, the band is so tight throughout the album that the production style highlights precision.

Although the audience sounds are not intrusive in the reissue's remix, audience members can still be heard, and they erupt when Brown enters the stage, as well as when he starts some of his big hits. The first song proper is "I'll Go Crazy," which was a hit for Brown back in 1960. Like most of Brown's other hits that are represented on this album, this is a truncated version. The inclusion of so many shortened versions of well-known songs—including a medley of nine songs that lasts less than seven minutes—makes it a punchy album. It also helps to put into perspective how many hits James Brown produced early in his career; these are just his pre-1963 songs.

Brown introduces "I'll Go Crazy" with his familiar "You know, I feel alright" Pentecostal preacher–style exhortations. The separation of the instruments—drums, organ, brass section, bass—in the mix brings out one reason Brown's ensemble was such an engaging live group: each individual or subgroup plays its own rhythmic role (steady eighth notes on the organ, heavy backbeat on the drums, a quarter-note walking bass line, punctuations in the horn section, and backing vocal harmony). It is a multilayered approach in which each component is clear, concise, and simple. Taken as a whole, this provides a truly interesting and infectious complex of polyrhythms, all in support of Brown's emotional lead vocal line.

The next song, "Try Me," finds Brown looking even further into his past catalog: the song was a hit in 1958. The audience screams make it clear, however, that even four years later, Brown's fans still loved this ballad. Structurally, the song is typical of late-1950s doo-wop and is even built around the so-called oldies chord progression (I-vi-IV-V). What makes the Apollo performance—as well as the original single from 1958—transcend a fairly standard late-1950s' period piece is the sincerity with which Brown sings. His pleas sound heartfelt and honest, without ever going over the top.

A 10-second instrumental interlude separates "Try Me" and the next song, "Think" (a 1960 pop and R&B chart hit, not to be confused with the later Aretha Franklin hit of the same name). The interludes on *Live at the Apollo* play a far more important role than their brevity suggests: they make it clear that the album is about—as the cover art states—"The James Brown Show." James Brown's performance is not just about singing past and current hits and engaging in a little repartee with the crowd in between songs. Brown's "Show" was a carefully choreographed composite event.

A fresh listen to the next track, "Think," suggests that regardless of how innovative James Brown was—redefining soul music, writing and recording songs that topped the charts and influenced both other American artists and British Invasion bands, being one of the earliest mainstream artists to take up the Black Power cause, and so on—he used certain stylistic signifiers at various points of his career. "Think" finds the horn section punctuating the end of each statement of the refrain with the famous ninth chord that also figured prominently in the arrangements of other Brown classics, perhaps most notably "Papa's Got a Brand New Bag," a song that had not yet appeared at the time of the Apollo recording.

One of the highlights of *Live at the Apollo* is the nearly 11-minute-long performance of "Lost Someone." Harmonically, the piece is based primarily on an oscillation between two chords, tonic and subdominant. In the extended middle section of the piece, when Brown pleads, expresses his heartache, and gets the audience involved with screamed "Yeahs," the horn section incorporates minor variations on their answering figures—just enough that the listener is never completely sure when they occur or in what subtle ways the figures will be varied. It is one of the reasons that the piece keeps the listener's attention, despite being deprived of the visual aspect of the performance as well as the collective feel from a crowd of 1,500 audience members. For his part, Brown tells his story like a preacher, with one phrase repeated with variations leading into another, all the while maintaining an ebb and flow to the emotional intensity, until the audience is about at the breaking point. The track—and the entire flow of the album, for that matter—is an excellent aural introduction to how James Brown worked a crowd perhaps better than any other performer of the late 20th century. The track is also as good an introduction as there is to the close ties between the sacred gospel genre and the secular soul genre. This track also highlights—particularly because of its length, the sometimes inexplicable crowd reactions, and because Brown seems to move off microphone from time to time—is the extent to which listening to *Live at the Apollo* is a little like listening to old pretelevision-era radio programs. There is so much going on besides a run-through of greatest hits that using one's imagination allows the listener to create visual cues. In that respect, experiencing *Live at the Apollo* as an album can be a richer experience than watching concert footage on video or DVD.

After Brown stretches his audience nearly to the breaking point of anticipation with the lengthy "Lost Someone," he comes back with a quick-hitting medley of hits, eight different songs (with short versions of "Please, Please, Please" forming the opening and closing bookends) in approximately six and a half minutes. The punchiness of the medley format serves to highlight how many memorable classics Brown had recorded up to that time. To the fan of Top 40 music of the late 1950s and early 1960s, some of the songs might not be familiar, but soul fans know them all—as, obviously, did Brown's audience at the Apollo on that October 1962 night.

The final track on the original vinyl release, "Night Train," was a more recently recorded hit. Although it is not an original James Brown composition, he put his personal stamp on it, especially as performed at the Apollo. The performance features Brown's band to a greater extent than most of the other songs on the album. Brown's arrangement and performance essentially deconstructs "Night Train," stripping it down to the barest essentials and making it a groove piece that points the way to the extended funk pieces that would define Brown's work of the late 1960s and the 1970s.

The CD reissue of *Live at the Apollo* (Leeds 2004) includes alternate mixes of "Think," part of the medley of previous Brown hits, "Lost Someone," and "I'll Go Crazy." Although the increased loudness of the audience reactions on these mixes adds some superficial excitement, it tends to dominate the real stuff that one buys this album for: the raw excitement and truly exceptional musicianship of James Brown and his backing ensemble.

Since 1962, there may have been better-recorded live albums—certainly later technology improved over what was possible in the early 1960s—but James Brown's *Live at the Apollo* continues to stand as a testament to one of greatest live performers in the history of American popular music.

JAMES BROWN: TWO MID-60S HITS: "I GOT YOU (I FEEL GOOD)" AND "PAPA'S GOT A BRAND NEW BAG"

Two of what are arguably James Brown's most persistent hits dated from right in the middle of the 1960s: "I Got You (I Feel Good)" and "Papa's Got a Brand New Bag." Both were popular singles, and both still receive airplay on oldies radio well over a half-century after their release. In terms of their standing within the soul repertoire, at least one popular music-appreciation book (see, for example, Ferris 2014) examines "Papa's Got a Brand New Bag" as the textbook's sole example of soul music. Although Brown's recordings going back to the 1950s were hits on the R&B charts, and although his work in the late 1960s and 1970s helped define funk and took on timely social issues, "I Got You (I Feel Good)" and "Papa's Got a Brand New Bag" brought him to or near the top of both the R&B and pop charts and established him with a significantly wider audience than his other work. In addition, "Papa's Got a Brand New Bag" won Brown his first Grammy Award, for Best Rhythm and Blues Recording.

"Papa's Got a Brand New Bag" is part of an era when new dance crazes seemed to appear on the scene every day. The Twist might have been the most famous, but there were numerous others, including the Watusi, the Swim, the Dog, and so on. The concept of new dance crazes was such that Brill Building songwriters Gerry Goffin and Carole King penned "The Loco-Motion" about a new dance craze that did not even exist at the time of the song's release. By all accounts, the dance moves described in "The Loco-Motion" were inspired by Little Eva, Goffin and King's babysitter, who sang lead on the famous recording of the song. In this era of well-defined new dances, Brown creates a scenario in which an older man (the "Papa" of the title) takes to the dance floor, unexpectedly grooving to several of the recent trendy dances.

Brown name checks the Fly, a dance associated with Chubby Checker's 1961 recording of the same name; the Monkey, popularized in Major Lance's 1963 recording "The Monkey Time"; and the Mashed Potato, another early 1960s craze based, in part, on Brown's own dance moves of the late 1950s. He also released "(Do the) Mashed Potatoes" pseudonymously in 1960 and, in 1962, released "Mashed Potatoes U.S.A." As a side note, there were several other Mashed Potatoes–related songs making the rounds in 1962, including Dee Dee Sharp's recording of "Mashed Potatoes Time."

Brown's "Papa's Got a Brand New Bag" can be read in multiple ways, depending on the interpretation of Papa's choice of dances. On one hand, Papa seems to be conversant with dance moves that were in vogue closer to the present (1965) than to the days of his youth. In this interpretation of the scenario, Papa would seem to be, in Brown's words, "hip." However, because Papa was conversant with these styles several years *after* their initial popularity—and, some of these were short-lived crazes quickly superseded by new dances—and because dancing in discotheques was becoming more free form as the 1960s wore on, Papa can also be understood as perhaps desperately trying to be "hip," but not quite hitting the mark.

On the other hand, a recording such as "Papa's Got a Brand New Bag" can be understood as being more about the overall experience—the arrangement, the performance style, the recording mix, and so on—than about the lyrics themselves. Understood in this way, "Papa's Got a Brand New Bag" might be one of the best examples of how composer, guitarist, singer Frank Zappa defined musical compositions in the recording age when he wrote:

> On a record, the overall timbre of the piece (determined by equalization of individual parts and their proportions in the mix) tells you, in a subtle way, WHAT the song is about. The orchestration provides *important information* about what the composition IS and, in some instances, assumes a greater importance than *the composition itself* [Italics and capitalizations from the original]. (Zappa and Occhiogrosso 1989, 188)

"Papa's Got a Brand New Bag" is instantly recognizable from the opening horn-section chord. The jangling electric guitar figure that immediately follows the title line every time Brown sings it and the recurring horn-section figure that answers each brief line of Brown's singing are other examples of the recording's strong instrumental hooks. In short, one could argue that changing or removing any of these components would create something that is not really "Papa's Got a Brand New Bag." It might be close, but it would not be what we know as the piece.

The crucial nature of record production in defining what the listening public understands as a full representation of a song that Zappa described is easily apparent for another reason in "Papa's Got a Brand New Bag" and the recording's enduring popularity and influence. Polydor's 1991 CD box set of Brown's recordings between 1956 and 1984, *Star Time*, contains the original studio recording of "Papa's Got a Brand New Bag." The recording begins with a small amount of studio chatter before Brown says, "This is a hit," and kicks of the song. Rather than the music starting with the familiar horn-section blast, it opens with a brief drum lead-in. The recording is also nearly seven minutes long and includes more sung material and a more extensive saxophone solo than the later well-known single release. In addition to editing out a few seconds of Brown speaking, the drum lead-in at the opening, and some of the middle of the original recording, the piece was sped up so that the key of the single was approximately a half-step higher than that of the original recording. All this made the single punchier, more focused, and more energetic than what James Brown and the JB's had put on tape in the studio. It led to the definitive version of the song.

Although the lyrics of "Papa's Got a Brand New Bag" might be open to interpretation, or misinterpretation, the lyrics of Brown's "I Got You (I Feel Good)" are more straightforward. However, as is the case with "Papa's Got a Brand New Bag," the title line basically sums up the song's theme. This is an up-tempo love song, with strong melodic and instrumental hooks (e.g., the brief, simple, but infinitely memorable alto-saxophone break). The form of "I Got You (I Feel Good)" represents an interesting hybrid of 12-bar blues and standard pop song, as the verses are in blues form, but the song contains a bridge section (the "when I hold you in my arms" part of the piece) that starts on the subdominant chord (IV) and ventures outside the 12-bar blues structure. As is the case with so many of Brown's hits, including songs as musically diverse as "Please, Please, Please," "It's a Man's Man's Man's World," and "Say It Loud—I'm Black and I'm Proud," the musical setting enhances the meaning of the lyrics.

Although the story of "Papa's Got a Brand New Bag" revolves around studio editing, the history of "I Got You (I Feel Good)" is also interesting. The song seems to have started out as "I Found You," a Brown composition recorded in 1962 by Yvonne Fair and the James Brown Band. Although this recording is obscure, at the time of this writing, it can be heard on several YouTube channels (see, for example, https://www.youtube.com/watch?v=ucSdbuccFJc, accessed January 29, 2020). Yvonne Fair includes some shouts in the song, but her recording does not exhibit the same degree of believable soulfulness as Brown's version. In considering Brown's slight lyrical changes to his composition—from "I found you" to "I got you"—it is also interesting to note that Brown first recorded the revised song on his 1964 album *Out of Sight*. For contractual reasons, *Out of Sight* listed the songwriter as Ted Wright, a pseudonym used by Brown. The horn riff is more focused on repeated notes in the album version, the rhythm section is considerably lighter, and Brown's voice does not exhibit quite as high a level of intensity. So, once again, as suggested by Frank Zappa's definition of what defines a song in the recording era, the revised instrumental arrangement, the greater prominence of the rhythm section, and the way in which Brown's lead vocals were recorded turned the 1965 version of "I Got You (I Feel Good)" into a fundamentally different—and more soulful—piece than either of its earlier incarnations.

The importance of these two 1965 singles in bringing Brown to the cannot be overstated, as they, more than any of Brown's earlier R&B

hits brought Brown's highly charged brand of soul to a nationwide audience that crossed racial lines. "I Got You (I Feel Good)" became James Brown's highest charting pop hit, and, like several of his other singles from the 1950s and 1960s, including "Papa's Got a Brand New Bag," it topped the R&B charts.

The quality and popular culture significance of these two James Brown singles was confirmed in *Rolling Stone* magazine's 2011 list of "500 Greatest Songs of All Time," in which "I Got You (I Feel Good)" was ranked No. 78, and "Papa's Got a Brand New Bag" was at No. 71 (*Rolling Stone* 2011).

MARIAH CAREY[2]

Reputed to have been the best-selling female artist of the 1990s and quite possibly of all time (Ankeny n.d.-b), Mariah Carey also has one of the most unusual vocal instruments in the history of the recording industry, with an exceptionally wide pitch range extended by her use of what many call a "whistle register." Despite her fame for the use of this register, however, Mariah Carey was not the first soul singer to use it; it was one of Minnie Riperton's vocal signatures during her brief career in the 1970s. As was the case with Riperton, the extremely high coloratura soprano register with the whistle register is something of a signature for Carey; however, she has proven herself to be anything but a one-dimensional singer. Although Carey is perhaps best considered a soul/R&B singer, she has enjoyed unprecedented success on the pop singles charts for a solo artist.

Carey first came to the attention of the public in 1990 with her self-titled debut album and the commercially successful singles that it spawned. *Mariah Carey* eventually hit No. 1 on the album charts, and "Vision of Love," "Love Takes Time," "Someday," and "I Don't Know" all made it to No. 1 on the pop charts. The album and its singles also met with critical approval: Carey won Grammy Awards for Best New Artist and Best Pop Vocal Performance (for "Vision of Love"). Notably, Carey cowrote all the songs on the album. As a female R&B/soul singer who focused on her own material, she helped set the stage for artists such as Beyoncé, Adele, Amy Winehouse, and others. The hits on Carey's debut album (e.g., "Vision of Love") helped establish her as a singer whose work was marked by the extensive use of improvisatory melismas, the use of several successive pitches on any given syllable. This stylistic trait can be traced back to the black gospel tradition through predecessors such as Whitney Houston and Aretha Franklin.

Carey's 1995 album *Daydream* is notable for the even greater commercial and chart success of its singles. Although "Fantasy" is a must-hear Carey track, "One Sweet Day" is perhaps her most notable mid-1990s song. This collaboration with the soul vocal group Boyz II Men, in fact, remained at the top of the singles charts for 16 weeks, a record at the time. The song was a true collaborative effort, with Boyz II Men and Carey contributing to the writing of the song and with lead vocal lines passed between Carey and members of Boyz II Men. The song's lyrical theme of being reunited with a deceased loved one in heaven in the afterlife connects "One Sweet Day" to some early soul music (e.g., some of the work of the Staple Singers) that straddled the fence between gospel and soul, or, to put it another way, between the sacred and the secular.

As hip-hop culture and musical style became more thoroughly integrated into black popular music through the 1990s and into the early 2000s, Carey's music reflected the changes. Mariah Carey's albums such as the 2005 collection *The Emancipation of Mimi* include the rhythmic elements of hip-hop and the paradigm of "featuring" various artists on individual tracks that seemed to be almost a requisite part of rap and hip-hop recordings. "Shake It Off" (not to be confused with the perhaps better-known Taylor Swift song of the same name), a No. 2 pop hit for Carey, is one of her more successful songs that integrated elements of hip-hop rhythmic and production style.

"Shake It Off" also serves as a suitable introduction into the lyrical themes typically used by Carey: her best-known songs focus on male-female romantic relationships. Within this milieu, however, the specific circumstances run the gamut from new loves, cheating partners, and so on. Arguably, Mariah Carey's songs are as obviously filled with lyrical, accompaniment, or melodic hooks as some of her predecessors, contemporaries, or singers who have followed her. However, Carey's voice itself drives the songs more than the arrangement, production, melody, harmony, or other aspects of the recorded song.

Carey's vocal style has influenced other singers. Writing in *The Philippine Star* in advance of a 2014 Carey performance in Manila, entertainment columnist Rosalinda L. Orosa listed artists whose singing style suggest Mariah Carey's influence, as well as those who have credited Carey with influencing their style. The list includes Beyoncé, Kelly Clarkson, Ariana Grande, Christiana Aguilera, Rihanna, and others (Orosa 2014). Carey's influence on 21st-century singers appears to be more pervasive than that list suggests. This pervasiveness, however, is not always viewed in a favorable light. For example, in a feature report about the tendency for female performers on *American Idol* to overuse dramatic, virtuosic melismas, National Public Radio's Mike Katzif interviewed gospel music expert Anthony Heilbut on the use of improvisatory melismas and the technique's transition from the black church into popular secular music. According to Heilbut, the main problem with the use of the technique by contestants is that "often, there isn't any musical justification of what they are doing. [Their flourishes] interfere with the flow of the melody, of the lyric, or the harmonies, sometimes of the rhythm itself. It's frequently a very vulgar and ugly display. [That is] the style of *American Idol* singer, most of whom are amateurs. [They] are simply mimicking the devices of the style's most famous practitioners—singers like Mariah Carey, who indulge in runs" (Katzif 2007). The use of the word "indulge" suggests that Heilbut did not mean the remark to be particularly complimentary to Carey.

One of the challenges for fans looking for a list of must-hear tracks is that Carey is a prolific artist, and several of her recordings from the 1990s through the present have been hits. Fortunately, Columbia Records has issued several greatest-hits-type collections. Any of these, or virtually any combination of her nearly 20 No.1 pop singles, can provide a representation of Carey's style and the reasons behind her commercial appeal.

Although Mariah Carey's primary impact on the R&B and pop charts came in the 1990s, she has continued to tour, record, and be part of popular culture. To a large extent, she has been successful; however, Carey's performance at the December 31, 2016, *Dick Clark's New Year's Rockin' Eve with Ryan Seacrest* show made headlines for all the wrong reasons. Carey barely sang during what was supposed to be a three-song set, because, apparently, she could not hear the backing instrumental track through her earpiece. Perhaps most damaging to her reputation as a vocal virtuoso, however, was that viewers of the television program could tell that the whistle tones were on the prerecorded backing track and not performed live. The incident created a great deal of controversy for a time in early 2017, with Carey claiming that Dick Clark Productions had sabotaged her performance. Fortunately for Carey, she was booked for the December 31, 2017, *New Year's Rockin' Eve* show, and her performance was a success, despite a minor controversy that arose over requested hot tea not being available for her. The tea incident illustrated how firmly ensconced Mariah Carey is in American popular culture, as it generated numerous social-media/internet memes. (For press coverage of the early 2018 memes, see, for example, Lang 2018.)

Also significant for Carey, in late 2017, for the first time, her 1994 recording "All I Want for Christmas Is You" made the Top 10 singles chart. Interestingly, despite it taking over 20 years for the seasonal single to place that high in the charts, "All I Want for Christmas Is You" is reputed to be one of the best-selling singles of all time. Mariah Carey's continuing relevance and popularity over a quarter century after her recording debut were confirmed in October 2019 by a report that Carey's recording of "All I Want for Christmas Is You" had reentered iTunes top downloads chart. The song set a record Christmas Eve 2018 on Spotify for the most downloads on a single day (Harvey 2019). Finally, on December 16, 2019, CNN reported that *Billboard* tweeted that "All I Want for Christmas Is You" hit No. 1 on the magazine's singles chart for the first time (Garvey 2019).

RAY CHARLES: "I GOT A WOMAN"

Several of Ray Charles's hits from the 1950s mixed sacred and secular influences and played significant roles in defining what soul music was all about. These songs also helped define rock and roll and other rock musicians took them up for years after Charles first recorded them. Audiences did not necessarily readily accept the mixing of gospel and R&B—or the sacred and the secular.

The 2004 Taylor Hackford biopic film, *Ray*, suggests that "Hallelujah, I Love Her So" caused dissention among conservative music fans who did not approve of gospel being secularized. In actuality, the principal mixture of the sacred and secular in this song arises with the song itself being a celebration of romantic love that includes the word "hallelujah" as an exclamation, something generally reserved for sacred music. In the film, a couple of conservative churchgoers interrupt Charles's band in the middle of the song, declaring that Charles and his musicians will be damned to hell for secularizing gospel music.

In terms of taking sacred material out of the black church and putting it into an entirely secular setting, however, "This Little Girl of Mine" and "I Got a Woman" are, perhaps, better examples of Charles's secularization of gospel music. In fact, "I Got a Woman" might be considered the first widely commercially successful soul song, a merger of gospel and R&B. "This Little Girl of Mine" is based on the Harry Dixon Loes song "This Little Light of Mine." As suggested by the similarity of the two titles, Charles retained some of the lyrical structure and the actual lyrics of the original sacred song.

The connection between "I Got a Woman" and its source material is a bit more complicated. Even a casual listen to the Southern Tones' recording of the Bob King composition "It Must Be Jesus," available at the time of this writing on several YouTube channels (see, for example, https://www.youtube.com/watch?v=mDoEhA6jh6I, accessed January 15, 2020), demonstrates that the Ray Charles-Renald Richard song "I Got a Woman" is largely based on the music and form of the King piece. The only significant differences in the melody and melodic rhythm occur because of different numbers of syllables in some of the lines. The lyrics of the two songs, however, are entirely different. About the only lyrical connection between the two is that each song focused on one individual: Jesus of Nazareth in the gospel song and the woman "way over town, that's good to me" in the Ray Charles-Renald Richard song. Interestingly, the Kennedy Center, from which Charles received the Kennedy Center Honors from U.S. president Ronald Reagan in 1986, includes a biography of Charles on its website that identifies Charles and Richard's source material as "My Jesus is All the World to Me" (*The Kennedy Center Website* n.d.), a gospel song that actually has little in common with "I Got a Woman," especially compared with "It Must Be Jesus."

Although the structure, melody, rhythm, and harmonic progression of "It Must Be Jesus" are shared by "I Got a Woman," the performance styles are not. The Charles-Richard song is significantly more energetic, thus representing its ties to the commercial R&B of its time. It is infinitely danceable, which may, in part, explain the success of Charles's recording of "I Got a Woman." The danceability, the energy, and the simple structure of the song perhaps contributed to "I Got a Woman" being a frequently covered song. During the heyday of Beatlemania in Great Britain, the Beatles recorded the song for BBC radio programs in 1963 and 1964. The extensive list of other artists who either recorded "I Got a Woman" or included the song in their concert repertoire includes Elvis Presley, the Everly Brothers, Roy Orbison, Bill Haley & His Comets, and numerous others. I highlight these performers because of their significance in helping define white rock and roll and rockabilly in the 1950s and into the early 1960s.

Although perhaps not as iconic as Charles's recording of "Georgia on My Mind" or his recording of his own "What'd I Say" (profiled in this chapter), "I Got a Woman, nevertheless, received honors over the years. For example, in 2011, *Rolling Stone* ranked the song at No. 239 in the magazine's list of "500 Greatest Songs of All Time."

"I Got a Woman" also lived on in the 21st century as a sample for Kanye West's 2005 song, "Gold Digger." The West song featured Jamie Foxx singing the Ray Charles song, reprising a role that Foxx played in the Charles biopic *Ray*. West's "Gold Digger" appeared on the album *Late Registration* and was also a hit single, reaching No. 1 on the pop and R&B charts.

RAY CHARLES: "WHAT'D I SAY"

Arguably, two of the best-known and most persistent call-and-response songs of the rock era both date from 1959: the Isley Brothers' "Shout" and Ray Charles's "What'd I Say." "What'd I Say," sometimes given as "What I Say," is one of those classic songs with an apocryphal story concerning its genesis. Whether or not the story portrayed in the biopic *Ray* or as told by Charles in his autobiography (Charles and Ritz 2004, 190–191) is entirely historically correct, the popular account of the genesis of "What'd I Say" is that Charles and his band improvised it when they were playing a dance gig and contractually had more time to go after they had completed the set list. Soon after, Charles recorded the song pretty much as it had allegedly come into being in the club. If the genesis of the song was not enough to make it a historically important work, then its long-range popularity and it becoming a widely covered example of 1950s' rock and roll cemented this as one of Charles's signature pieces.

Atlantic Records released "What'd I Say" edited down and split between the two sides of a 45-rpm single. The song eventually topped the R&B charts and made it solidly into the Top 10 of the pop charts; however, it was not an immediate smash hit. It appears that part of the reason for the single's slow takeoff was that some radio stations initially refused to play it. In particular, the moans that Charles traded back and forth with his backing vocalists, the Raelettes, were considered too sexually suggestive. Two-sided singles, too, were something of a rarity and were not necessarily conducive to the popular AM radio format of the day.

That give and take, or call and response, between Charles and the Raelettes, though, is one aspect of "What'd I Say" that helps define the song's connections to gospel music. The lyrical content (e.g., "she knows how to shake that thing") and the sexually suggestive moans might be anything but sacred, but the call and response, as frenetic as it is, remains a clear tie to the gospel tradition. So, this is a song that clearly has its feet planted squarely in both camps: the sacred and the secular.

"What'd I Say" was also an important part of the rock and roll repertoire, particularly in the late 1950s and early 1960s. Rock and roll artists of the 1950s, such as Roy Orbison, Jerry Lee Lewis, Elvis Presley, and others, covered Charles's call-and-response classic. Later, Liverpool, England, bands associated with the British Invasion, including the Searchers, the Big Three, the Beatles, and Gerry and the Pacemakers, included "What'd I Say" in their live sets and/or commercially recorded the song. The range of artists who covered the song, though, is even wider than this list suggests. For example, Clifton Chenier, arguably the most important and most legendary artist in the Zydeco genre, also covered "What'd I Say."

"What'd I Say" became firmly ensconced in popular culture and was one of Ray Charles's signature works throughout the rest of his lengthy career. As just one example of the iconic nature of the song in American popular culture, consider the November 12, 1977, episode of NBC's *Saturday Night Live*, which Charles hosted. Cast members and comedians Dan Aykroyd, John Belushi, Jane Curtin, Bill Murray, Laraine Newman, and Gilda Radner portrayed a fictional late-1950s singing group called the Young Caucasians. In the sketch, the group meets Charles with enthusiasm and sings their version of what they pronounce as "What Did I Say." Incidentally, in another *Saturday Night Live* episode, John Belushi, dressed as classical composer Ludwig van Beethoven, snorts cocaine, and then proceeds to don sunglasses and start playing and singing the beginning of "What'd I Say."

This soul and iconic rock and roll recording was added to the Library of Congress' National Recording Registry in 2002 (National Recording Preservation Board of the Library of Congress n.d.). In the magazine's list of "500 Greatest Songs of All Time," the editors of *Rolling Stone* ranked "What'd I Say" at No. 10 (*Rolling Stone* 2011), marking it as one of the greatest recordings of the rock era.

THE COMMODORES AND LIONEL RICHIE

Unfortunately, some music fans might overlook the Commodores and singer-songwriter Lionel Richie when compiling a list of the most commercially successful artists of the 1970s and 1980s. After all, the world of the 1970s included disco, funk, punk rock, and new wave, all of which generated significant sales and attention from the listening public. The 1980s also seemed to be dominated by, among others, the "King of Pop," Michael Jackson, Madonna, and others whose work lent itself to the medium of the music video. Throughout this period, however, the Commodores and their lead singer, songwriter, and saxophone player, Lionel Richie, scored hit after hit as a group and then during Richie's subsequent solo career, incorporating funk, easygoing soul, and pop along the way. Through his songwriting work with the Commodores and later as a solo artist, Richie was one of the most commercially successful composers of the period.

During the Lionel Richie years, the commercial impact of the Commodores can be seen in the fact that between 1976 and 1979, four

Commodores albums in a row (*Hot on the Tracks*, *Commodores*, *Natural High*, and *Midnight Magic*) topped the R&B charts, and between 1975 and 1979, the songs "Slippery When Wet," "Just to Be Close to You," "Easy," "Three Times a Lady," and "Still" all topped the R&B singles charts. Significantly, Lionel Richie authored the latter three songs; Commodores guitarist Thomas McClary wrote "Slippery When Wet." Another widely known and well-remembered Commodores song from the 1970s was "Brick House," which is credited to the group. The Commodores' drummer, Walter "Clyde" Orange, sang lead on "Brick House," which, although not a chart topper, has been used in the soundtrack of several Hollywood films and television programs and is still considered a classic example of 1970s' funk.

After Lionel Richie left the Commodores for a solo career, the band continued and enjoyed another chart-topping hit in 1985 with "Nightshift," written by Walter Orange, Dennis Lambert, and Franne Golde. The song's lyrics pay tribute to soul singers Marvin Gaye and Jackie Wilson, both of whom died in 1984. Orange and Richie's replacement, J. D. Nicholas, trade lead vocals on the song, which includes lyrical and brief musical references to songs associated with Gaye and Wilson.

Lionel Richie's solo career got off to an auspicious start with "Endless Love," a Richie-written duet with Diana Ross that topped the R&B and pop charts. The impact of the song was confirmed in a special 2011 Valentine's Day list of "The 40 Biggest Duets of All Time" in *Billboard* magazine; "Endless Love" topped the list. The magazine's editors identified "Endless Love" as the biggest No. 1 hit for either artist and cited the fact that the song remained on the charts for 27 weeks as extraordinary (*Billboard* 2011).

Between 1982 and 1986, Richie continued to enjoy significant chart success with "Truly," which topped the pop charts and rose to No. 2 on the R&B charts; "You Are" and "My Love," which topped the adult contemporary charts; "All Night Long (All Night)," which topped the pop and R&B charts; "Hello," a No. 1 adult contemporary, pop, and R&B hit; "Stuck on You," "Penny Love," "Love Will Conquer All," and "Ballerina Girl," all of which topped the adult contemporary charts; and "Say You, Say Me," which topped the adult contemporary, pop, and R&B charts.

In addition to this impressive list, in 1985, Richie cowrote "We Are the World" with Michael Jackson. The recording of "We Are the World" included a veritable who's who of solo singers, including Richie, Jackson, Stevie Wonder, Cyndi Lauper, Bruce Springsteen, Paul Simon, Al Jarreau, James Ingram, Huey Lewis, Kim Carnes, Daryl Hall, Dionne Warwick,

Willie Nelson, Tina Turner, Kenny Rogers, Kenny Loggins, Billy Joel, Ray Charles, Diana Ross, Steve Perry, and Bob Dylan, all billed as USA for Africa. By 2006, the song had helped raise over $60 million for short-term famine relief and for long-term future famine avoidance in Ethiopia and other African countries (*USA Today* 2006). The commercial success of "We Are the World" was such that the bulk of that total was raised within a year of the 1985 release of the single. "We Are the World" also won multiple Grammy Awards and is still considered one of the greatest charity recordings of all time.

Although the solo career of Lionel Richie reached its zenith at the midpoint of the 1980s, he returned to the top of the R&B charts in 1992 with "Do It to Me." He wrote the song, as was the case with all of his hit ballad recordings. Despite Lionel Richie's commercial success as the one-time lead singer of the Commodores and as a duet and solo singer, he is perhaps best remembered as a songwriter. In large part, this is because so many of his compositions have become standards. Because of his contributions as a composer and lyricist, the Songwriters Hall of Fame presented Richie with the prestigious Johnny Mercer Award in 2016.

Perhaps one of the most interesting aspects of Lionel Richie's approach to soul is that he was so successful as both a singer and songwriter on the R&B, pop, and adult contemporary charts. It would be difficult to identify another artist who was as successful on the three charts. Certainly, Michael Jackson dominated the pop and R&B charts for a time, as have subsequent artists such as Mariah Carey. Carey, too enjoyed several triple-chart crossover hits; however, those were primarily in the first several years of her recording career, before her music became more dance oriented. Richie's success on all three charts in the 1970s and 1980s suggests the extent to which his romantic soul ballads crossed over demographic lines, appealing to black and white listeners and younger and older listeners. The best remembered of his songs, too, tend toward optimism, even in a song about a broken relationship, such as the Commodores' hit "Easy." Richie is not one dimensional as a singer-songwriter. For example, a song such as "All Night Long (All Night)," which is part ballad and part dance tune, incorporated Afro-Caribbean influences in the musical setting as well as in Richie's vocal approach. On the other hand, Richie has also integrated American country music into other songs, thus demonstrating his range as a songwriter.

Although part of the crossover appeal of Richie's brand of soul is the melodic nature of his compositions and his focused lyrical messages—generally revolving around near-universal feelings and emotions—Richie's singing style is also part of the equation. Generally, he sings with a gentle, engaging expression. His voice does not take a great deal of getting used to. There is a soulfulness to some extemporization; however, Richie's improvisations on the song's basic melody tend to be restrained. That Richie appears to be genuinely enjoying singing his songs in his official music videos probably also adds to the appeal of his music.

Because Lionel Richie wrote so many of the Commodores most successful hits, and because several of Lionel Richie greatest-hits-type collections include not only his solo hits but also the Richie-composed songs that topped or came close to topping the various charts for the Commodores, these collections can form a solid basis for a Commodores and Lionel Richie must-hear body of music. Add to one of those collections USA for Africa's "We Are the World" and the Commodores' "Brick House" and "Nightshift," and both the group and its one-time lead singer would be fully represented.

SAM COOKE: *AIN'T THAT GOOD NEWS*

It is possible to engage in a considerable amount of discussion about what the most important and iconic parts of Sam Cooke's career were. Certainly, his early work with the Soul Stirrers and his early solo recordings were important in bridging the gap between gospel and secular music and, in doing so, with helping establish soul as a genre. In light of how young Cooke was at the time he was shot and killed (age 33) and presuming that he might have continued performing and recording for many years beyond 1964, it is also interesting to look at his last recordings, in part, because they represent a still-vital part of Cooke's legacy, and, in part, because they hold clues as to the direction Cooke might have gone had he lived longer. *Ain't That Good News*, released early in the last year of Cooke's life, might have sported a title that strongly suggested ties to Cooke's early gospel roots, but it was Cooke's last-recorded studio album.

Ain't That Good News opens with the nearly identically titled "(Ain't That) Good News," basically, a rewrite of Ray Charles's "I Got a Woman," which itself was a rewrite of the gospel song "It Must Be Jesus," written by Bob King and recorded by his group, the Southern Tones (available on YouTube at https://www.youtube.com/watch?v=mDoEhA6jh6I, accessed February 6, 2020). Cooke's "(Ain't That) Good News" incorporates some of the horn section accompaniment figures of "I Got a Woman." These, however, are closely related to the backing vocal punctuations in the Southern Tones' recording, albeit with more syncopation in the rhythms. Like the Ray Charles song, the Cooke piece is performed at a faster, more danceable tempo than the purely gospel original. One of the notable differences between the arrangements of "(Ain't That) Good News" and "I Got a Woman" is that the Cooke piece sports a prominent acoustic rhythm guitar part that drives the song along. This provides "(Ain't That) Good News" a touch of the feel of folk revival style, a musical movement that helped some African American blues, gospel, and soul musicians make greater inroads with white audiences in the late 1950s and early 1960s.

Cooke's lyrics, although secular, are closer to a prayer of praise and celebration for the return of Cooke's lover. Unlike "I Got a Woman," which has references to the "woman, way over town" providing Ray Charles's character with financial support and "lovin,'" Cooke's song is more oblique about the relationship, although it is clearly celebratory about her return and Cooke's character learning that she is still in love with him.

Although the nature of the party that will occur "at Mary's place" in Cooke's "Meet Me at Mary's Place" is left open in the lyrics, the old-time gospel style and hints of instrumental jazz in René Hall's arrangement calls to mind the rent parties of the early and mid-20th century. Interestingly, though, Cooke's description of the party suggests a level of refinement that is completely absent from the goings-on described in other songs about rent/house parties—for example in Louis Jordan's well-known "Saturday Night Fish Fry," a party that, ultimately, a police raid breaks up.

The album's next track is Cooke's hit "Good Times." When released as a single, "Good Times" topped the R&B charts and nearly made the Top 10 in the pop charts. Once again, Cooke's lyrics are somewhat oblique and open to interpretation. Although his character wants to continue to "let the good times roll" until he and his companion's souls are satisfied, more specifics are left to the listener's imagination.

Another aspect of this song that is important to note is Cooke's use of harmony. One of the standard chord progressions of 20th-century popular music, dating back to Hoagy Carmichael's "Heart and Soul" is the so-called oldies progression: I-vi-IV-V (in which the Roman numerals represent the scale tones on which each chord is built, and in which the uppercase Roman numerals indicate major chords and the lowercase Roman numeral "vi" indicates a minor chord). Cooke uses these four chords in the chorus of "Good Times"; however, he reserves the use of the vi chord until the end of the progression, during the lyric "If it takes all night long." Some listeners might associate the minor harmony within the context of a major-key song with a feeling of bittersweet happiness or longing. Cooke's harmonic usage might also suggest a restfulness. In any case, Cooke's placement of the minor harmony outside its almost-stereotypical location just after the tonic (I) chord is one of the distinctive aspects of "Good Times."

"Good Times" was covered shortly after the success of this album and Cooke's single release by a number of artists, including the Rolling Stones (who also performed it in some of their television appearances from the period, see, for example, https://www.youtube.com/watch?v=OCS3r1ToPHA, accessed January 29, 2020), and Ike and Tina Turner. However, "Good Times" has also proven to be one of Sam Cooke's most persistent compositions, subsequently having been covered by Dan Seals, Phoebe Snow, and Aretha Franklin, among others.

Just as the prominent use of the minor submediant chord (vi) helps define "Good Times," it is also at the core of the chorus section of "Rome (Wasn't Built in a Day)." The chorus of this brief track is largely built of oscillations between the I and vi chords. One interpretation is that this is a musical depiction of Cooke's character continuing to wait for the woman to whom he sings to build up a love for him that is equal to the love he has for her. Again, it gives the song a bittersweet quality.

The bittersweet quality that some listeners might detect in "Good Times" and—especially—"Rome (Wasn't Built in a Day)" is particularly ironic in that the next track is Cooke's famous and persistent song "Another Saturday Night." This piece finds Cooke portraying a character who is "in an awful way." Here, however, the musical setting is rhythmically upbeat and the harmony almost studiously avoids minor-quality chords. Like "Good Times," the single release of "Another Saturday Night" topped the R&B charts and touched on the pop Top 10. Cat Stevens released a hit version of the song approximately a decade after Cooke's version, demonstrating the timeless nature of some of Sam Cooke's material.

Cooke, arranger and conductor René Hall, and producers Hugo & Luigi next turn to the 1940s' country song "Tennessee Waltz." On the surface, this song, which, incidentally, soul artist Otis Redding also later covered, might not seem to be a natural for the soul genre. However, the René Hall arrangement turns the moderate-tempo triple-meter Pee Wee King waltz into a significantly faster, quadruple-meter pop-soul piece. It is not as successful as Ray Charles's 1962 *Modern Sounds in Country and Western Music*. One aspect of the arrangement and production that has not aged well is the sameness to some of the earlier tracks (e.g., "(Ain't That) Good News" and "Good Times"). In addition, the acoustic rhythm guitar in this track sounds like it might have been incorporated to help the song and the album more easily find acceptance with fans of middle-of-the-road pop music and possibly folk-revival music.

Charlie Gillett, the author of *The Sound of the City: The Rise of Rock and Roll*, wrote that Cooke's song "A Change Is Gonna Come," "took a phrase out of the black culture and returned it loaded with even more meaning than it had previous implied, so that the song and the expression took on personal, religious, and political suggestions in the mood of growing confidence that had come to the black communities during the sixties" (Gillett 1996, 204). The song has an interesting structure in that the verses clearly follow in the spiritual and gospel traditions. However, in the pop music tradition, the song contains a bridge section. Although Cooke expresses hope that "a change is gonna come" in his personal life, in the racist system that denies African Americans opportunities for employment, for hotel accommodations, for entertainment, and so on, this expression of hope is, unfortunately bathed in an orchestra-based setting that suggests 1950s' pop perhaps more than 1960s' soul. The arrangement is quite complex, with the textures of the accompaniment changing from verse to verse. Although this arrangement might have suggested the brightness and grandeur of the vision of hope for racial equality and respect at the time of the album's release, some later listeners might find it dated or at least something that draws their attention away from Cooke's poignant lyrics. As a song, however, "A Change Is Gonna Come" is perhaps Cooke's greatest contribution to soul music. Numerous artists have covered it on recordings and in live performances. The song also played a prominent role in Spike Lee's 1992 film *Malcolm X*. "A Change Is Gonna Come" plays as Malcolm travels by car to the Audubon Ballroom, where he was later murdered.

Still, by the time the song was released as a single after Cooke's untimely death, violence against blacks was on the rise again, and Cooke's optimism was not entirely topical. The intervening years, too, have not brought the kind of fundamental social changes Cooke envisioned. As *New Yorker* writer David Cantwell reflected on the 50th anniversary of the release of the single, "If Cooke were alive to update 'A Change Is Gonna Come' for the current political scene, he might be tempted to rename it 'The More Things Change'" (Cantwell 2015).

The orchestra-heavy arrangement on Harold Battiste's "Falling in Love" works well, particularly because of the song's context as a slow love ballad. Battiste's writing could have come out of the pop-jazz styles of the 1940s and 1950s. Although perhaps not one of Cooke's best-known recordings, "Falling in Love" adds a dimension to his singing that is not otherwise represented on the album.

Dating back to the early 1930s, a widely diverse list of artists recorded Harry Clarkson, Geoffrey Clarkson, and Peter van Steeden's "Home (When Shadows Fall)" before Cooke recorded it, including the Mills Brothers, the Dorsey Brothers, Nat King Cole, Louis Armstrong, and even the surf guitar–based band the Ventures. Like "Falling in Love," "Home (When Shadows Fall)" casts Cooke as a jazz-pop song stylist, somewhat in the style of Nat King Cole. Similarly, Cooke's performance of Irving Berlin's "Sittin' in the Sun" owes more to pop music than soul. The lyrics of the song, in which Cooke portrays a character "sitting in the sun, counting my money," in particular, are far removed from the soul tradition. The image also creates a strong rhetorical dissonance with the thoughtfulness and social significance of Cooke's "A Change Is Gonna Come."

The album's penultimate song, "There'll Be No Second Time," came from the pen of Sam Cooke's guitar player, Clifton White. In form, style, and arrangement, this is another track that moves Cooke in the direction of pop and lounge jazz. *Ain't That Good News* concludes with the traditional folk song "The Riddle Song." Befitting the material, the arrangement by Joe Hooven and the production by Hugo & Luigi (Hugo Peretti and Luigi Creatore) combines folk revival and pop. Although the arrangement itself does not necessarily reflect soul sensibilities, the middle section of the track—the material that Cooke added to the old folk song—finds him singing with a soulful expressiveness.

The real meat of *Ain't That Good News* is in Cooke's songs, which populate roughly the first half of the album. "A Change Is Gonna Come" is easily the most famous and the most critically recognized of these; it was elected part of the Grammy Hall of Fame by the Recording Academy (The Recording Academy n.d.), and the National Recording Preservation Board of Library of Congress added it to the National Recording Registry in 2007 (National Recording Preservation Board of the Library of Congress n.d.). In 2011, "A Change Is Gonna Come" was ranked at No. 12 on *Rolling Stone* magazine's list of "500 Greatest Songs of All Time" (*Rolling Stone* 2011). But, Cooke's "(Ain't That) Good News, "Good Times," and "Another Saturday Night" remain R&B and pop staples, and the first two of these clearly exhibit Cooke's ties to the soul and gospel traditions.

D'ANGELO: *BROWN SUGAR*

Several artists emerged in the 1990s as examples of the neo-soul genre, a genre that reconnected with the soul music of the 1960s and 1970s and brought soul into the hip-hop age. As Cheo Coker wrote in *Rolling Stone* of D'Angelo, one of the most visible of the neo-soul artists of the era, "He's no trailblazer—Stevie Wonder, Smokey Robinson and Prince have all walked down the same musical paths where D'Angelo meanders. Yet he manages to build on the examples of the masters" (Coker 1995).

D'Angelo's 1995 album *Brown Sugar* represents the neo-soul genre well, as does Lauryn Hill's *The Miseducation of Lauryn Hill* (also profiled in this chapter), but the two albums come at the subgenre in different ways. Arguably, one of the things that sets *Brown Sugar* apart from other albums that integrate soul and hip-hop influences is its clearer ties to the past.

Brown Sugar opens with its title track. The song is tuneful but includes a rap-inspired verse melodic structure in which D'Angelo uses many repeated pitches. The effect in the verses, then, is almost that of rapping on pitch. The brief chorus hook, "I want some of your Brown Sugar," is instantly memorable and stylistically calls to mind the tradition of some of the classic soul hits of the 1960s. "Brown Sugar" was written by D'Angelo and Ali Shaheed Muhammad, who also coproduced the track. All vocals—lead and multitracked backing—are by D'Angelo, which is true throughout the album. Other musicians are credited only for the woodwinds, brass, strings, and percussion that appear on several tracks, as well as the drum-machine programming. D'Angelo's falsetto vocalizing also suggests ties to 1960s and 1970s, all while a hip-hop drum machine beat underscores the song. Using food as a metaphor for love and sex is also part of the tried-and-true R&B tradition that goes back to early 20th-century blues and hokum songs.

In the second song, "Alright," D'Angelo incorporates a more aggressive drum part, which provides a strong contrast with the impressionistic, atmospheric opening. In this ballad, D'Angelo's character tries to coax back his lover after the pair was torn apart by disagreements. Although the drum arrangement and rhythms practically scream 1990s' hip-hop, the improvisational melodic style of the lead vocal and the use of multitracked D'Angelo backing vocals suggests the inspiration of a mix of 1960s and 1970s soul artists, including Al Green, Marvin Gaye, and Curtis Mayfield and the Impressions. D'Angelo's incorporation of scratchy turntable effects reinforced the old-school connections. Unfortunately, some listeners might find the needle-on-well-used-record effects to be somewhat overdone in this song, which deflects attention from D'Angelo's singing.

The opening of "Jonz in My Bonz" continues the trend of opening songs with impressionistic, atmospheric, largely synthesized sounds, and then breaking into a contrastingly hip-hop-oriented beat in the drum machine. Here, D'Angelo and cowriter, Angela Stone, explore the theme of following one's heart. The lyrics, however, are widely open to interpretation. Specifically, the "thing" that he knows he should pursue could be just about anything or anyone. The groove nature of the accompaniment makes "Jonz in My Bonz" part of a tradition in soul music that goes back to the work of artists such as Isaac Hayes and Al Green.

In "Me and Those Dreamin' Eyes of Mine," D'Angelo sings an improvisatory falsetto lead that suggests Al Green's 1970s hits, updated for the hip-hop era. Although lyrically, this is a conventional soul love ballad, it is perhaps the most notable track on *Brown Sugar* for the backing vocal arrangement, composed and executed by D'Angelo. The arrangement takes the male quartet concept from gospel and from the vocal groups that became popular in R&B in the late 1940s and through the 1950s, and expands it out to a full-male-chorus backing texture.

In "S***, Damn, Mother***ker," D'Angelo explores to the extreme how one might react to discovering an affair between his wife and his best friend. Because of the song's title—the sole lyrics in the piece's chorus—and because the song is framed around D'Angelo's confrontation with his friend, it might be surprising that it is slow-paced and that D'Angelo delivers the title line more with an air of sadness than with anger. Ultimately, D'Angelo's character sees that his wife and best friend are covered in blood, although he does not understand why. He also expresses disbelief that he might be responsible for their murder as he is led from the scene in handcuffs. One of the highlights of the album, "S***, Damn, Mother***ker," then finds D'Angelo exploring widely contradicting emotions musically and lyrically, as well as exploring the seething rage and violence that, on the surface, is hidden by his quiet sadness.

Based on the juxtaposition of intensely different emotions—and apparent courses of action—on *Brown Sugar*, this is not a unified-feeling concept album, except to the extent that most of the material clearly revolves around romantic relationships. So, although the transition from an apparent double homicide to a song about how "smooth" one's lover is can be quite a shock, it does not seem to interrupt a larger narrative. Throughout *Brown Sugar*, D'Angelo tends to start the songs with impressionistic instrumental music that provides little hint of what is to come once the hip-hop rhythms kick in. Such is the case with "Smooth," a piece that opens with drum and guitar licks that suggest a jazz group warming up. Ultimately, the song becomes almost a hip-hop reimagining of Al Green's work during his early run of popularity with songs such as "Let's Stay Together." "Smooth" provides the listener with perhaps the best opportunity on the album to hear how D'Angelo's falsetto lead singing matches the seductiveness of Green's work.

D'Angelo's cover of Smokey Robinson's "Cruisin'" might be problematic for some listeners familiar with the 1979 original. Although D'Angelo's arrangement resulted in a Top 10 R&B chart single that was truncated from the album version, it is dense with numerous texture changes in a way that Robinson's earlier hit recording was not. Some listeners might find that the texture changes, particularly with respect to the backing vocals, take some of the emphasis off the lyrics, particularly as compared with Robinson's original. Still, by covering the song, D'Angelo demonstrates part of what his brand of soul—or neo-soul—was about: taking materials from the soul artists of the 1960s and 1970s and putting a hip-hop-era spin on them. Arguably, the approach works best in D'Angelo's original songs.

The next track, "When We Get By," is a straightforward love song and the most retro-sounding piece on the album. In sharp contrast to the hip-hop-inspired style of rhythm and rhythmic syncopation that runs through other tracks, here D'Angelo uses a form of shuffle beat. Although this was common enough, say, in some of the Motown soul and R&B of the mid-1960s, D'Angelo's usage does not sound derivative. The horn section arrangement, too, would not have been out of place in early-1970s' soul. The horn section is quiet enough in the recording's mix, though, so that it does not immediately sound like an imitation of, say, the Memphis studio musicians who backed up artists such as Al Green.

D'Angelo and Raphael Saadiq's "Lady" is a love song and a groove piece reflective of late-1960s and early 1970s' soul. In contrast to the other tracks, "Lady," one song on which D'Angelo does not play all or nearly all the instruments, has a clearly band/ensemble sound. One negative of *Brown Sugar* that some listeners might detect right around the time of "Lady" is that although D'Angelo explores several different aspects of love and romantic relationships in the first half of the album, a thematic sameness creeps into the second half.

The album concludes with "Higher," a collaboration of D'Angelo, Luther Archer, and Rodney Archer. The song's sentiments are summed up in the line, "You take me higher, higher than I've ever, ever known." Romantic love takes on almost a religious air in the piece as D'Angelo replaces overt hip-hop rhythmic references with a drum part that would have been entirely at home in the early 1960s, and the organ figures prominently in the instrumental accompaniment. The song can be understood as a spiritual descendant of the 1960s' Jackie Wilson hit "(Your Love Keeps Lifting Me) Higher and Higher."

One significant way in which *Brown Sugar* differs from a plethora of other albums of the hip-hop era is that the tracks—with one exception—are either written by D'Angelo alone or in collaboration with one other writer. To put it another way, there is no long litany of writing credits that one often finds in rap/DJ-oriented hip-hop: the songs are not built around samples. This is original material and, although it is decidedly studio music (how could it be any other way with one musician providing all the lead and backing vocals as well as most of the instrumental tracks?). It is a magnificent example of the vocal, composing, and arranging talents of D'Angelo and an example of how D'Angelo managed to fuse the old and the new.

THE DRIFTERS

The history of the Drifters is perhaps the most interesting and convoluted of any solo artist or group represented in this chapter. Since 1953, there have been numerous incarnations of this vocal group, legal intrigues related to the ownership of the group name, numerous personnel changes, and so on. However, the great hits that the Drifters recorded, including "This Magic Moment," "Money Honey," "Save the Last Dance for Me," "Up on the Roof," "I Count the Tears," "Under the Boardwalk," "Some Kind of Wonderful," and "On Broadway" easily are among the best representations of male vocal groups of the early 1950s through the early 1960s. Additionally, the group included two prominent lead singers who went on to substantial solo careers—Clyde McPhatter and Ben E. King, with McPhatter being one of the pioneers in blending sacred and secular styles into the soul genre, and King becoming a substantial star after he left the group.

Both Clyde McPhatter, who had been lead tenor in Billy Ward and his Dominoes, and Atlantic Records executive Ahmet Ertegün were responsible for building the original incarnation of the Drifters around McPhatter's vocal talents. Despite this, McPhatter was with the group only for a small part of its career. The McPhatter era included the hits "Money Honey" and "Honey Love." After McPhatter left the group in 1955, ownership of the name "the Drifters" caused the next incarnation to be known as Bill Pinkney's Original Drifters. The most commercially productive period for the Drifters, however, began in 1958, when the Five Crowns, an entirely different vocal group that featured Ben E. King (born Benjamin Earl Nelson) on lead, were rebranded as the Drifters. Such were the peculiarities of the ownership of the "Drifters" name.

During the Ben E. King era, the Drifters' best-remembered hits included "There Goes My Baby," "This Magic Moment," and "Save the

Last Dance for Me." After King left the group, Rudy Lewis became the primary lead vocalist, and the Drifters released "Up on the Roof," "On Broadway," and "Some Kind of Wonderful." Lewis's premature death in 1964 led to group member Johnny Moore—who previously had sung lead occasionally on some Drifters tracks—becoming the featured lead vocalist. Moore was featured on the Drifters' last great hit, "Under the Boardwalk." Just as lead singers came and went, so did other members of the Drifters over the years, so, in some respects, it might be most accurate to think of the Drifters as a franchise rather than as a well-defined group.

All the comings and goings, not to mention the wholesale substitution of personnel under the same group name, was highly unusual for the era. It can be interpreted in several ways. For one thing, it suggests the sheer number of highly talented lead singers and male vocal groups active at the time and that, under the moniker of the Drifters, several could be commercially accepted and successful. The success of this never-stable "group" also suggests the importance and strength of the material the Drifters recorded, as well as the commercially appealing production on Drifters' recordings.

Throughout the most commercially successful part of the Drifters' career, 1958 to 1964, part of the strength of the resonance of their recordings with the R&B and pop audiences came from the Brill Building songwriters and producers, such as the team of Jerry Leiber and Mike Stoller collaborating with the team of Barry Mann and Cynthia Weil ("On Broadway"), the team of Doc Pomus and Mort Shuman ("This Magic Moment," "Save the Last Dance for Me," and "Sweets for My Sweet"), and the then-husband-and-wife team of Gerry Goffin and Carole King ("Up on the Roof" and "Some Kind of Wonderful"). The success of some of these songs even years after the Drifters' versions were on the charts clearly shows the lasting quality of the material, even taking the Drifters themselves out of the equation. For example, the group Jay and the Americans took "This Magic Moment" into the pop Top 10 in 1968; singer-guitarist George Benson's live recording of "On Broadway" made it into the pop Top 10, came within one spot of topping the soul charts in 1978, and was featured in the 1979 Bob Fosse film *All That Jazz*; the Cryin' Shames made the pop singles charts with "Up on the Roof" in 1968; critically acclaimed songwriter Laura Nyro enjoyed her only chart single as a recording artist with "Up on the Roof" in 1970; and James Taylor made the pop Top 40 with his version of "Up on the Roof" in 1979.

The group also benefited during the Ben E. King years from him being active as a songwriter. The Drifters' 1960 hit "There Goes My Baby" is credited to King (under his real last name, Nelson); the Drifters' road manager, Lover Patterson; and the Drifters' manager, George Treadwell. This recording, produced by Jerry Leiber and Mike Stoller, features a highly emotional lead vocal from King and is notable for the incorporation of Brazilian rhythms and a Stan Applebaum string arrangement that goes beyond the norm of the day in terms of its virtuosity and textural contrast from section to section.

The 1959 hit "There Goes My Baby" is constructed around the so-called "oldies chord progression": I, vi, IV, V, where the Roman numerals represent the scale degrees on which the chords are built, with the uppercase numerals representing major chords, and the lowercase Roman numeral (vi) representing a minor chord. This progression had been in usage in American popular music for a couple of decades, going back to Hoagy Carmichael's composition "Heart and Soul." During the late 1950s and early 1960s, however, this became something of a go-to chord progression for songwriters in the vocal group area. Another important soul song from the period that was built on the progression, "Please Mr. Postman," a 1961 hit for the Marvelettes, was notable for being the first single from Berry Gordy's new Motown collection of labels (this song was released on Tamla Records) to reach No. 1 on the pop charts.

More to the point, however, regarding songwriter Ben E. King and "There Goes My Baby," King's use of the oldies progression here anticipates his use of it in his later, best-known composition from his solo career and one of the most persistent songs of the entire 1960s, "Stand By Me." The chord progression, the distinctive string arrangement, and the use of Brazilian rhythms in "There Goes My Baby" both helped to define the sound of the Drifters for several years. For example, Doc Pomus and Mort Shuman's "This Magic Moment," released by the Drifters in 1960, includes verses built around the progression, includes a string arrangement that is particularly distinctive and dramatic in the introduction, and features a Latin-inspired pulse. Pomus and Shuman's "Save the Last Dance for Me," the group's only single to top the pop singles charts, broke free of the oldies-progression harmonic paradigm but ratcheted up the integration of Latin rhythms into the sound of the Drifters. Pomus and Shuman's "Sweets for My Sweet" continued the Latin rhythmic feel on Drifters recordings into 1961. This song found its way into the early repertoire of the British Invasion band the Searchers, and British reggae singer C. J. Lewis covered it in 1994.

In these and other hits, in the voices of the Drifters, the group members explored the beauty of love, hopes and dreams of stardom in the big city, loss in love, the importance of having a space in which one can simply be and forget one's troubles, and so on. In short, they set a wide range of emotions and experiences to memorable melodic and arrangement hook-filled music. And, regardless of who was singing in the group at any time during their heyday, the vocals on the Drifters' hits were consistently soulful and balanced.

In the magazine's list of the "500 Greatest Songs of All Time," *Rolling Stone* ranked the Drifters' recording of "Under the Boardwalk," which the magazine described as "a staple of beach-town jukeboxes every summer since its release" at No. 489, "Money Honey" at No. 254, "There Goes My Baby" at No. 196, "Save the Last Dance for Me" at No. 184, and "Up on the Roof" at No. 114 (*Rolling Stone* 2011). With a full 1 percent of all the songs on the list, the Drifters are one of the most-represented artists in *Rolling Stone*'s compilation of the top singles and album tracks of the 1950s through 2010.

In addition to the hits that the various incarnations of the Drifters produced from the mid-1950s to the mid-1960s, the group was also important in the history and legacy of soul music as the launching point for Ben E. King, who recorded several classics of 1960s' soul, including "I (Who Have Nothing)," "Spanish Harlem," and "Stand By Me," the latter of which is profiled in this chapter. King returned to the top of the soul charts in 1975 with his song "Supernatural Thing." As a group, the Drifters were inducted into the Rock and Roll Hall of Fame in 1988 and the Vocal Group Hall of Fame in 1998.

ARETHA FRANKLIN: *I NEVER LOVED A MAN THE WAY I LOVE YOU*

Aretha Franklin's recording career in popular secular music began in 1960 and her first releases on Columbia Records, although she had recorded gospel music as early as 1956 on the J.V.B. label. Although Franklin made several successful recordings up to 1966 when she left Columbia, she, arguably, established and cemented her reputation as the Queen of Soul or Lady Soul with her first Atlantic album, *I Never Loved a Man the Way I Love You*. As *Rolling Stone*'s Jon Dolan wrote of this collection just after Franklin's death, "This was the album that made her a legend, inaugurating a run of LPs for Franklin on Atlantic that's up there with any other series of records by any solo artist ever" (Dolan 2018).

Ironically, given the importance of this album and the prestige it achieved, the history of its recording and production was anything but straightforward. Producer Jerry Wexler held the initial session at the FAME Studios in Muscle Shoals, Alabama, with Franklin backed by a group of white Southern studio musicians, known informally as the Swampers. These musicians had an uncanny ability to bridge gaps between a wide variety of musical genres, primarily country and soul. The only song completed at FAME, however, was "I Never Loved a Man (The Way I Love You)." After conflicts between Franklin's husband, Ted White, FAME's Rick Hall, and Jerry Wexler regarding an incident in which a member of the horn section allegedly acted inappropriately toward Franklin, Wexler brought the Muscle Shoals musicians to New York to resume recording the rest of the sessions at Atlantic's studios. For the New York sessions, additional horn players were added—including the great blues and R&B saxophonist King Curtis—as well as Cissy Houston and Franklin's sisters Carolyn and Erma as backing singers, so the bulk of the album was recorded by a fully racially integrated collection of instrumentalists and singers.

The completed album opens with Franklin's cover of Otis Redding's "Respect." Because this chapter contains a separate entry for "Respect" that details the impact of both Redding's and Franklin's recordings, particularly in how Franklin's recording provides a narrative that resonated especially strongly within the social movements of the late 1960s and early 1970s (e.g., the civil rights movement and the women's movement), suffice it to say here that "Respect" is perhaps the most potent track on the album. Like the rest of the album, too, "Respect" found Aretha Franklin fully bringing the expression, improvisation, and vocal technique of gospel music into the secular world to produce some of the strongest soul music ever recorded.

Although the Muscle Shoals musicians figure prominently in the tracks recorded in New York, one of the major instrumental stars of "Respect" was the great tenor saxophonist King Curtis. As an example of Curtis's impact on the sessions, Matt Dobkin's study of the making of the album quotes producer Jerry Wexler and engineer Arif Mardin crediting King Curtis with the idea of using the bridge section of Sam & Dave's "When Something Is Wrong with My Baby" for the saxophone solo section in "Respect" (Dobkin 2004, 170–171).

"Drown in My Own Tears," a Henry Glover composition that Ray Charles most famously recorded a decade earlier, continues the gospel-inspired expression. Here, too, the piano part adds to the ties to gospel. Jerry Wexler later expressed trepidation about the female backing-vocal arrangement for Carolyn Franklin, Erma Franklin, and Cissy Houston focusing largely on single syllables so as to make the trio sound like a horn section (Dobkin 2004, 176–177). However, the backing-vocal arrangement provides a nice contrast to that of "Respect," particularly in that the previous track includes so much overlap and overlayering of the lead and backing vocals.

On Franklin's death, *Rolling Stone* ranked "I Never Loved a Man (The Way I Love You)" at No. 2 in its list of "The 50 Greatest Aretha Franklin Songs" (Browne et al. 2018). Not only a hit single, "I Never Loved a Man (The Way I Love You)" is also highly distinctive because of its triple-meter feel. Because the texture is somewhat sparser than that of some of the other tracks on the album, Franklin's instrumental contributions on acoustic piano, which enters in the second verse and adds a pronounced gospel feel to the piece, are relatively easy to hear.

Franklin's piano playing is also a distinctive part of "Soul Serenade." Based on the instrumental piece of the same title most closely associated with King Curtis, this is basically a groove piece that is notable for Franklin's improvised vocals. To put it another way, the lyrics were not fully constructed with distinctive verses and a recurring chorus. The impact, then, is not as much in the words as in the soulful expression with which Franklin sings.

Franklin's composition "Don't Let Me Lose This Dream" is a Latin-style piece. As such, it stands out from the other tracks on the album. The style of the song itself is closer to the pop music that Franklin recorded for Columbia earlier in the 1960s (and to which she returned from time to time later in her career) or to the kind of more-pop-oriented material associated with singers such as Dionne Warwick. A close listen to the recording, however, reveals an intensity to Franklin's singing—particularly in her vibrato—that almost seems to want to break free of the laid-back style. The backing vocals, too, use clipped phrases that seem more appropriate for a higher-energy setting.

A collaborative composition of Aretha and Carolyn Franklin, "Baby, Baby, Baby," is reminiscent of compound quadruple-meter (12/8 time) ballads from the late 1950s and early 1960s. The chord progressions, too, of the verses and the bridge absolutely would not have sounded out of place up to a decade before the release of *I Never Loved a Man the Way I Love You*. Rhetorically, the song adds another dimension to the tales of heartache that run through the album. In this case, Franklin sings about how much she misses her man now that *she* is gone. In earlier songs, the subject seemed to revolve around the male character who did not give Franklin's character her "proper respect" or who was "no good." Based on the situations that Franklin explored in the earlier songs, the listener might infer from "Baby, Baby, Baby," that her character has finally had enough and left.

Franklin and then-husband Ted White wrote "Dr. Feelgood (Love Is a Serious Business)." Described by reviewer Thomas Ward as "one of the singer's most impassioned vocal performances on the album" (Ward n.d.), the song perhaps most clearly demonstrates Aretha Franklin's ties to the gospel-music tradition. From Franklin's gospel-style piano, to the sustained organ chords (with characteristic vibrato), and an early brief saxophone fill from King Curtis, the song's roots are clear. However, Franklin's improvisatory singing probably represents the song's strongest ties to the gospel tradition. An interesting feature in the arrangement is the inclusion of a stop-time section, which begins approximately two minutes into the track. This, and the basic AAB structure of the lyrics of each stanza suggest at least a weak influence of the blues, although Franklin and White's harmonic vocabulary is much more gospel than blues. And, although "Dr. Feelgood" is in the same 12/8 meter of "Baby, Baby, Baby," the texture, the rhythmic drive, and the harmonic vocabulary make them sound like they come from two entirely different worlds.

Sam Cooke's "Good Times" brings a sense of optimism and a party-like atmosphere to the album that contrasts with all the previous tracks. The song itself is a moderate-tempo shuffle-feel piece, in contrast to the rhythmic feel of other tracks. It is also a short song, clocking in at just over two minutes. This, the lack of lyrical meat to the song, and the unusually abrupt fade-out, make "Good Times" seem somewhat superfluous. Certainly, the album's closer, "A Change Is Gonna Come," is a better representative of an Aretha Franklin reworking of a Sam Cooke song.

The next song, "Do Right Woman—Do Right Man," came from the pens of two members of the Muscle Shoals contingent: Chips Moman and Dan Penn. The lyrical theme of treating a lover with respect echoes back to the first track on the album. The recording opens with some of Franklin's most restrained singing on the entire album. This is important, because the sharp contrast might give some listeners the impression that the lyrics are of great significance. Some listeners might also interpret the restraint as symbolic of sadness or resignation, which would be in keeping with much of the album's other material. Another notable aspect of the song is that the form is less clear-cut than in many songs of the era. The melody is not as distinctive as those of the best-known songs on the album, although some of the phrases suggest the possible influence of Sam Cooke's "Bring It on Home to Me." When released as a single, the recording did not resonate with the public nearly as well as "I Never Loved a Man (The Way I Love You)" or "Respect," both of which were smash hits.

A collaborative effort of Aretha and Carolyn Franklin and King Curtis, "Save Me" is mono-harmonic groove piece built over a brief riff. The nature of the song provides Franklin with much room for extemporization based on—and extending well beyond—the basic tune. The basic melody, incidentally, calls to mind a stripped-down version of the verses of Isaac Hayes and David Porter's composition "Soul Man," a 1967 hit for Sam & Dave. Although the piece might seem like something of a trifle on the album, Franklin's cry for salvation after a lost love demonstrates the sometimes-awkward ties between the sacred and the secular at the heart of soul music.

Sam Cooke's "A Change Is Gonna Come" closes the album. Although a thoroughly 20th-century gospel-style song, the expression of sorrow and hope that "a change is gonna come" can be linked to the spirituals and sorrow songs of 19th-century experience of slavery. While it can be interpreted as a statement about a wide variety of different painful experiences, it is widely recognized as a central part of the civil rights movement that was in full swing when Cooke wrote it in the early 1960s. Aretha Franklin's version is more fully gospel oriented than Cooke's original, largely as a result of Franklin's piano contribution and the absence the commercial-sounding orchestral strings of Cooke's recording.

Because of the multiple interpretations of the album's opener, Otis Redding's "Respect," in Franklin's rendition of the song (*e.g.*, a call for respect from one individual in a relationship to another, a call for respect for African Americans, a call for men to respect women, and so on), its bookend, "A Change Is Gonna Come," is also open to alternative interpretations. As mentioned earlier, the text is related to the sorrow songs and spirituals of the 19th century, which were born out of slavery. However, although "A Change Is Gonna Come" resonates with the 1960s' struggle for freedom and equality of African Americans, the song can also be understood as an early expression of the call for equality across gender lines that became more visible in the women's movement of the early 1970s.

All in all, then, Aretha Franklin's *I Never Loved a Man the Way I Love You* is a quintessential soul album, largely focused on struggle and overcoming obstacles ranging from personal relationships to larger national and world issues, albeit in an oblique, almost coded way. It is also the album on which Franklin's ties to the black church came through more fully than on any of her previous recordings, and, in the process, established her as a leader in the soul genre.

ARETHA FRANKLIN: "THINK"

Unfortunately, it is easy to lose sight of the fact that, in addition to her very visible work as a singer who took full control over other writers' songs and made them her own (e.g., "(You Make Me Feel Like) A Natural Woman," "Respect," "A Change Is Gonna Come," and so on), Aretha Franklin was a talented and active pianist and songwriter. Her piano contributions to her recordings reinforced her music's ties to the gospel tradition but were such a natural-sounding part of the texture of the accompaniment that they can be overlooked. Although several of Franklin's solo and collaborative compositions were strong album cuts, some, such as "(Sweet Sweet Baby) Since You've Been Gone," were successful singles. Cowritten with her then-husband Ted White, "Think" became the most iconic Aretha Franklin composition. In addition to the 1968 recording, Franklin rerecorded "Think" for the 1980 movie *The Blues Brothers* and for her 1989 album *Through the Storm*.

The lyrics are at times somewhat impressionistic, with the suggestion that the character Franklin addresses has tried over and over to manipulate her character and get her to do things that she does not want to do. The listener never learns, however, exactly what the nature of this manipulation is. What we do know is that the two characters have known each other since childhood, and, most importantly we know in no uncertain terms that Franklin's character can see right through the attempts to manipulate her.

By all accounts, the relationship between Aretha Franklin and Ted White was contentious. The couple married in 1961 and divorced in 1969. Although some associates and friends of Franklin claim that White was abusive, writer Mark Bego pointed out in his biography of Franklin that White denied those allegations and that, over the years, Franklin and White themselves provided little detail about the relationship or how and why it ended (Bego 2012, 102–103). Given that the lyrics suggest a contentious relationship and are open-ended enough that the relationship could be between a musician and a manager/spouse, it is easy to interpret "Think" as a chronicle of the cry for "freedom" that would come through the Franklin-White breakup and divorce. This is particularly true when one considers that Franklin reportedly first saw White several years before they first became romantically involved (for an account of their apparent first meeting see, for example, Ritz 2014, 44–45), a direct connection with the timeline of the relationship between the two characters in the song.

Musically, "Think" is a quintessential soul song, with strong, instantly identifiable and memorable hooks. The line that Franklin sings at the beginning, "You better think, think what you're trying to do to me," lays out the song's basic premise, the warning from Franklin's character to the other character not to continue trying to manipulate and dominate her. Also notable are the backing vocals' punctuations, in which statements of "think" echo Franklin's statement of the word in the phrase "You better think."

"Think" is built largely around the standard I, IV, and V7 chords (A, D, and E7 in the key of A major). In the "Freedom" section, however, the listener is apt to feel surprise in the harmonic progression I, bIII, IV I (A, C, D, and A). Franklin's use of the unusual bIII chord in this section provides a rising feel on the repetitions of the word "freedom." Some listeners might interpret this rising figure as a statement of Franklin's empowerment after she finally warns her counterpart against trying to manipulate and control her.

Like Franklin's cover of Otis Redding's "Respect," "Think" was a commercial success at the time of its release. The single topped the R&B charts and made it solidly into the Top 10 of the pop charts. In addition to Franklin's later recorded versions of the song for *The Blues Brothers* movie and for her *Through the Storm* album, "Think" has been covered by several other recording artists and has been used in a number of films, television programs, and television commercials, making it the most persistent and popular of any of the songs Franklin wrote or cowrote. In the wake of Franklin's death in 2018, "Think" was published in marching band arrangements and as part of concert band medleys of her hits, thus keeping the memory of this soul classic alive for the next generation of music fans.

MARVIN GAYE: *LET'S GET IT ON*

To say that Marvin Gaye's 1971 album *What's Going On* and the singles it spawned—"What's Going On," "Mercy Mercy Me (The Ecology)," and "Inner City Blues (Make Me Wanna Holler)"—was a commercial and critical success would be a massive understatement. *What's Going On* is still regarded as one of the greatest concept albums of all time. While it focused on contemporary social issues, Gaye's 1973 follow up, *Let's Get It On*, focused on love and sex. Gaye's liner notes explain the basic premise of the album. He wrote, "I can't see anything wrong with sex between consenting anybodies." Gaye also wrote, "I contend that SEX IS SEX and LOVE IS LOVE," and he continues by writing that although sex and love can work well together between compatible individuals, "they are really two discrete needs and should be treated as such" (Gaye 1973).

Let's Get It On did not achieve the fame and reputation of its predecessor, but it was Marvin Gaye's most successful recording on the album charts. In light of the development of subsequent soul and R&B

subgenres and Gaye's murder, *Let's Get It On* has a significance that goes well beyond mere commercial success. Although it was recorded over a period of several years, included four tracks produced by Gaye alone and four tracks coproduced by Gaye and Ed Townsend, had arrangements written by several orchestrators, and included one track in which—for all intents and purposes—Gaye's lead vocals were substituted for the lead vocals on a pre-existing recording, *Let's Get It On* is remarkably consistent, not only in its lyrical focus but also musically.

The album opens with its title track, jointly composed and produced by Gaye and Ed Townsend. As one might reasonably suppose from the title, "Let's Get It On" is a sensuous call to lovemaking and sex. The real meat of the song is not, however, just in that message: it is in how the musical setting supports the lyrics and the lyrical intent. In the manner of much of the music on *What's Going On*, the setting of "Let's Get It On" is hypnotic, with the song largely built around an ostinato-like I-iii7-IV-V7 chord progression. There is little distinction within the accompaniment between sections, and Gaye's lead vocals have an almost completely improvised feel to them. "Let's Get It On" sets the stage for most of the rest of the album in this regard: the album largely focuses on improvised-sounding lead vocals over instrumental and backing vocal grooves. This song and several other tracks also mostly stick to the medium and medium-slow sides of the tempo spectrum.

The almost through-composed, improvisational style of "Let's Get It On," as well as the easygoing groove and the focus on lovemaking can be understood as the antecedents of the groove, slow jam, and quiet storm subgenres of R&B. However, "Let's Get It On" is more than just a preview of coming attractions in the world of R&B and soul music—despite lyrics that caused some consternation among radio programmers, it was a hugely successful single and topped pop and R&B singles charts in the United States.

Another compositional and production collaboration of Gaye and Townsend, the next song, "Please Stay (Once You Go Away)" sports a curious title, particularly as throughout the track, Gaye pleads with his lover *not* to go away. The title may provide a subtext, suggesting that if she does indeed leave him, she ought not to return; however, the surface-level lyrics solely represent a plea for her to stay. Again—but not quite to the same extent as the opening track—"Please Stay (Once You Go Away)" is built around harmonic repetition. Unlike in a conventional pop song, Gaye, as lead vocalist, largely improvised the verses. The backing track instrumental arrangement (arranged by René Hall) resembles the basic texture of several of David Van DePitte's arrangements on

What's Going On (e.g., the sustained notes played by the upper orchestral strings and so on).

The third Gaye and Townsend collaboration, "If I Should Die Tonight," is a more-conventionally structured (e.g., well-defined phrases and sections) soulful ballad. The lyrical theme is best summed up by the line "I wouldn't die blue, sugar, 'cause I've known you." So, in the thematic continuum that Marvin Gaye set forward in his liner notes—love, sex, and their intersection—"If I Should Die Tonight" is squarely focused on romance.

Although it is tempting to view Gaye and Townsend's "Keep Gettin' It On" as a mere reprise or extension of the album's title track, it is much more, albeit in subtle ways. Here, Gaye incorporates some of the social commentary of his *What's Going On* album—for example, asking his listeners if they would rather make love or war. The piece overall, though, is a call to keep making love in the physical sense. The backing chorus of "keep gettin' it, keep gettin' it on," the rhythmic groove and the repetitive I-iii7-IV-V7 harmonic progression all work well in support of Gaye's enticement. One of the interesting little details is that at one point, Gaye sings that Jesus encourages people "to come on; to get it on." Although this is a decidedly fleeting part of the song, it demonstrates the connection between the sacred and the secular in soul music. It also anticipates the philosophy that would run through much of Prince's vast output of songs about love and sex in the 1980s and beyond: that sex is a gift from God for humans to enjoy.

Although Gaye and Ed Townsend cowrote and coproduced the album's first four songs, Gaye produced the last four. Two of these were solo Marvin Gaye compositions, and two he wrote with other collaborators. Gaye's "Come Get to This" featured an arrangement by David Van DePitte and Gene Page that was composed before Van DePitte's exit from Motown in 1972. This brings up the fact that the songs on *Let's Get It On* were written and recorded over the course of several years.

Lyrically, "Come Get to This" is a call to sex from Gaye's character after he has "been gone such a long time." Unlike the slower, more musically and vocally seductive smooth songs on the album, "Come Get to This" is built around Gaye's version of the compound quadruple-meter Motown-shuffle feel. Arguably, this rhythmic feel does not work as well as the sleekly slinking slow groove feel of, say, "Let's Get It On" as a pairing to the sentiments of the lyrics.

"Distant Lover," a collaboration of Gaye, Gwen Gordy, and Sandra Greene, is a gentle ballad in which Gaye reminisces about a transitory lost summer love. Although the rhythmic and harmonic feel is entirely different, "Distant Lover" finds Gaye singing the same kind of improvisational melody during the verses. The improvisational melodic style makes the performance sound more personal and more fully as though it is straight from the heart—just as in other songs on the album, it makes the lyrics sound like they come straight from the loins.

With backing vocals by Madeline and Fred Ross, "You Sure Love to Ball" is the most overtly sexually charged song on the album. A solo Gaye composition, this is a call to physical lovemaking and includes vocalization of sounds of enjoyment (e.g., moaning and so on) that one might expect during sex. Fred and Madeleine Ross provide the vocalizations. "You Sure Love to Ball" is more harmonically varied than some of the other songs and is built almost completely of seventh chords, ninth chords, or triads over nonchord tones in the bass. Gaye's treatment gives the song a lush, full harmonic feel, which seems to represent almost a musical glorification of sex.

Let's Get It On concludes with "Just to Keep You Satisfied," a collaboration of Gaye, Anna Gordy Gaye, and Elgie Stover. The song opens with Gaye singing that fighting and "bitchin'" in a relationship can melt away and be cured "once in bed with you." However, the relationship is now broken, ended, and that is the focus of Gaye's singing in the verses. Curiously, "Just to Keep You Satisfied" was a song that dated from several years before the recording of the album. The *Let's Get It On* version of the song was essentially an earlier recording by the Originals, with Gaye's reminiscences of the relationship and his feelings about its end substituted for the original lead part.

As critic Jason Ankeny wrote "Perhaps no other record has achieved the kind of sheer erotic force of *Let's Get It On*, and it remains the blueprint for all of the slow jams to follow decades later" (Ankeny n.d.-a). The erotic nature of the album highlights one of the great conflicts in the life and career of Marvin Gaye, the singer who grew up in the church only to record one of the most overtly sexually oriented albums. And this conflict can be understood as representative of the great divide between Gaye and his father, a Pentecostal minister with deep conflicts himself, a divide that eventually led to Marvin Gay Sr. killing his son.

MARVIN GAYE: *WHAT'S GOING ON*[3]

Among American record companies in the 1960s and early 1970s, Berry Gordy Jr.'s Motown was noticeably quiet about the various social issues of the day, including drug usage, teen pregnancy, the war in Vietnam, racial discrimination, and others. A few statements did emerge, such as

Stevie Wonder's recording of the Bob Dylan song "Blowin' in the Wind," in which the teenaged singer changes the line "How many years must some people exist before they're allowed to be free" to "How many years must a *man* exist before he's allowed to be free," which placed a special emphasis on the struggle of blacks for freedom and equality in the mid-1960s. And Diana Ross and the Supremes recorded "Love Child," a 1968 hit about poverty, ghetto life, premarital sex, and teen pregnancy. For the most part, however, until Edwin Starr turned Norman Whitfield and Barrett Strong's song "War" into a lasting icon of American pop culture with his 1970 hit recording, social and political issues did not figure into the output of any of Gordy's record labels. Marvin Gaye, one of the most successful male singers in the long history of Motown, collaborated with Al Cleveland and Obie Benson to write "What's Going On," a song that documents just what was going on in 1970: poverty, racial discrimination, protests against the Vietnam War, drug addiction, urban blight, labor strife, and police brutality. The song was recorded on June 1, 1970 (Edmonds 2002), but Motown initially refused to release it. When Gaye threatened to stop recording for the label, Motown head Berry Gordy Jr. relented, and the single became a pop and R&B smash hit. Gaye then expanded on "What's Going On," collaborating with several different writers and producers to perform (as lead singer and on piano) an entire album devoted to seeking solutions to global problems. The result, *What's Going On*, remains one of the most popular, influential, and iconic concept albums ever.

Starting with street noise and conversation, the title track kicks off *What's Going On*. The opening suggests that the song and, for that matter, the entire album, is designed to inform someone who has been away for a while just "what's going on" in the urban United States of the time. Part of the inspiration for this seems to have come from Gaye's younger brother, Frankie, who had been serving in Vietnam just prior to the recording of the album.

Once the song proper begins, it is clear this is not typical protest music of the period. In sharp contrast to the majority of late 1960s' and early 1970s' protest music, Gaye, as a singer, instrumentalist, and producer, and his arranger, David Van DePitte, never become strident. The spacious production, Gaye's gentle multitracked soulful singing, the clarity of the instrumental arrangement, the sustained string lines, and the saxophone solo make "What's Going On" a completely disarming protest song.

In "What's Going On," cowriters Gaye, Cleveland, and Benson deal with police brutality, warfare, picket lines, age and racial discrimination, and poverty. As a singer, Gaye presents the issues and offers that the answer to these social ills is "love." The engaging setting and performance create a curious effect. Conventional wisdom might suggest that the snappy rhythms, beautiful singing style, and spacious production would combine to tell the listener that the singer does not take the issues seriously. In other words, the listener might question how Gaye can bring up the various problems and not express anger about "what's going on." To many listeners, it is clear he does, in fact, take the issues seriously. He just believes so firmly in the power of the simple solution he proposes—love—that there is no place for anger.

What becomes evident as one experiences *What's Going On* is that not only is it a concept album insofar as the lyrics of the songs deal with the theme of contemporary social issues and Gaye's proposed solution to them, but many of the songs also share musical connections. This is perhaps clearest at the start of "What's Happening, Brother." The song opens with a 30-second introduction that, with its conga drums, sustained unison violin lines, tempo, and laid-back feel might initially suggest a remake of "What's Going On." Although one might not take notice at first, the percussion instruments come from the opposite channel that they did on the album's title track. Whether or not it is intentional, this change in the mix is of rhetorical interest, for "What's Happening, Brother" comes from the viewpoint of the man—presumably someone such as Frankie Gaye—who has been away. The two songs can be understood, then, as a conversation; however, it is curious that the questions about recent news come after "What's Going On."

In the next track, "Flyin' High (In the Friendly Sky)," Gaye (and cowriters Anna Gordy Gaye and Elgie Stover) deals with the issue of drug addiction. Gaye portrays an addict who has also "hooked [his] friend to the boy who makes slaves out of men." Gaye incorporates jazz-inspired extended chord, which links the song to several others on the album; however, the overall texture is quite different from any of the other tracks. The rhythm section sets up atmospheric ostinato figures, while the strings play mostly unison extended phrases, and Gaye improvises as he sings. The musical setting—particularly the harmony—creates an otherworldly effect and supports the impressionistic lyrical references to "flyin' high."

"Save the Children" continues the experimental feel of "Flyin' High." Here, though, the lyrics implore the listener to "save the world for the children." Using multitracking, Gaye alternated between speaking and singing each line of the lyrics in the first part of the song. Because he speaks a line of text, and then sings it, the effect is that of a melodic improvisation on each line. While this is effective, perhaps even more striking is the fell of two simultaneous tempi—one steady tempo within the instruments and a second slower and more flexible feel in Gaye's singing.

The conga drums of the album's first two tracks return in "God Is Love," as do the chromatic harmonic motion and emphasis on major sevenths and ninths in the melody. This musical connection reinforces what seems to be the rhetorical connection between "What's Going On," "What's Happening, Brother," and "God Is Love," as well as the progression of the album up to this point. The first two songs establish the problems of American society at the start of the 1970s. "Flyin' High (In the Friendly Sky)" focuses in on one deadly way in which the disenfranchised try to deal with those problems; "Save the Children" tells the listener that solutions to social problems must be found not only for members of Gaye's generation but also for future generations; and "God Is Love" suggests that the solution to the various social ills is God, through Jesus Christ. Significantly, Gaye and cowriters Anna Gordy Gaye, Elgie Stover, and James Nyx include the text "For when we call on him for mercy, mercy...He'll be merciful, my friend." The repetition of the word "mercy" anticipates the title line of the next song, "Mercy Mercy Me (The Ecology)."

In "Mercy Mercy Me (The Ecology)," the only song on the album attributed solely to Marvin Gaye, the singer laments about ecological disasters, such as underground radiation; urban overcrowding; poisoned oceans; and dying birds, fish, and other animals, all caused by humankind's abuse of the natural environment. While "Mercy Mercy Me" is very much a product of its time—the first Earth Day was celebrated in 1970—it remains one of Gaye's best-known and continuingly relevant recordings. The musical setting is even more laid-back and disarming than that of "What's Going On"; however, these two classics share a feeling of spaciousness in the production, emphasis on the conga drums, and jazz-inflected harmonies.

Perhaps the most interesting aspect of "Mercy Mercy Me" is the sense of tension that Gaye creates between the disconcerting scenes of environmental degradation and the laid-back syncopation and engaging melody. Gaye pulls off this rhetorical/musical conflict, in part, because he sounds simultaneously resigned and optimistic. In the context of the album, arguably, the song works more effectively than it does as a stand-alone piece. The "mercy, mercy" link between "God Is Love" and "Mercy Mercy Me (The Ecology)" can be interpreted as a suggestion that, as bad as things might be, there is hope in the Almighty. This hope in the Almighty returns in the track that follows "Mercy Mercy Me," "Right On."

One of the aspects of *What's Going On* that keeps listeners on their toes is that Gaye (as producer) arranged the tracks so that there is not a logical progression over the course of the entire album from despair to hope. For example, after he offers hope for solving humanity's problems through faith in "Right On and "Wholy Holy," he comes back with "Inner City Blues (Make Me Wanna Holler)." Here, Gaye and cowriter James Nyx connect widespread poverty and the resulting crime and consequent police brutality, with the U.S. government channeling money into such things as space exploration and the military. As was the case with the album's earlier songs, in which Gaye expresses dissatisfaction with the state of America—"What's Going On" and "Mercy Mercy Me (The Ecology)," in particular—he keeps his anger fully in check. Similarly, as with old pre-television-era radio programs, the listener to this track is forced to read and interpret the tension that is always lurking below the surface. This serves several purposes: it forces the listener to engage with the entire gestalt of the recording in order to work out the contradictions, it allows the song to connect with a wider demographic than might be the case if it were angry and preachy sounding, and it better connects the song with the sentiments of the album's religious material. Again, then, "Inner City Blues (Make Me Wanna Holler)" probably makes more sense in the context of *What's Going On* than it does as a stand-alone song. This is especially the case when one considers the unexpected harmonic and stylistic shifts that occur just past the 3:30 mark and at approximately at the 4:20 mark. The ending of the song, in particular, with the return of the conga drums coming out of one channel of the stereo soundscape and with the line "Who are they to judge us, simply 'cause our hair is long," connects "Inner City Blues" directly back to the album's title track.

What's Going On made an immediate and lasting impact on U.S. popular culture. The album spent nine weeks at the top of *Billboard* magazine's R&B charts and made it to No. 6 on the pop charts. Although issued before the album, the single release of "What's Going On" reached No. 1 on the *Billboard* R&B charts and No. 2 on the magazine's pop charts. The two singles that were issued after the release of the album, "Mercy Mercy Me (The Ecology)" and "Inner City Blues (Make Me Wanna Holler)," also resonated well with the black community, with both hitting No. 1 on the R&B charts. The album continues to be listed as one of the best albums of all time. For example, in 2012, more than 40 years after the album's debut, *Rolling Stone* ranked *What's Going On* at No. 6 on its list of "500 Greatest Albums of All Time" (*Rolling Stone* 2012).

AL GREEN: *GREATEST HITS*

In the first several years of the 1970s, one could not avoid hearing the voice of Al Green on the radio. Such was the commercial impact of songs such as "Tired of Being Alone," "Let's Stay Together," "I'm Still in Love with You," "Sha La La (Make Me Happy)," and others, on both the R&B and pop charts. Although Green's albums of the period also made an impact, it is, arguably, through these hit singles and through his live shows that he made his greatest imprint on popular culture.

Much more than a biography of Al Green (despite its title), Jimmy McDonough's book *Soul Survivor: A Biography of Al Green* (McDonough 2017) includes important details about how HI Records functioned, what made its soul releases stand out from other Memphis labels, such as Stax and Stax's sister label, Volt. These distinctions can easily be heard in the hits that Green recorded at HI between 1970 and 1977, the tracks contained on this album. Principally, clarity in the arrangements and production distinguished HI recordings from some of the more heavily produced contemporary recordings released on the other major soul labels based in Memphis, Stax and Volt. So, even on a later (1974) piece such as "Sha La La (Make Me Happy)," which includes brass; strings; the Sandra Rhodes, Charles Chalmers, and Donna Rhodes backing vocals; and Green's customary HI rhythm section, the component parts of the overall texture each has individual role to play, and they do not get in each other's way the way they might seem to compete in some of the more-heavily produced recordings of the period from HI's Memphis competitors.

Arguably, however, this feeling of clarity can best be experienced in Green's most commercially successful hit, "Let's Stay Together." The minimalistic approach allows all the instrumental parts, the backing vocals, and the lead vocal to be clear. This song, too, is an excellent example of Green's unique vocal approach. He moves between falsetto and regular, lower-range singing, and sings in an improvisatory manner. Each verse, or each statement of the chorus, is slightly different than the rest melodically. Although Al Green grew up in gospel music, his singing style—once it became fully established at HI—was gentler than that of some of the more overtly expressive male soul singers who preceded him. Listeners might think of Green as a microphone singer, almost an improvisatory soul crooner, as opposed to some of his counterparts, vocalists who the microphone captured, but who sang with the kind of volume they might have used when singing unamplified in a church.

What the listener can overlook in experiencing the hit songs that Green cowrote with the various combinations of producer/engineer/HI Records executive Willie Mitchell, guitarist Maron "Teenie" Hodges, and drummer Al Jackson, is how deceptively complex they are. For example, the harmony of a song such as "Let's Stay Together" includes seventh chords, ninth chords, three-note chords with a nonchord tone in the bass, and unusual chord-root motion. In addition, Green's lead vocal melody sometimes finds him on the dissonant upper extensions of the chords. It is difficult to sing, say, the major-seventh of a chord or extensions above that accurately, so, although the melodies tend to have a natural and easy feel, they often require a keen ear and vocal execution to match. This songwriting and singing approach certainly is not limited to the smash hit "Let's Stay Together"; it runs through the bulk of the songs on *Greatest Hits*.

Although perhaps not widely known at the time, HI Records was one of several Southern soul record companies and/or recording studios that was racially integrated. In Muscle Shoals, Alabama, white studio musicians and producers backed up black singers on numerous soul and R&B recordings at FAME Studios and Muscle Shoals Sound Studio, and at Stax Records in Memphis, Tennessee, the integrated Booker T. & the M.G.'s not only enjoyed crossover pop and R&B instrumental hits (e.g., "Green Onions), they were also the house band that performed on countless soul recordings. HI Records differed fundamentally, however, in that the white trio of Sandra Rhodes, Charles Chalmers, and Donna Rhodes, who came out of the country and white gospel music traditions, were the studio's backing vocalists. Rhodes, Chalmers, and Rhodes can be heard prominently on Green's entire catalog throughout his tenure at HI.

Green wrote or cowrote eight of the nine tracks that HI included on *Greatest Hits*. The one exception is a cover of Norman Whitfield and Barrett Strong's "I Can't Get Next to You," a 1969 hit that Whitfield and Strong wrote for their Motown labelmates, the Temptations. In place of highly danceable and funky syncopations at the sixteenth-note level of the Temptations' chart-topping version, the Green recording turns "I Can't Get Next to You" into a 12/8-meter ballad. The Green version, though, has an off-kilter rhythmic and metrical feel, in part because of the metrical placement of the backing vocal "I can't get next to you" refrain and the principal horn figure, which tends to defy the meter. The slow tempo and the fact that the lead vocals do not jump from singer to singer as they do in the Temptations' version emphasizes the lyrics' theme of unrequited love. Green, Willie Mitchell, and the HI house band and backing vocal trio take what was a dance-oriented sad song and turn it into a soulful sad song.

About the only other major song associated with Al Green during this important part of his career that is left off the *Greatest Hits* album is

"Take Me to the River," which Green cowrote with Teenie Hodges and which was a hit R&B chart single for Syl Johnson. For Green, "Take Me to the River" was an album track on *Al Green Explores Your Mind* in 1974. Although the song was not included on *Greatest Hits*, it has been one of Al Green's most persistent compositions. In 1978, new-wave rockers Talking Heads included the song on their album *More Songs about Buildings and Food*. Talking Heads' single version made it squarely into the pop Top 40 the following year, and the song played prominent roles in several of the band's tours and live films. From around the start of the 21st century, "Take Me to the River" was sung by the kitschy (some would say, tacky) animatronic Big Mouth Billy Bass, a novelty that was popular and widely parodied for several years.

Green's style influenced subsequent soul singers in how he incorporated falsetto within his singing range, arguably making it more seductive and sexier than, say, Smokey Robinson, whose falsetto vocals were a staple of Motown in the 1960s. The clarity of the arrangements and production on Green's hits during his HI Records period also paved the way for the kind of production heard in some of the blue-eyed soul music of the 1970s and beyond.

ISAAC HAYES: *HOT BUTTERED SOUL*

In many respects, Isaac Hayes's 1969 album *Hot Buttered Soul* was one of the most unusual soul collections ever: the bulk of the playing time for the four tracks was allotted to covers of songs that were originally middle-of-the-road and country-pop hits, respectively, "Walk on By" and "By the Time I Get to Phoenix." And why only four tracks in approximately 45 minutes? Because "By the Time I Get to Phoenix" clocked in at almost 19 minutes, and "Walk on By" tipped the scales at over 12 minutes. The other tracks, "Hyperbolicsyllabicsesquedalymistic" and "One Woman," were not exactly lightweights either, at $9\frac{1}{2}$ and 5 minutes, respectively. And what possible reason was there for a disc with such lengthy, hypnotic, repetitious tracks that seem to keep building and building? As Robert Gordon writes in his history of Stax Records, Hayes's label at the time, "this was a boudoir record" (Gordon 2015, 235). More than that, *Hot Buttered Soul* was an album that, more than virtually any album of its time, focused on arrangements and studio production.

The story of how this album came to be, particularly because Isaac Hayes was primarily active at Memphis-based Stax as a songwriter and record producer, and because his first album as a solo artist was not a commercial success is interesting. The short version of the story is that up until 1968, Atlantic Records distributed Stax releases; however, the distribution agreement ended in 1968. After the split, Atlantic owned the distribution rights to Stax's catalog up until 1968, a tremendous blow to a company that had been associated with blues and Southern soul music for approximately the previous decade. It was in an atmosphere of the Stax label desperately needing new product that Hayes went back into the studio and recorded this highly unusual—and highly commercially successful—album.

Hot Buttered Soul opens with Burt Bacharach and Hal David's "Walk on By," which had been a hit single for singer Dionne Warwick in 1964. It might not be entirely fitting to call the Isaac Hayes version a deconstruction of the original, although the song's original melody is mostly in the backing female vocals and not in Hayes's more improvisatory lead vocal. Given the recording's length; its variety of instrumental tone colors; the sense that, at times, it only hints at Bacharach's original tune; and how the instrumental setting seems to play out the sentiments of the lyrics, it might be best to think of this as a reconstruction or recomposition of "Walk on By."

Most of the tone colors of the lengthy introduction come from the realm of an R&B/soul rhythm section and the realm of orchestral instruments. In the latter category, the Bar-Kays, the Stax studio musicians, served as the rhythm section for the entire album. The one part of the aural spectrum that stands out from the rest of the instrumental tone colors is the fuzz-tone electric guitar. As the song progresses, the guitar plays an increasingly prominent role. In the introduction, the guitar plays a riff figure that begins the same way as jazz great Cannonball Adderley's "Work Song."

As Hayes and the backing vocalists sing, several orchestral woodwind instruments play brief fill figures to round out the phrases. These include contributions from a solo oboe and another figure played by a pair of flutes in harmony. The fuzz-tone guitar continues to play a role throughout this part of the piece. Because the electric guitar tone contrasts so highly with that of the orchestral woodwinds, and because Hal David's text revolves around a relationship that is so broken that the singer's character tells a former partner to "just walk on by" if they see each other on the street, some listeners might interpret the edgy fuzz-tone guitar as representing one of the characters, and the more mellow woodwinds as representing the other.

"Walk on By" concludes with a lengthy groove section in which the full orchestra and the rhythm section play hypnotic repetitious figures over march-like drumming, while the fuzz-tone guitarist improvises.

When released as a single, "Walk on By" was heavily edited. The full-length version, however, is much more intense, and, so, it captures the feeling of a relationship that is totally and completely unreconcilable.

"Hyperbolicsyllabicsesquedalymistic" combines elements of funk and electric blues in a playful call to lovemaking in which Hayes sings a text built on somewhat disconnected, impressionistic notions involving numerous multisyllabic words. Much of the effect of the piece comes from the sound of these multi-syllabic words, and not necessarily their meaning within a narrative. This calls to mind a quote widely attributed to jazz saxophonist Charlie Parker when he was asked about the meaning of the title of one of his compositions, "Klactoveedsedstene." Parker is reputed to have said something on the order of, "It's a sound, man; it's just a sound." So, Isaac Hayes's "Hyperbolicsyllabicsesquedalymistic," too, is about the sounds of the words, from the title, which is sung by the backing chorus, to the likes of "modus operandi," "sweet phalanges," "gastronomical stupensity," and so on, as sung by Hayes.

"One Woman," a song from the pens of Charles Chalmers and Sandra Rhodes, is a far more conventional soulful ballad. Although the orchestration utilizes the oboe and celesta on solo lines, the overall arrangement is not nearly as elaborate—some might say "over the top"—as those of the other tracks. Although the setting and the musical aspects of the song and the recording are entirely fitting for a gentle love ballad, the lyrics paint this as anything but the conventional love ballad. Hayes sings of his love for the one woman who "is making [his] home," as well as his love for another woman who is "making [him] do wrong." The song's structure—supported by the musical setting and the lead vocals of Hayes—suggests that his character feels genuine love for both his wife and the woman with whom he is having an affair. It might be going too far to suggest that Hayes's character becomes a sympathetic figure for the listener; however, the entire package of the song paints him as more sincere than a mere good-for-nothing cad.

As a stand-alone song, "One Woman" might seem, to some listeners, like a weak excuse for an extramarital affair; however, the song functions very well in the context of the second side of the original LP. Here, it stands in sharp contrast to Jimmy Webb's composition "By the Time I Get to Phoenix." In the Webb song, Hayes provides a lengthy and detailed spoken account of the situation between a loving and loyal man and a cheating wife that goes well beyond Webb's actual lyrics. To put it another way, Hayes takes Webb's premise and riffs on it. The piece becomes a tale of morality and how the lack of morality on the part of the cheating spouse utterly breaks the heart of the husband.

The pairing of "One Woman" and "By the Time I Get to Phoenix," then, raises several questions, such as does Hayes support extramarital affairs by men, but not by women (using a literal read of both songs), or is there a deeper subtext, a two-song morality play? The first song seems to set\ the listener up for the expectation that the Hayes' character's relationships with the two women are justified because (as he claims) he loves them both. Then, the second song shoots down whatever sympathy the listener might have had for Hayes's character in the first. To distill this down to its essence: the pairing of the songs seems to cause a pull and tug of emotional responses.

Regardless of whether the listener interprets the pairing of the songs on the second side of the album (as originally released on LP) as a two-part morality play, there is one other important point to consider regarding Hayes's monologue. By expanding greatly on Jimmy Webb's premise and providing elaborate details about the husband's situation and his evolving emotional responses to his wife's serial cheating with different men, Hayes demonstrates the emotional intensity associated with much soul music. To put it another way, he takes Webb's story and lyrics and gives the listener a clear feel for what the young man is going through. When Hayes sings the song proper, then, we can empathize with him in a more complete way than we can with Glen Campbell in his multi-Grammy-winning recording, and it is this emotional connection that is necessary for soul music to work at its best.

From the musical standpoint, "By the Time I Get to Phoenix" pulls out all the proverbial stops that Hayes and his compatriots used on the other three *Hot Buttered Soul* tracks. However, this piece is marked by an easier-to-perceive long-range structure. The instrumental backing for Hayes during his monologue and during the sung part of the piece gradually and continually increases in volume. In this respect, the piece is something like a soul version of Maurice Ravel's famous orchestral composition *Bolero*, famously associated with lovemaking in popular culture by virtue of the movie *10*. After Hayes and the backing vocalists finish singing, "By the Time I Get to Phoenix" concludes with a lengthy instrumental section. Here, the rhythm section maintains the momentum, while various orchestral string, woodwind, and brass figures are layered over the top of the rhythm section.

As writer Robert Gordon described how Hayes approached the album, "Immersed in the studio's possibilities, and his own, with instructions to do as he pleased, he'd opened a door that other singers hadn't seen, and legions followed him through it, fans and artists alike" (Gordon 2015, 235). That is certainly a more-than-fair assessment of one of the most unusual LPs ever released in the soul genre or in any other popular music genre.

LAURYN HILL: *THE MISEDUCATION OF LAURYN HILL*[4]

Onetime member of the hip-hop trio the Fugees, Lauryn Hill began her solo career in 1998. Her debut solo album, *The Miseducation of Lauryn Hill*, created a sensation in the world of hip-hop and R&B and is now considered a neo-soul classic. The album garnered Grammy Awards for Album of the Year and Best R&B Album, and the song "Doo Wop (That Thing)" earned Grammys for Best Female R&B Performance and Best R&B Song. The album sold well enough to top virtually every imaginable record chart and was seen as a formidable personal statement, as Hill wrote or cowrote every track, produced or coproduced every track, and served as the entire collection's executive producer. However, there was a problem: Hill's unique blend of hip-hop, R&B, and soul was followed by virtual silence into the 21st century, not to mention a jail term for tax evasion. Although that this album is nearly a singular example of Lauryn Hill's work as a solo artist, *The Miseducation of Lauryn Hill* still stands as perhaps the best document of what it was like to be black, urban, and female in the United States at the end of the 20th century.

The brief opening track, "Intro," sets the stage for what follows. This piece includes a slow acoustical background from which the sound of a teacher's voice taking attendance gradually emerges. As the album progresses, Hill returns to the sound of the classroom but, more importantly, conjures up images of what urban black youths find when they move from the world of the school to the street.

The album's first song, "Lost Ones," establishes Hill's philosophical basis and her eclectic musical style. Her rap addresses someone who has "gained the whole world for the price of your soul." Throughout the song, Hill contrasts the need to follow one's heart and ethical and religious rules with the insular self-serving lust for power, control, sex, money, and fame that she sees in her counterpart(s). The piece has been interpreted as Hill's put-down of the commercial motivations of Wyclef Jean and Pras Michel, her former partners in the Fugees (see, for example, Bush n.d.-b). Rarely does Hill maintain the same style or texture throughout any given song on the album. In "Lost Ones," for example, she juxtaposes Jamaican-style rap with soul. Another notable feature of the production is Hill's exploration of rhythmic phrases in the chorus section, in which the background rap seems to go ever so slightly out of phase with the backing instruments. This creates a feeling of unbalance that, whether intentionally or not, supports the tension of Hill's lyrics.

A production element that binds some of the songs on *The Miseducation of Lauryn Hill* together is the sound of a scratchy, old-school vinyl record spinning on a turntable in the background. This effect seemed to be in vogue in the second half of the 1990s in the neo-soul genre, as D'Angelo also used it on his contemporaneous album *Brown Sugar*. On "Lost Ones," the effect is subtle; however, the sound of the scratchy record is more pronounced on other tracks. It seems to support the contrasts that Hill draws in her lyrics, particularly the opposition between what children learn in school versus the experience on the streets and the opposition between the love of money versus the love of people and relationships. Because Hill uses the effect as a unifying factor throughout the album, it becomes part of the album's narrative, in contrast to how the effect might seem to be grafted on needlessly in the work of some other artists of the era.

In "Ex-Factor," Hill's character addresses a former lover with whom she is still deeply in love. No matter what she does, she receives no "reciprocity." Although the track includes the incessant subwoofer pounding bass drum that instantly identifies the recording as a product of the late 20th-century hip-hop era, the lyrical theme and style and the melodic and harmonic aspects of the song owe a great deal to old-school soul. This is part of the beauty of *The Miseducation of Lauryn Hill*. While Hill explores various aspects of pain, disappointment, loss, deceit, and conflict between the values of the heart and the values of the material world—as well as other life experiences—throughout the album, she does so by successfully walking a musical tightrope between romantic soul/R&B and edgier rap.

The next track, "To Zion," mixes biblical imagery with images drawn from the real-life story of undoubtedly countless women of more modern times. In contrast to "Ex-Factor," here Hill sings in the lower part of her range, which may suggest that she portrays a different character. Her text explores a situation in which her character is pregnant, with friends suggesting that she "think of [her] career." The unspoken implication is that they counseled her to terminate her pregnancy. The title of the song refers to the sense of joy that Hill's character feels when her son is born. Hill's minor-key musical setting, while firmly placed in the modern R&B/hip-hop realm, weaves in the influence of Hispanic music. In part, this comes from Hill's use of harmony and the minor mode, but it is also suggested by the inspired guitar playing of guest artist Carlos Santana.

"Doo Wop (That Thing)" is the best-known song on the album. Here, Hill turns to the theme explored by several female singer-songwriters over the course of at least the past several decades before the release of *The Miseducation of Lauryn Hill*: that one cannot truly love another unless one learns to love oneself. In the past, several songs of Carole King's album *Tapestry*—particularly "Beautiful"—expressed the importance of a feeling of self-worth to young women of the early 1970s, and Whitney Houston's recording of "Greatest Love of All" brought the same general theme to the young women of the second half of the 1980s. Because of its commercial and critical success, "Doo Wop (That Thing)" is a worthy successor. However, Hill's recording is not the product of a longtime well-established songsmith or the work of a diva. "Doo Wop (That Thing)" is more to the point and enjoys a certain "street cred" because of the gritty and graphic nature of the lyrics (particularly Hill's rap). The musical setting includes references to earlier R&B and soul, a touch of jazz, and street-corner doo-wop.

Hill's next song, "Superstar," can be understood as a put-down of her former Fugees or, more generally, of any musicians who turned their focus from music designed "to inspire" to thoughts of superstardom. "Final Hour" is more experimental—and more memorable than "Superstar"—but sharpens the lyrical focus more on spirituality and the consideration of what one really possesses in "the final hour." Hill raps that at the end of one's life, "power" and "money" mean nothing. The piece is particularly interesting as a recording and production because of the phasing of the vocals and the layering effects.

In "When It Hurts So Bad," Hill moves into the world of smooth, romantic, soulful R&B. Like the other rap-free songs on the album, however, there are production touches—here principally in background percussion lines that work against the prevailing beat and subdivision of the beat—that paint the song as a product of the late 1990s. As impressive as Lauryn Hill's vocals and those of her backup singers are on the track, in retrospect, the production add-ons seem somewhat gimmicky on this song. The main problem is that the production effects draw the listener's attention away from the singing.

The next track, "I Used to Love Him," does not suffer from the same drawback. The piece works better than "When It Hurts So Bad" because, overall, it does not reference older styles as much. As a result, Hill gets away more easily with the experimental production effects. The other thing that makes "I Used to Love Him" stand out is the lyrical depth of the song. If the previous pieces seem like a collection of somewhat-connected tracks that do not entirely reach a concept-album level of coherence, then "I Used to Love Him" pulls several of them together. Hill's character sings about a man she "used to love" but no longer does. More importantly, she prays to "the father" (her "creator," in a subsequent stanza) to forgive her for her past sins. This might cause the listener to reflect on "To Zion," which also included religious and spiritual references.

Not only does Hill's character pray for forgiveness for herself in "I Used to Love Him," she broadens her prayer to include all sinners in "Forgive Them Father." However, her focus is on "backstabbers," and, as historical examples, she cites Cain, Judas, and Brutus. The mix of rap (essentially constituting the verses) and singing (the tuneful chorus) is particularly effective in this piece, which makes it a highlight of the album. The imagery in Hill's rap, too, is a bit more diverse than in some of the other songs and includes references to apartheid and the Soweto area of Johannesburg, South Africa; Pinocchio's creator, Geppetto; the previously mentioned biblical/historical figures; and more general themes, such as the desire to build oneself up by tearing another down.

In "Every Ghetto, Every City," Hill reflects on growing up and suggests that the experiences of youth remain with her, even now that she has found fame and success in the music industry. Clearly, not all things that Hill witnessed and experienced in "every ghetto, every city, and every suburban place" of her youth were happy ones; however, each is indelibly etched on her. On the surface, "Every Ghetto, Every City" does not appear to be as much of a message song as some of the others on the album. In the context of those earlier tracks, however, the song's overarching background theme seems to be that people must do everything they can to raise children in loving and caring environments, because their childhoods will help shape who they will be and what they will accomplish for the rest of their lives.

The next track, "Nothing Even Matters," is easy to overlook, particularly if one listens to *The Miseducation of Lauryn Hill* for its overt social commentary. "Nothing Even Matters" is a pure love song and sounds like a late 1990s' descendant of the slow soul ballads of the quiet storm genre. The gist of the lyrics is that no matter what problems befall Hill's character, "nothing even matters" because of the strength of the relationship she is in. The thing that really makes this track stand out from hundreds of other soulful love ballads is the musical arrangement, which includes a recurring off-kilter percussion effect in what sounds like synthesized finger snaps. The music, then, simultaneously plays out the quiet stability that Hill's character finds in her relationship and the unsettling problems that can otherwise be found in everyday life.

Hill's rap in the next song, "Everything Is Everything" provides perhaps the best description of her intent in the piece and throughout the album: "where hip hop meets scripture." She provides a message of hope (e.g., "after winter must come spring") that speaks to the audience of

Hill's time and place, just as other pop musicians from George Harrison to Stevie Wonder did in the 1970s and 1980s. In fact, the theme of the negative leading by necessity to the positive reflects Harrison's "All Things Must Pass." The spirit of Stevie Wonder's work can be heard in Hill's singing style; in the synthesized string arrangement, which sounds as though it could have been inspired by deconstructing Wonder's "Village Ghetto Land"; and in the focus on spirituality providing a sanctuary from deprivation and discrimination.

In the album's title track, Hill reaffirms the belief that, in order to achieve fulfillment, one must follow the lead of one's heart and not the demands of others. Some listeners may come at *The Miseducation of Lauryn Hill* with the view that, generally, effective singers are not necessarily effective rappers and vice versa and that the two vocal performance media require such different skill sets that it would be difficult to find someone equally skilled as a singer and as a rapper. This song, perhaps better than anything else Hill has recorded, exhibits her talent as a pure singer. Her technique and expression are so effective that it seems nearly impossible that this is the same Hill who delivers rhythmically complex, finely developed rap elsewhere on the album.

Next, Hill turns to the old 1967 hit for Frankie Valli, "Can't Take My Eyes off of You." Although this might seem an unlikely cover, the rhythm track and the production techniques paint the setting as pure 1990s' hip-hop. The sequential nature of the melody of the verses of this Bob Crewe and Bob Gaudio song sound as contemporary in a late 1990s' context as it did in the pop/jazz context of the Valli recording. Musically, however, the chorus sounds a bit dated and does not translate into the hip-hop medium as well. Rhetorically, the piece is a fitting companion for Hill's own "Nothing Even Matters." The album concludes with another view of love, "Tell Him," a song with lyrics based largely on the famous "Love is patient, love is kind . . . " text of 1 Corinthians 13.

The nature of love and the importance of love and understanding, forgiveness, and nurturing young people are the basic themes that connect the songs of *The Miseducation of Lauryn Hill*. The spirituality that runs through the album reflects on some of the earlier artists who straddled the gospel/soul divide, and the album proved that one person could excel at singing, rapping, and producing. The album still stands as one of the greatest integrations of soul and hip-hop.

WHITNEY HOUSTON

Arguably, the age of the diva in modern popular music began with Whitney Houston's ascent to stardom in the middle of the 1980s. It is difficult to imagine artists from the world of soul and beyond such as Mariah Carey, Céline Dion, Jennifer Hudson, Alicia Keys, Beyoncé, Adele, and numerous others without the influence of Houston. With her mother, gospel and soul singer Cissy Houston, and her cousin, pop and soul singer Dionne Warwick, her godmother, singer Darlene Love, and her close family friend, soul superstar Aretha Franklin, Houston seemed to be destined to be a presence in the world of gospel music and soul from childhood. Ultimately, Houston became one of—if not the—best-selling female artist in the history of sound recording.

Houston grew up singing in church and began her professional career as a backing singer. Her first two albums, *Whitney Houston* and *Whitney* were released in 1985 and 1987, respectively. Both albums topped the charts and immediately established her as a star. Houston's success was equally impressive on the singles charts: "You Give Good Love" from Houston's debut album topped the R&B singles charts, and her cover of "Saving All My Love for You," also from Houston's debut album, topped the pop charts. Without question, one of Whitney Houston's most iconic performances on her debut album was of the Michael Masser and Linda Creed song "Greatest Love of All." This work started out life as "The Greatest Love of All." Under its original title, the public first heard the song in the 1977 film *The Greatest*, in a rendition recorded by jazz/soul singer-guitarist George Benson.

As well-remembered as "Greatest Love of All" remains, arguably Whitney Houston's best-known recording came from the soundtrack of the 1992 film *The Bodyguard*. Her cover of country singer-songwriter Dolly Parton's composition "I Will Always Love You" was the most significant hit from among the half-dozen Houston recordings in the film. Although Parton had topped the country charts twice earlier with her song—upon her first single release of "I Will Always Love You" in 1974 and with a new version of the song for the 1982 film *The Best Little Whorehouse in Texas*—Houston's version was even more commercially and critically successful. In fact, Houston's cover of the Parton song is reputed to be one of the best-selling singles in the history of the recording industry. The soundtrack for *The Bodyguard* earned Houston a Grammy Award for Record of the Year, Soundtrack Album, and a Grammy Award for Album of the Year.

Babyface, whose work with Boyz II Men help that vocal group reach the top of the R&B charts several times during the 1990s, contributed "Exhale (Shoop Shoop)," a hit for Houston from the soundtrack of the 1995 film *Waiting to Exhale*. As she had done in *The Bodyguard*, Houston starred in *Waiting to Exhale*. The following year, she starred in the film *The Preacher's Wife*, a remake of a five-decades-old movie. The soundtrack album for *The Preacher's Wife* is reputed to be the best-selling gospel album of all time. *The Preacher's Wife: Original Soundtrack Album* topped the R&B album charts and made it into the Top 10 of the pop album charts. Despite its commercial success, the film's soundtrack was not an unqualified critical success. For example, AllMusic's Stephen Thomas Erlewine gave the album a decidedly mixed review, describing the soundtrack as "a fairly awkward attempt at gospel-soul" (Erlewine n.d.-b).

Throughout her career, Whitney Houston was one of the most successful crossover artists in the music industry. In fact, like Motown's highly successful 1960s vocal group the Supremes, Houston's singles generally performed slightly better on the pop charts than on the R&B charts. Many of her singles from the 1980s and 1990s also rose high in the adult contemporary charts. As a result, Houston is sometimes considered a pop singer; however, her broad crossover appeal established her as perhaps *the* voice of soul of the second half of the 1980s into the early 1990s.

The songs that Whitney Houston took to the top of the charts came from as disparate sources as even the most diverse soul artist included in this volume, including covers of songs originally associated with Dolly Parton and George Benson to stand-alone songs specifically written for Houston. What marked all the recordings, be they pop ballads, soulful ballads, or dance songs, was Houston's voice. In fact, it was the bigness of Houston's voice, her use of vibrato, and her use of melismas that marked her as the vocal diva of her generation. In the wake of Houston's premature death, the *BBC News Magazine*'s Lauren Everitt wrote of Houston's use of melismas, "An early 'I' in Whitney Houston's 'I Will Always Love You' takes nearly six seconds to sing. In those seconds the former gospel singer-turned-pop star packs a series of difference notes into the single syllable. The technique is repeated throughout the song, most pronouncedly on every 'I' and 'you.' The vocal technique is called melisma, and it has inspired a host of imitators. Other artists may have used it before Houston, but it was her rendition of Dolly Parton's love song that pushed the technique into the mainstream in the 90s" (Everitt 2012).

The commercial and critical success that Houston enjoyed helped ensure that she would influence the next several generations of soul and pop singers, including Mariah Carey, Adele, Jennifer Hudson, and others. As mentioned by Everitt, some singers, such as Carey, extended Houston's melismatic melodic variations; however, others, such as blue-eyed soul singer Adele, were influenced by the sheer power of Houston's vocal delivery.

Writing in the U.K. publication *The Telegraph*, Tracey Thorn described the appeal of "big-voiced" singers. Regarding Whitney Houston, Thorn wrote, "Like many listeners I was wowed by the accuracy and punch of her singing, and the apparent ease. Critic Simon Frith described her 'swinging through a ballad like a trapeze artist,' which conveys something of the panache of a great singer. But it seems we were all taken in. The years took their toll on her voice, but it wasn't just smoking and drugs that did the damage—it was the very way in which she sang. I've seen several vocal experts talk about the wrongness of her singing, the absence of technique, and it astonished me" (Thorn 2016). Indeed, Houston's approach damaged her instrument, as it has Adele's and other singers who belt out a song using improper vocal technique. Houston developed a reputation as a demanding star, an attribute some subsequent soul and pop divas have adopted. However, as easily the most commercially successful artist of her generation and one of the best-selling artists in the history of commercial sound recording, Whitney Houston virtually defined a major aspect of soul music, particularly from the late 1980s through the 1990s.

THE IMPRESSIONS: "PEOPLE GET READY"

Although they underwent a couple of name changes and numerous personnel changes, the Impressions' career spanned 60 years. Arguably, the most significant part of this career was in the 1960s, particularly during the period in which the group's Curtis Mayfield served as principal songwriter. Not only were the Impressions notable for their smooth harmony vocals, several of their recordings during the Mayfield era played important roles in the civil rights movement. Mayfield's 1965 song "People Get Ready" is perhaps one of the clearest examples of the connection of soul back to gospel and back to the spirituals and sorrow songs that provided solace and hope and expressed sadness during slavery. The song was also a commercial success, but, more importantly, it has been covered by numerous artists, and became an anthem of the U.S. civil rights movement, as well as social movements in other countries.

Mayfield's lyrics find the singer inviting humanity to "get ready" for an approaching train to freedom and brotherhood and sisterhood. A little more than a century earlier, the train metaphor could have been understood literally as code for the underground railroad. Even after the Civil War era, however, the symbol of a train to freedom remained part of the lexicon, even if it became more symbolic. References to "the train to Jordan" and Mayfield's offering that all that is required for admittance to the train is "to thank the Lord" also paint the song as a descendant of the 19th-century tradition of spirituals that used Judeo-Christian imagery and stories as symbols of contemporary struggles for freedom. However, the images continued to give hope in the struggle against Jim Crow laws, the struggles with poverty and unequal treatment during the Great Depression, the specter of lynchings, and so on. Mayfield's theme of a train that is open to all except for unrepentant sinners also calls to mind the old gospel song "This Train," sometimes called "This Train Is Bound for Glory." So, Mayfield's lyrics not only directly tied "People Get Ready" to an important mid-19th-century song tradition as well as to the early 20th-century gospel tradition but were also part of a thriving ongoing tradition. As Mark Anthony Neal described the social importance of the Impressions in *What the Music Said: Black Popular Music and Black Public Consciousness*, "Mayfield originals like 'People Get Ready,' 'Keep on Pushing,' and Jester Hairston's 'Amen,' effectively secularized black spirituals for mainstream audiences, though unlike Ray Charles, the Impressions did so while maintaining some semblance of religious discourse" (Neal 1999, 52).

Notably, one of Mayfield's references breaks the clear ties to the past with the train imagery and the spiritual-like music: the type of propulsion that moves the train. The text includes references to hearing "the diesels humming," which paints the song as a 20th-century protest song. In fact, because diesel locomotives became widespread in the United States after World War II, Mayfield's reference marks "People Get Ready" as a song of its time, even as otherwise connected as it is to past rhetorical and musical traditions.

Despite the clear ties of "People Get Ready" to the past, it is not a musical re-creation of black spirituals of an earlier century. True, Curtis Mayfield's melodic and harmonic vocabularies demonstrate ties back through gospel to the spirituals, but the musical setting and the singing style of the Impressions is contemporary. an important aspect of the recording is that it largely features Mayfield on lead vocals singing in a high falsetto register. Mayfield's gentle falsetto and the soul ballad-like instrumental arrangement are thoroughly disarming, a contrast to some of the more confrontational realities of the civil rights movement. Perhaps this and the easy-to-remember tunefulness of the melody are part of the reason the song took on life as part of the movement; it was a peaceful song of hope and protest that seems to have aligned particularly well with Rev. Dr. Martin Luther King Jr.'s tactics of nonviolent protest.

In fact, King actively used the song within the civil rights marches and rallies (Erickson n.d.).

This disarming quality of "People Get Ready" also anticipated the later post-1970, gentle antiwar protest songs that graced the pop and/or R&B charts, songs such as Marvin Gaye's "What's Going On" (which takes on several social issues of its time), Freda Payne's "Bring the Boys Home," Mayfield's "We Gotta Have Peace," Cat Stevens's "Peace Train," and so on. Although some of the spiritual descendants of "People Get Ready" were successful commercially and in galvanizing focus on their movements' pushes for social change, some were not, and some were met with critical reaction that suggested that the gentle, soft-sell approach was meant more to sell records than to make a political point.

It would be difficult to make that accusation of "People Get Ready," the song that started it all. Although Mayfield and his fellow Impressions' vocal styles re disarming and easily accessible to a wide variety of listeners, it sounds sincere. There is a sense of pain from the hurts—the unspoken racism and the economic and social disaffection and oppression—of the past, but also a sense of hope in the singers' voices. This is what makes "People Get Ready" authentic in its expression, even though it was a commercial success.

A variety of artists have covered "People Get Ready," including Bob Dylan, Glen Campbell, Aretha Franklin, Al Green, Rod Stewart, Bob Marley, John Denver, Dusty Springfield, and numerous others. This suggests both the song's universal message of love and acceptance and its religious connotations and how important "People Get Ready" was sociologically in the 1960s and beyond.

In 2011, *Rolling Stone* magazine ranked "People Get Ready" No. 24 in its list of "The 500 Greatest Songs of All Time" (*Rolling Stone* 2011). In 2015, the Library of Congress added "People Get Ready" to its National Recording Registry (National Recording Preservation Board of the Library of Congress n.d.).

THE ISLEY BROTHERS: *THE HEAT IS ON*

Readers may be familiar with the Isley Brothers' 1959 song "Shout," which is one of the best-remembered and most persistent call-and-response party songs of the late 1950s. In the words of Ernie Isley, the younger brother of the group's founders and later a full-time member of the group, "Shout" "was gospel designed as rock-and-roll, and a lot of people in my mother's church were not too pleased when it came out" (Wilner 1977). This song was not necessarily an overwhelming hit at the time of the single's release, but it has remained in the repertoire of rock and R&B bands throughout the intervening decades, a cover version by the fictional band Otis Day and the Knights was featured in one of the best-remembered scenes from the 1978 film *National Lampoon's Animal House* (perhaps one of the best comedies about college life ever), and a lyrically modified cover version of "Shout" has been used as a theme song by the NFL's Buffalo Bills ever since the late 1980s. The Isley Brothers are also well remembered for being the first group to enjoy a hit with the song "Twist and Shout," although today, the Beatles' cover version is more likely to be heard than the original. The Isley Brothers evolved musically from the late 1950s and early 1960s to the mid-1970s. Their 1975 album *The Heat Is On* found the Isleys mixing soul, funk, and elements of psychedelic blues-rock. *The Heat Is On* featured material written entirely by the group, usual overall structure, and important political commentary in the form of "Fight the Power." Surprisingly, for a family-based group as well-known as the Isley Brothers had been for years, *The Heat Is On* was also the Isley Brothers' first album to top the pop charts. Starting with the album's predecessor, *Live It Up*, *The Heat Is On* was also part of a string of five R&B chart-topping albums in a row.

The Heat Is On opens with "Fight the Power." When the song was released as a two-part single, it topped the R&B charts and made it well into the Top 10 of the pop charts, albeit with one expletive beeped out for radio airplay. Easily the best-remembered and most influential track on the album, "Fight the Power" is a call to "fight the powers that be," those that are behind "all this bulls*** going down" in society. The funky style of the song resembles some of the late 1960s' and early 1970s' work of Sly and the Family Stone. The rhythm-section style and the riff-based nature of the bass line also suggest a link between, say, the work of Sly and the Family Stone and the popular late-1970s and early-1980s recordings of funk stars such as Rick James. The singing style is grittier and more forceful than some of the other funk/soul songs of the era that also dealt with social ills such as discrimination against young people, racism, poverty, and the silencing of dissent, particularly when compared with Marvin Gaye's songs on *What's Going On* and Stevie Wonder's socially conscious music of the first half of the 1973 to 1976 period.

The funk-style bass line is instantly recognizable, as is the melody, which is built of brief phrases in an antecedent-consequent relationship. Although the melody, the bass line, the rhythmic feel, and so on, are filled with hooks that are clearly behind the song's commercial success, it is interesting to note how much the Isley Brothers' musical and lyrical vocabulary had evolved since the group-composed "Shout" over a decade and a half earlier.

"Fight the Power" not only was popular as a single release but also can be viewed as one of the songs of the 1970s that helped open lyrics up to include expletives. In "Fight the Power," the word "bulls***" might have required a beep for radio airplay and might have offended some listeners, but it does seem appropriate as a description of the kinds of social ills about which the Isleys sing. Of course, frank language about social ills became considerably more common and more explicit with the rise of rap, and the Isley Brothers' "Fight the Power" has a clear connection to that genre. According to rapper Chuck D, the Isley Brothers' "Fight the Power" was the inspiration for Public Enemy's song of the same title, a piece written for the 1989 Spike Lee film *Do the Right Thing* (Myrie 2008, 122). In fact, in 2018, National Public Radio's Phil Harrell interviewed Chuck D and Ernie Isley about the origins and relationships of the two songs (see Harrell 2018 for a transcription of the interview, as well as for a link to the audio recording). Just as the Isley Brothers' "Fight the Power" addressed social issues of the mid-1970s, the Public Enemy song of the same name dealt specifically with late-1980s issues that were of concern in urban black communities.

An interesting structural feature of *The Heat Is On* is that each one of the tracks is given as "Pts. 1 & 2" (e.g., "Fight the Power, Pts. 1 & 2"). This reflects the unusual length of the songs on the album. In fact, the two parts of "Fight the Power," which is really one song, represents the shortest track on *The Heat Is On*, clocking in at just under five and a half minutes. The way the songs are constructed, the first part of each is a unit that is self-contained enough and short enough (e.g., 3 minutes, 20second in the case of "Fight the Power, Pt. 1") that it is suitable for the single-release format of the day. After one listens to the entire album, it also becomes apparent that the collection is designed around the LP format of its time, with the first side consisting of fast-paced songs and the second side consisting of ballads that are more characteristic of earlier work by the group.

The second track, "The Heat Is On," although not exactly the mature disco music that soon emerged, is a potent dance track. In particular, the instrumental figures all give the song a strong rhythmic drive. The extensive use of the wah-wah pedal on the electric rhythm guitar is perhaps one aspect of "The Heat Is On" that has not aged particularly well. This effect on Ernie Isley's lead guitar and the rhythm-guitar part reflects back to Jimi Hendrix's iconic wah-wah pedal work in the late 1960s. However, on "The Heat Is On," the extent to which the effect dominates the instrumental part of the texture makes the track seem somewhat dated. Arguably, though, the Isley's soloing style sounds contemporary at the same time.

The last track on the first half of the album, "Hope You Feel Better Love," is another relatively fast-paced song; however, unlike its two predecessors, it is constructed around more of a rock rhythmic feel than funk. In fact, the general feel and style of the rhythm guitar part suggest a tie to the Doobie Brothers' hit "Listen to the Music," which dates from a few years before the Isley Brothers' song. Although the lyrics are not particularly specific, the song seems to be a statement of well-wishing to a former lover after a breakup. This brings up another interesting aspect to the overall structure of *The Heat Is On*: the album opens with strong political and social observation and commentary ("Fight the Power"), moves in the direction of high-energy dance music absent social commentary ("The Heat Is On"), and decreases the lyrical and musical level a bit more ("Hope You Feel Better Love"), before moving to a second-half focus on slower ballads.

The single release of "For the Love of You" was not as commercially successful as "Fight the Power"; however, this ballad did make it into the pop Top 40 and reached No. 10 on the R&B charts. The song features gentle falsetto singing from Ron Isley, whose singing style, as well as his wordless vocal extemporizations, reflect the contemporary style of Al Green, who enjoyed a string of soul ballad hits in the early 1970s. Stylistically, the main difference between "For the Love of You" and the more traditionally scored ballads of singers such as Green is that the arrangement is synthesizer—as opposed to horn section—based. The song's lyrics are an impressionistic expression of love. The impressionistic nature of the lyrics and Isley's lead vocal style give "For the Love of You" a feeling of spontaneity.

With its added note chords and melody tones that include some of the chord extensions, "Sensuality" is a lush track. Like its immediate predecessor, "Sensuality" fits squarely within the quiet storm subgenre of soul. Although this was not one of the single releases from the album, the ballad has an appealing melody and is not so heavily synthesizer driven (the most prominent instrumental part is that of the electric piano) as to make it sound dated.

The Heat Is On concludes with the seven-and-a-half-minute-long "Make Me Say It Again Girl." The verses feature repetitions of the chord progression F#m7, G#m7, Amaj7. The added sevenths give the harmonic texture a lush sound, similar to that of "Sensuality." The repetitious nature of the harmonic riff suggests the groove style associated with Marvin Gaye during his *What's Going On* and *Let's Let Get It On* period, a few years before *The Heat Is On* was released. The unexpected to move to a Cmaj7 chord at the end of the line, "You're all I need" emphasizes the line, which is the overarching theme of the entire text. Again, this move to the bIII chord is reminiscent of the sudden harmonic shifts in some of Marvin Gaye's songs slightly earlier songs. This is not to suggest that "Make Me Say It Again Girl" necessarily sounds derivative of Gaye—the texture and production style is so different that the song does not sound imitative—it is to suggest that the Isley Brothers were still creating music that reflected the aesthetics of the time period well after the group's early style (e.g., "Shout") had ceased to sound modern.

Some later digital reissues of *The Heat Is On* include the A-side version of the single release "Fight the Power, Pt. 1." This is an interesting track to hear because of the inclusion of the radio-friendly beep on the word "bulls***" and because the truncated version of the song is punchier than the album version. Unlike a fair number of the songs and albums profiled in this chapter, neither "Fight the Power" nor the album itself won any major awards or appear on lists of the most significant recordings of the commercial sound recording era. Because "Fight the Power" captured some of the political dissent of its time and later inspired the Public Enemy song of the same name, *The Heat Is On* was the Isley Brothers' first No. 1 pop album and part of a string of five soul chart-topping albums, and the ballads captured so well the quiet-storm format, this album remains essential listening.

MICHAEL JACKSON AND THE JACKSON 5

Without a doubt, the Gary, Indiana, Jackson family played a significant role in American popular music from the late 1960s into the 21st century through the work of the Jackson 5 and the solo work of Michael, Janet, Jermaine, and LaToya Jackson. In so far as the work of Janet Jackson is largely dance-based and the solo work of Michael's other siblings made far less commercial and critical impact than did Michael's work, let us focus on the imprint on soul in the work of the Jackson 5 and Michael Jackson.

The Jackson 5, later known as the Jacksons for reasons explained later, consisted of Jackie, Tito, Jermaine, Marlon, and Michael Jackson. Although they had been active performers for several years and had released a couple of early singles, the Jacksons' career took off in the late 1960s when they signed with Motown Records. The Jackson 5's work of the late 1960s and early 1970s included everything from fast-paced dance music to ballads. Generally, however, on the soul continuum, the Jackson 5's work fell on the pop side. In fact, once the group was signed by Motown, even their first releases, such as 1969's "I Want You Back," their debut Motown single, and their follow-up 1970 singles "ABC," "The Love You Save," and "I'll Be There," topped both the pop and the R&B charts. Their success across a wide audience demographic, particularly among young female music fans, made the Jackson 5 perhaps the top crossover act of the day.

These early singles, as well as the single from the group's 1970 *Jackson 5 Christmas Album*, "Santa Claus Is Coming to Town," emphasized young Michael's high-pitched lead vocals. Although several of the group's early hits are played on oldies radio early in the third decade of the 21st century, it is "Santa Claus Is Coming to Town" that is perhaps most likely to be heard, particularly during the holiday season. "ABC," too, seems to be among the more persistent pop-soul-dance hybrids of the early 1970s. And, although it is not as well remembered, "Never Can Say Goodbye" was one of the Jackson 5's better, more mature-sounding works from the early part of their career.

In 1972, Michael Jackson was still performing with his brothers but released his debut solo album. *Got to Be There* included Jackson's cover of the old Bobby Day song "Rockin' Robin." Jackson's recording is now the one that is most frequently heard on oldies radio, his "Rockin' Robin" having surpassed Day's original version in popularity. Starting with Michael Jackson's ascent into solo stardom, the group began to lose some of its commercial luster. This was particularly true after bitter legal wrangling with Motown that found the group owing the record label a substantial sum of money when their Motown contract expired. In addition to ultimately paying Motown approximately $2 million dollars, the group lost the rights to royalties for their Motown recordings and had to be rebranded as the Jacksons; Motown owned the legal rights to the name "Jackson 5" (Borja 2016, 327). The Jacksons signed with the CBS label Epic. Notably, at Epic, instead of the staff producers at Motown, the Jacksons worked with the team that can be considered the principal architects of the Philadelphia soul style: Kenny Gamble and Leon Huff. Although the Epic recordings of the Jacksons are not as well remembered as their Motown work, it is interesting to compare the way in which Gamble and Huff set the brothers' recordings and how they moved the group in the direction of the period's Philadelphia soul sound.

Although Michael Jackson's 1972 solo debut performed well on the pop and R&B charts, his solo career really took off in 1979 with the release of *Off the Wall*. "Don't Stop 'til You Get Enough," a song written by Jackson, was a potent dance track that was highly success at a time when disco music was still huge commercially. The song resulted in a Grammy Award for Jackson for Best R&B Performance, Male. However, *Off the Wall* was not a one-dimensional album; it allowed Jackson to demonstrate a wide stylistic range. The Tom Bahler composition "She's Out of My Life," for example, was arguably one of Michael Jackson's best ballad performances of his entire career as a recording artist. In 2012, *Rolling Stone* recognized *Off the Wall* as No. 68 in the magazine's list of "500 Greatest Albums of All Time" (*Rolling Stone* 2012).

As a solo artist, Michael Jackson toured extensively in support of his albums, which generally were released at sufficiently lengthy intervals, particularly in the 1980s and 1990s, that their release dates became highly anticipated events. During this period, Jackson was known as the "King of Pop," such was his domination of the R&B and pop record charts. Michael Jackson, along with Madonna, was one of a small group of artists who also dominated the world of music videos. In fact, Jackson's videos during the 1980s have aged well and demonstrate his attraction as an all-around performer.

Michael Jackson's career reached a zenith in 1982 with the release of *Thriller*. Tracks such as "Thriller," which featured a spoken-word appearance by veteran horror-film star Vincent Price, "Billie Jean," "P.Y.T. (Pretty Young Thing)," "Human Nature," "The Girl Is Mine," "Wanna Be Startin' Somethin'," and "Beat It" established Jackson as a major superstar. The album won eight Grammy Awards, including Album of the Year, and *Rolling Stone* ranked it at No. 20 on the magazine's list of "500 Greatest Albums of All Time" (*Rolling Stone* 2012). The music videos for "Thriller," "Billie Jean," and "Beat It" are among the best-remembered works of the decade in the video medium. These videos, particularly "Billie Jean" and "Beat It," have aged well, too, and seem as fresh as they did at the time of their release, something that some of the popular videos of the 1980s cannot claim.

Although "Billie Jean" and "Beat It," arguably the most important songs from the album, are infectious, they also demonstrate the extent to which Jackson had matured as a musician and as a person. In place of "ABC" and the innocent songs of his childhood, "Billie Jean" found Jackson portraying a character who apparently has a one-night stand with a woman he met in a dance club and who later confronts him with the allegation that her child is his son. Jackson's character struggles to reconcile the woman's allegations, his belief that "the kid is not my son," and the fact that the child's eyes look "just like mine."

Although the "Billie Jean" video is a must-experience part of the Michael Jackson story, the video for "Beat It" is far more elaborate, as well as one of the most iconic such works of the entire music video age. Enlisting actual street gang members as dancers and actors, "Beat It" can be understood as an early 1980s re-interpretation of the famous gang scenes of the film version of the musical *West Side Story*. However, as I wrote in *Listen to Pop!*, "it is not so much the premise" of these two solo Michael Jackson compositions, "that is the most important feature; it is the combination of music, lyrics, arrangement, and Jackson's highly rhythmic vocal approach, which includes wordless inhalations and exhalations and vocables used for rhythmic emphasis" that really make the pieces work as well as they do. Jackson's signature vocal approach in these recordings extends a technique that Stevie Wonder used in his funk recordings of the 1973 to 1975 period (Perone 2018, 106).

Michael Jackson's next major achievement was the song "We Are the World," which he cowrote with Lionel Richie. The 1985 recording of the song, which included a virtual who's who of the pop and soul music world of the 1980s, resulted in one of the most successful charity singles to date. A report in *USA Today* claimed that by 2006, the song had helped raise more than $60 million for short-term famine relief and for long-term future famine avoidance in Ethiopia and other African countries (*USA Today* 2006).

Although Jackson's 1987 album *Bad* did not have quite the same commercial impact on the singles charts as *Thriller*, "I Just Can't Stop Loving You," "Bad," and "Man in the Mirror" were successful and continued Jackson's string of pop and R&B hits. "Man in the Mirror" is particularly notable for Jackson's acknowledgment that only by working to improve oneself can one improve the world. Although not a Jackson composition, the song suggests a further maturing of the still-under-30 Michael Jackson and can be understood as a continuation of the general theme of Jackson and Richie's "We Are the World."

Certainly, part of the commercial and critical success of both *Thriller* and *Bad* can be attributed to the work of Quincy Jones as Jackson's coproducer. For example, the sparse textures in a recording such as "Billie Jean" allowed all the vocal and instrumental details to make the song a musically rich experience. As coproducers, Jackson and Jones also enlisted guest artists such as jazz saxophonist Tom Scott, who played electronic wind controller on "Billie Jean," and, most famously, rock guitarist Eddie Van Halen, who contributed a searing solo to "Beat It."

Beginning primarily in the late 1980s, Michael Jackson's personal life became fodder, whether rightly or wrongly, for the tabloids. Increasingly, the songs he recorded—such as some of the material on the 1991 album *Dangerous* and the 1995 collection *HIStory: Past, Present and Future*,

Book I, turned in the direction of paranoia and also found him taking on the paparazzi and tabloid journalists who, by then, were constantly hounding him. At the same time, *Dangerous* included songs such as "Keep the Faith" and "Will You Be There" that are so closely tied to the gospel music tradition that they are among Michael Jackson's most conventionally soul-focused performances.

At the time of his death in 2009, Michael Jackson was preparing for a concert series to take place in London. After Jackson's death, the documentary *This Is It*, which included footage of Jackson's rehearsals for the concerts, as well as an album by the same name, provided suggestions of Jackson's musical and performance direction at the end of his career. In addition to six new songs, the *This Is It* album included a retrospective of Jackson's career and debuted at No. 1 on album charts around the world, confirming standing as the "King of Pop."

ETTA JAMES

To some music, fans Etta James is largely defined by one song, the ballad, "At Last," so iconic was her recording of it, and so frequently has the James recording appeared in film and television soundtracks. Etta James's career spanned the mid-1950s to the early 21st century. More than just spanning time, however, James's recordings ran the gamut from early racy R&B to her hit jazz-influenced ballads to gospel-inspired songs, to work in the 1970s and beyond that integrated funk and rock.

Early in her career, James was defined as an R&B singer. Her recording of "Roll with Me Henry," which was also known as "The Wallflower," was a response to "Work with Me Annie," a recording by Hank Ballard and the Midnighters. Both songs were understood at the time—the mid-1950s—to be risqué. Certainly, some of the lyrics can be understood as references to dancing, but in the Etta James song, the "oooh eees" that she sings can also just as easily be understood as expressions of pleasure while making love.

By the time of the release of her album *At Last!* five years later, James was singing soulful ballads. "All I Could Do Was Cry," one of the ballads on the album, might meet with mixed reactions from a 21st-century audience because of the overdone orchestration and backing vocal arrangement, but James proves herself to be a powerful soul singer on the track.

Because the 1960 release, "At Last," is so iconic in popular culture, let us consider this recording beyond its sheer popularity in recent years. James's recording made it to No. 2 on the R&B charts of the day but did not fare particularly well on the pop charts. The song was written by Harry Warren and Mack Gordon and first appeared in the 1941 film *Sun Valley Serenade*. The Glenn Miller Orchestra and its vocalist Ray Eberle enjoyed a hit with the song in 1942, and the former Miller Orchestra trumpeter and singer Ray Anthony recorded another pop hit version in the early 1950s. The point is that "At Last" was not originally a soul song, or even a song primarily associated with African American performers. The Riley Hampton arrangement and production by Phil and Leonard Chess for the Etta James recording does not necessarily scream "soul," although the bluesy figures in the string parts suggest a connection to jazz and blues. What really makes the Etta James recording of "At Last" a soul classic is James's vocal style. She uses dynamic changes and rhythmic inflections to alter the mood as the song progresses, and one of the greatest bluesy single lines in soul music can be found at the end of the recording, when James extemporizes on the line, "And you are mine at last."

Etta James's recording of "At Last" moved from being an R&B chart classic to being part of general American popular culture beginning in the late 1980s. The recording was used in the soundtrack of the popular film *Rain Man* and subsequently featured prominently in television shows such as *Northern Exposure* and *Criminal Minds*. It was also featured in the 1995 film *Father of the Bride II*. In 1999, the Recording Academy selected James's recording of "At Last" for its Grammy Hall Fame. More recently, it has been used in television commercials for a range of products. James herself also became better known for her portrayal by Beyoncé in the 2008 film *Cadillac Records*.

By the time of the more mid-career 1968 release "I'd Rather Go Blind," James's soul singing was given a more conventional but more contemporary accompaniment. Gone, for example, were the overwrought strings of recordings such as "All I Could Do Was Cry." Instead, a rhythm section, lead electric guitar, and female backing singers accompanied James. Although much of her post-1960 work flew somewhat under the proverbial radar—singers such as Aretha Franklin having become more highly visible and more dominant on the singles and album charts—the settings for James's work continued to progress and reflect the times.

Such is the case with the 1973 album *Etta James*. The opening track, "All the Way Down," which was also released as a single, is very much a composition, arrangement, and production of the time. The lyrics, too, are in line with the era's songs about the poverty, casual sex, drug abuse, unemployment, and so on, in the urban ghetto. James sings quietly, sings loudly, sneers, and screams some of the lyrics. The range of expression makes this a must-hear track. Stylistically, it is a world apart from mid-1950s' R&B

and early 1960s' over-arranged soul ballads. Even a quick comparison of "All the Way Down" with the work from Etta James's earlier recordings suggests that perhaps no other soul singer went through nearly as great a metamorphosis between the mid-1950s and the mid-1970s.

A late Etta James album that deserves attention is the 2006 cover collection *All the Way*. It is a wide-ranging album, including jazz standards (such as the title song), Prince's "Purple Rain," John Lennon's "Imagine," Marvin Gaye's "What's Going On," and so on. On each of these, James provides somewhat restrained but consistently soulfully expressive vocals. On tracks that are not quite as successful as the original, such as "Purple Rain," the reason is not so much James's singing as the iconic nature of the original. And specifically, in the case of "Purple Rain," the intensity of the famous live performance at the end of Prince's *Purple Rain* film, as well as Prince's virtuosic guitar work, would be virtually impossible to match. I mention the restrained nature of Etta James's singing throughout the album, and it is in this that one can feel her connection to jazz.

From somewhat risqué 1950s R&B dance (ostensibly) numbers, to one of the most persistent ballads of the early 1960s in the form of "At Last," to powerful funk and late-career restrained soul, Etta James was perhaps one of the widest-ranging soul singers of the second half of the 20th century and the first years of the 21st century. A sampling of tracks from the 1950s, 1960s, 1970s, and 2000s will demonstrate her versatility and serve as a documentary of the changes that transpired in soul during the period that encompassed James's lengthy career.

ALICIA KEYS

Alicia Keys is truly a soul artist for the 21st century, as she hit the music scene running with her highly acclaimed 2001 debut album, *Songs in A Minor*. Unlike some artists who have stumbled after a popular and widely talked about debut, Keys followed it up with *The Diary of Alicia Keys*, another album that featured the singer-songwriter's blurring of the lines between soul, classical, jazz, and hip-hop and integrating them all in such a way as to define her as a singer, pianist, and songwriter. On her first two albums, by and large, the original songs were written either by Keys alone, or by Keys in collaboration with one or two cowriters. As Keys moved through the second decade of the 21st century, she increasingly has included "featured" artists—a very common practice in the hip-hop and rap subgenres—and has included samples to the extent that some of the songs on albums such as *Girl on Fire* (2012) and *Here*

(2017) credit 4, 5, 6, and up to 10 individuals as cowriters. Let us look at Keys's debut album and two of her 2010s' albums to see how work as a leading neo-soul artist evolved and how Keys has, at the same time, maintained a continuum as a singer-songwriter.

First, *Songs in A Minor*, technically, is not a musically accurate title for Keys's debut, as the songs—largely written by Keys alone or in collaboration with one or two others—are not all in the key of A minor. The reference to a key, a tonality, in part betrays Keys's training as a classical pianist, but it also suggests the theme of adversity and the struggle to overcome adversity on a variety of levels that runs through many of the album's tracks, because minor keys are frequently associated with sadness. As an example of the theme of adversity, in "Girlfriend," Keys ruminates on a friend of both her and her boyfriend; the friend shares a bond with Keys's character's boyfriend that she does not, and she is jealous. Keys does not express a fear that the other woman will replace her; she expresses the feeling that, in some regards, she is an outsider. As another example, in "Caged Bird," Keys uses the imagery contained in the title of Maya Angelou's 1969 autobiography *I Know Why the Caged Bird Sings*, itself borrowed from Paul Laurence Dunbar's late-19th-century poem "Sympathy," and expresses that she, too, feels like a caged bird who outside forces metaphorically keep from flying and thus can only turn to song to experience freedom.

The album's opening track, "Piano & I," hints at Keys's refuge from these feelings of alienation and repression: her piano. In fact, the lyrics suggest a bond between musician and instrument in which each needs the other to find meaning in life. The piano plays a role throughout the album, although most of the songs include the drum programming rhythms of hip-hop. "Caged Bird," however, which concludes *Songs in A Minor*, focuses solely on Keys's voice and piano. The bookends of the album, then, might not quite give *Songs in A Minor* a concept album–like wholeness, but they do present and reinforce the theme that it is through her music that Keys's character can survive life's trials and tribulations.

With the mix of singer-songwriter-style voice-and-piano texture, hip-hop production, and programmed drum rhythms, the entire album falls into the same basic ballpark as Lauryn Hill's *The Miseducation of Lauryn Hill*. Interestingly, though, some of the songs on Keys's debut had been years in the making and predate the release of Hill's 1998 debut. Despite the range of rhythmic feels and textures, all the songs on *Songs in A Minor* exhibit a vocal style with clear ties to the soul tradition. In particular, the depth of Keys's voice and her use of vibrato suggest that she is clearly part of a continuum that extends back through Aretha Franklin and Nina Simone to the world of gospel music. Keys's improvisation on melodic lines, too, clearly is part of the soul continuum. It is not that it stands in contrast to the hip-hop references in the production and heavy rhythms on some tracks, but it makes her singing seem like soul for a new generation.

I mention Nina Simone and Franklin, too, because those earlier figures also incorporated their piano playing into their recordings and live performances. Critics mentioned Keys's blurring of genre lines with her commercial recording debut. Arguably, Simone's piano playing broke free of the soul/gospel tradition more than any other singer-pianist with her clear references to jazz and classical styles. Franklin's piano work was generally more reflective of the black church, of gospel music. One could reasonably argue that on her debut album, the way Alicia Keys plays bring various and disparate influences together in a more integrated way than in the music of Simone. In this respect, it is a personal-sounding style and ties Keys to the singer-songwriter movement of the 1970s.

Although the focus here is not on Keys's second album, *The Diary of Alicia Keys*, several notable aspects of this collection are certainly worth consideration. First, the title might suggest such disparate images as *The Diary of Anne Frank* (also known as *The Diary of a Young Girl*) or *The Miseducation of Lauryn Hill*. Although it might seem presumptuous to even imply connections to those works in one's sophomore solo album release, the themes of discrimination and repression that run through Frank's account of the Nazi era and Lauryn Hill's album find their way into Keys's album and, indeed, through much of her output to date. So, there is a solid thematic connection, even if some listeners find the title presumptuous. The album also includes a more fully realized example of Alicia Keys's classical training on piano in the form of her composition "Harlem's Nocturne," the title of which suggests the swing-era jazz standard "Harlem Nocturne," a piece that, over the decades, had been a hit, both as an instrumental and, fitted with lyrics, as a song. Another notable track is "If I Was Your Woman/Walk on By," a combination of the 1971 Gladys Knight & the Pips' hit "If I Were Your Woman" and the 1964 Dionne Warwick hit "Walk on By." Although Keys is primarily known as a singer-pianist-songwriter, her performance and coproduction of the track (coproduced with Easy Mo Bee and Dwayne "D. Wigg" Wiggins) brings the pair of songs squarely into the hip-hop age. In this respect, this continues the tradition of earlier soul artists—perhaps most famously Isaac Hayes on his *Hot Buttered Soul* album—of taking material by other artists and essentially reworking the original genres, turning them into something substantially new.

By the time of *Girl on Fire* (2012) and *Here* (2016), Keys's most recent studio albums, the ties to hip-hop became more obvious. The use of sampling increased, such that tracks on *Here* include up to 10 names on the songwriting credits. Both albums also include important contributions from guest artists, such as A$AP Rocky, Nicki Minaj, Bruno Mars, and Maxwell. Both albums, also, have moved closer to the pure hip-hop paradigm by featuring a variety of track producers, who each lend their own personal touch to the overall sound of the tracks.

Still, despite the samples, multiple producers, and so on, Keys includes songs that clearly paint her as a singer and piano-based songwriter at her core. "Not Even the King," a *Girl on Fire* track, for example, focused on Keys singing and playing the piano. The texture of this song is particularly effective because it follows "Tears Always Win," a more conventional song about loneliness that in lyrics, melody, arrangement, use of backing vocals, and basic rhythmic feel clearly reflects back to the classic soul of the 1960s and 1970s (except for the hip-hop programmed drums). The intimacy of the texture of "Not Even the King" pulls the listener squarely into Keys's lyrics about the poverty of soul suffered by some people who are materially rich.

The social issues surrounding the life of urban blacks in the middle of the second decade of the 21st century run through both albums. Throughout *Here*, however, the lyrics are wider ranging and more pointed than on *Girl on Fire* and are more pointed than on Keys's earlier recordings. In fact, some critics commented on the profusion of images that come out in the songs of *Here*. For example, AllMusic critic Andy Kellman wrote that "at points, Keys' invigorated energy level and need to simply expel ideas, rather than refine them, lends the album a hollow quality" (Kellman n.d.-a). It is true that Keys paints images of poverty, brutality, racial discrimination, poor housing, drug abuse, abusive relationships, and so on without providing detailed solutions—perhaps the "hollow quality" that Kellman detects. However, the proliferation of images and the rapidity with which Keys expresses them, as well as the fact that she returns to "money" as a core issue, suggests the extent to which she believes the system is broken and the extent to which the social ills and personal brokenness can be traced back to wealth or a lack thereof. The implication also seems to be that the social problems that Keys identifies can only be solved through the investment of sufficient funds.

Keys provides hints of hope for the future, such as referencing Sam Cooke's lyrics "a change gonna come" in "The Gospel." However, the numerous images of pain, suffering, addiction, discrimination, and so on, can leave the listener wondering if there truly is hope. The final track on *Here*, "Holy War," provides an age-old solution to the world's ills, a solution that runs back through the soul tradition and into gospel music: love provides the hope and is the solution.

As the winner of over a dozen Grammy Awards, as well as awards from the Songwriters Hall of Fame; the American Society of Composers, Authors and Publishers (ASCAP); the National Association for the Advancement of Colored People (NAACP), and other organizations for her work as a singer-songwriter and for her humanitarian work, Alicia Keys has been one of the most honored musicians of the early 21st century. *Billboard* magazine named her one of the top artists of the first decade of the century and ranked her song "No One" at No. 6 on the magazine's "Hot 100 Songs of the Decade chart." Although a long-anticipated seventh studio album has not yet appeared at the time of this writing, Keys continues to release singles, make guest appearances on others' recordings, and perform at major festivals, and she was active for several years as a judge on the television program *The Voice*.

BEN E. KING: "STAND BY ME"

Cowritten by Ben E. King and the famous Brill Building team of Jerry Leiber and Mike Stoller, King's 1961 hit "Stand by Me" remains King's greatest achievement as a singer and one of the most well-loved, award-winning, and iconic songs of the pre-British Invasion 1960s. The song also demonstrates, perhaps better than most, the close intertwining of gospel and soul music.

"Lord, Stand by Me," also known simply as "Stand by Me," by the late 19th-century and early 20th-century gospel writer Charles Albert Tindley, was first published in 1905. The song includes several phrases that revolve around life's trials and tribulations—for example, "When the storms of life are raging." These phrases are answered by the words, "stand by me." Tindley's hymn asks the "Lily of the Valley," a commonly used expression for Jesus of Nazareth, to "stand by" the singer.

In terms of its structure, Ben E. King's "Stand by Me" works similarly; however, the person to whom he sings, the person he asks to "stand by me," is identified only as "darling," which might suggest a romantic relationship between the characters, but that is a matter of interpretation. Another distinction between "Stand by Me" and its apparent gospel inspiration is that King's character both relies on his "darling" for strength and also offers support near the end of the song ("Whenever you're in trouble, stand by me . . .").

Despite the possible romantic implications of "darling," the overarching theme of devotion and constancy in the lyrics is consistent with Tindley's old gospel song. Because the possible romantic references in the song are muted (e.g., "Stand by Me" could be about a parent-child relationship or about a platonic relationship, such as that in the 1986 Rob Reiner film of the same title), the relationship between King, Leiber, and Stoller's "Stand by Me" and its gospel is significantly closer than, for example, the relationship between the Ray Charles-Renald Richard composition "I Got a Woman" and the gospel predecessor with an almost identical melody, Bob King's "It Must Be Jesus." To put it another way, "Stand by Me" is less overtly secular and certainly less sexual than the Ray Charles adaptation of gospel music; it is infinitely more subtle.

Musically, "Stand by Me" is notable as one of the most famous songs built around the so-called "oldies progression." This succession of chords, I-vi-IV-V (C major, A minor, F major, and G major in the key of C major), is sometimes called the "oldies progression" or the "'50s progression" because it was so prominent in the popular music of that decade; however, the earliest well-known popular song built around it was Hoagy Carmichael's (lyrics by Frank Loesser) 1938 song "Heart and Soul."

Attributing extra-musical associations to melodic, rhythmic, and harmonic materials can be a tricky business, as individual listeners' interpretations might vary widely. To this writer, the pervasiveness of the progression in "Stand by Me" suggests the constancy of devotion that runs through the lyrics. At the same time, because the progression ends on the dominant chord (V), which usually resolves to tonic (I) for the music to have a feeling of completion instead of on tonic, the progression tends to feel like it never fully ends. Again, some listeners might interpret this as representative of the ongoing—some might say, eternal—devotion of the characters in the song.

The single release of Ben E. King's recording of his best-known song reached No.1 on the R&B charts and made it solidly into the Top 10 on the pop charts of the day. Subsequently, various covers of "Stand by Me" have made the R&B, pop, and Latin record charts. Such diverse artists as John Lennon; country singer Mickey Gilley; Earl Grant; Earth, Wind & Fire's Maurice White; Prince Royce; and Seal, among others have recorded it. King's original recording was also a chart hit in 1986 when it was reissued in conjunction with the soundtrack of the Rob Reiner film *Stand by Me*, the title of which the song inspired; the King song was used during the film's closing credits. Because of the success of Ben E. King's 1961 recording and the subsequent cover recordings, at the time of the song's recognition by the Songwriters Hall of Fame in

2012, "Stand by Me" held the distinction of having charted more times on *Billboard* magazine's Hot 100 than any other song in the history of the recording industry (Songwriters Hall of Fame 2012).

In 2014, the National Recording Preservation Board of the Library of Congress added King's "Stand by Me" to the National Recording Registry (National Recording Preservation Board of the Library of Congress n.d.). *Rolling Stone* magazine ranked "Stand by Me" at No. 112 on its list of "500 Greatest Songs of All Time" (*Rolling Stone* 2011), and, in 1999, Broadcast Music International (BMI) declared "Stand by Me" the fourth-most performed song of the 20th century on radio and television (BMI 1999). In 2012, the Songwriters Hall of Fame presented "Stand by Me" the organization's Towering Song Award and Ben E. King with the organization's Towering Performance Award for his recording of it.

GLADYS KNIGHT AND THE PIPS

One of the more highly visible popular soul vocal groups of the 1960s and 1970s, Gladys Knight and the Pips scored numerous Top 10 R&B and pop singles, including "Every Beat of My Heart," "I Heard It Through the Grapevine," "If I Were Your Woman," "Neither One of Us (Wants to Be the First to Say Goodbye)," "Midnight Train to Georgia," "I've Got to Use My Imagination," "Best Thing That Ever Happened to Me," "On and On," and "The Way We Were/Try to Remember," and these are just the singles that made the Top 10 of both charts. The group recorded six more singles that made the Top 10 of the R&B charts but not the upper reaches of the pop charts. In addition to this chart success, Gladys Knight and the Pips were staples of television music and television variety shows of the 1960s and 1970s. The harmony of the Pips—a male trio backing up a female lead vocalist— produced a truly unique texture, and the polished performances by the group were tailor-made for television. Several of the group's signature recordings were among the most memorable of the era.

Gladys Knight's first brush with fame came in 1952 when, as a child, she was a winner on the television program *Ted Mack's Amateur Hour*. The group that came to be known first as the Pips and then Gladys Knight and the Pips came into being in the 1950s and eventually consisted of Knight, her brother Bubba Knight, and their cousins William Guest and Edward Patton, and Langston George. This was the lineup that recorded "Every Beat of My Heart," the Pips' first hit.

After Langston George left the group and Gladys Knight returned from time off to start a family, the group, now officially using the name

Gladys Knight and the Pips, signed to Motown's Soul Records label. Their first Motown-era hit was "I Heard It Through the Grapevine." Although Marvin Gaye's later remake of the song was the most commercially successful version and is the one most frequently heard on oldies radio today, the Gladys Knight and the Pips recording reached No. 1 on the R&B charts and nearly topped the pop charts in 1967. Ironically—and arguably—the Marvin Gaye recording is more closely tied to the rock of the late 1960s than the original version by Knight and company. In fact, the style of the Gaye recording that seems to have been the inspiration for rock band Creedence Clearwater Revival's subsequent version. The version by Knight and the Pips features more soulful extemporizing on the melody. and the rhythmic setting reflects the double-time syncopations that marked funk later in the 1960s and into the 1970s. To put it another way, the Gladys Knight and the Pips version is, in some respects, more progressive than the subsequently more commercially popular versions of "I Heard It Through the Grapevine."

Gladys Knight and the Pips, however, were anything but one-dimensional. In addition to the up-tempo and funky "I Heard It Through the Grapevine," the group excelled at soul ballads. Curiously, one of the most memorable of these, "Neither One of Us (Wants to Be the First to Say Goodbye)," the group's last hit before leaving Motown for Buddah Records, was written by country songwriter Jim Weatherly. Knight suggested in her autobiography that the best material penned by Motown's staff writers was given to other big-name artists at the label (Knight 1997), so perhaps it is fitting that three of Gladys Knight and the Pips' most memorable ballads, "Neither One of Us," and the later post-Motown songs "Midnight Train to Georgia" and "Best Thing That Ever Happened to Me," came from the pen of Weatherly.

"Neither One of Us (Wants to Be the First to Say Goodbye)" concerns a relationship that is at the breaking point. Despite the apparent realization by both parties that the relationship holds no future, neither person wants to openly confront the relationship's end. Knight's lead vocals capture the sadness expressed in the lyrics. In addition to the outstanding tie of the lyrics to Knight's performance, it is a song with strong musical hooks, particularly in the memorable echo of the words "neither one of us" by the Pips. Not only was this ballad a success on both the pop and R&B charts, it also earned Gladys Knight and the Pips a Grammy for Best Pop Vocal Performance by a Duo, Group, or Chorus at the 1974 Grammy Awards ceremony.

In addition to the previously discussed must-hear recordings, the most iconic single produced by the group was Jim Weatherly's composition

"Midnight Train to Georgia, which was released late in 1973. Using interviews with the song's writer and material from Gladys Knight, author Marc Myers traced "Midnight Train to Georgia" from a country song inspired by a conversation Weatherly had with actors Lee Majors and Farrah Fawcett Majors, through Cissy Houston's soul cover of the song, to the recording by Knight and the Pips. For her part, Knight stated, "I listened to Cissy's version and loved it—but I knew I wanted something different. I wanted an Al Green thing going, you know?" (Myers 2016, 219). In fact, the instrumental introduction is curiously reminiscent of the horn writing in Al Green's "Let's Stay Together," and Knight adopts a Green-like understated vocal style in the verses. The commercial and critical success of "Midnight Train to Georgia," Gladys Knight and the Pips' signature song, suggests that Knight, the child star of the early 1950s and hit recording artist starting in 1961, recognized the direction in which soul music was going with the ascent of Al Green, and she was able to adapt to the changes that were underfoot in the genre.

The 1974 Grammy Awards was the high point of recognition for Gladys Knight and the Pips. In addition to the aforementioned Grammy for Best Pop Vocal Performance by a Duo, Group or Chorus for "Neither One of Us (Wants to Be the First to Say Goodbye)," they won the Grammy for Best R&B Vocal Performance by a Duo, Group or Chorus for "Midnight Train to Georgia." Although not as essential as those two songs, the group's 1974 singles, Jim Weatherly's "Best Thing That Ever Happened to Me" and Curtis Mayfield's "On and On," were also substantial hits. These songs also serve as examples of the fact that the group seemed to move effortlessly between ballads and funk songs. Unfortunately, Gladys Knight and the Pips enjoyed only a few subsequent hit singles, although they returned to the charts in 1987 with "Love Overboard," for which they won the Grammy Award for Best R&B Performance by a Duo or Group with Vocal.

On all these must-hear recordings, the texture of Gladys Knight's alto voice on the lead part with her three male relatives backing her up is fundamentally different than the texture of any of the other major soul artists of the era. The norms were: a same-gender ensemble with a lead singer backed by the others (e.g., the Supremes, Martha and the Vandellas, the Impressions, early and mid-1960s work of the Temptations, and so on); a male lead singer backed by female vocalists (e.g., Ray Charles with the Raelettes); or a female soloist with a generally unnamed female backing group (e.g., Aretha Franklin's recordings made with the supporting vocals of her sisters Carolyn and Erma and other backing singers). Al Green's backing by a gender-mixed trio of studio musicians was unusual, particularly because they were white vocalists from a country background, but the female-lead/male-backing ensemble texture of Gladys Knight and the Pips stood alone among the most commercially successful groups of the era.

Not only was the group defined by its unusual texture and its ability to reach the upper slice of the pop and R&B charts with the almost bipolar extremes of (1) slow ballads about relationship problems and lost love and (2) upbeat, funk songs (also, typically, about relationships, both good and bad) but the rich depth of Gladys Knight's lead vocals provided some of the strongest soul singing of the late 1960s into the middle of the 1970s. Gladys Knight and the Pips broke up in 1989, with Knight herself turning to a solo career. The group was elected to the Rock and Roll Hall of Fame in 1996 and the Vocal Group Hall of Fame in 2001. "I Heard It Through the Grapevine" and the group's early 1970s' ballad hits remain must-hear classics.

JOHN LEGEND

Named the "Sexiest Man Alive" in 2019 by *People* magazine, John Legend is a rare figure who has received accolades in a wide variety of media, including 10 Grammy Awards, an Academy Award, an Emmy, and a Tony Award to date. Born John Roger Stephens, Legend was first exposed to the public by playing piano on Lauryn Hill's song "Everything Is Everything," a hit single and a track on Hill's acclaimed album *The Miseducation of Lauryn Hill*. Hill's nickname for the pianist-singer-songwriter, Legend, eventually became Stephens's professional name.

When Legend began his solo career, he was under management by the highly successful hip-hop producer and rapper Kanye West. West, along with several other hip-hop luminaries, contributed to Legend's 2004 debut album, *Get Lifted*. This album eventually received eight Grammy nominations and earned Legend three Grammy Awards. One of the most popular tracks, and one that might surprise listeners familiar with Legend's collaborators on the album, such as Kanye West and will.i.am, is "Ordinary People." At the 2006 Grammy Awards ceremony, this hit single earned Legend a Grammy for Best Male R&B Vocal Performance. The texture of Legend's voice and piano, captured in the official video for the song (see, https://www.youtube.com/watch?v=PIh07c_P4hc, accessed January 31, 2020), is significantly more voice focused than what is common in hip-hop-era production. This makes a couple's struggles more poignant than what might have been the case in a setting that included numerous samples and electronic effects. This is not to say that it is entirely a retro-styled album. Other songs include more contemporary rhythms and effects; however, the emphasis is consistently on Legend's singing.

Writing in *The Guardian*, critic Caroline Sullivan addressed the difficulty that some popular artists have with their sophomore album, particularly after a successful first release. Sullivan said of the 2006 collection *Once Again*, in comparison to Legend's highly acclaimed debut, "There's no reason it shouldn't match it, though—unless his voice ends up on a list of banned substances because of its high-calorie creaminess. What worked so profitably for him before also works now: his tunes are little Motown-ish symphonies, lit from within by his quiet-storm intensity, itself beholden to Smokey Robinson" (Sullivan 2006).

The comparison to classic 1960s' Motown is appropriate throughout *Once Again*. For example, the opening track, "Save Room," opens with a gentle, nearly ostinato harmonic oscillation that is reminiscent of some of the *What's Going On*–era work of Marvin Gaye. The instrumental setting is absent the heavily syncopated bass drum so frequently heard in hip-hop-era music. Instead, the organ, keyboards, and rock-like drum part would not have been rhythmically or texturally out of place years earlier. One of the features that helps to make this melody stand out is Legend's emphasis on melodic notes from the chord thirds and fifths. Holding back a bit on revolving around the root notes of the chords gives the tune a sense of restlessness and a slightly unresolved feel that some listeners might hear as a completely appropriate setting for the pleading of the lyrics.

As was the case with Legend's debut album, the songs of *Once Again* tend to revolve around relationships—budding, broken, and everything in between. Romance, desire, and affection are common themes, and Legend generally treats them consistently with how predecessors such as Smokey Robinson, Marvin Gaye, Al Green, and other male singer-songwriters from the earlier days of soul treated them. To put it another way, Legend incorporates hip-hop-era musical touches, but without abandoning the lyrical sensibilities of the 1960s and 1970s.

John Legend has been a prolific musician and has engaged in collaborations with a variety of artists. Perhaps one of his most intriguing projects was the 2010 album *Wake Up!*, produced in collaboration with the Roots. The album includes only one new, original song, Legend's "Shine," a call to give the disenfranchised "prisoners of history" a chance to be heard and to have their hopes and dreams realized. The song sounds as though inspired by the gospel-inflected calls for social justice in classic 1960s' soul, as well as by Stevie Wonder's similarly themed songs of the

1973 to 1974 era. In fact, the musical style and Legend's lyrics would not have been at all out of place on Wonder's *Songs in the Key of Life* or its immediate predecessors, *Fulfillingness' First Finale* and *Innervisions*.

The rest of *Wake Up!* consists of songs originally associated with artists such as Marvin Gaye, Bill Withers, Nina Simone, Donny Hathaway, Baby Huey & the Babysitters, and others. All speak to the social issues of the 1960s and 1970s; however, all songs also speak to the social conditions of the United States at the time Legend and the Roots recorded the tracks. Scholar and writer Salamishah Tillet provided the context for *Wake Up!* in the album's liner notes: "the greatest economic downturn in the United States since the Great Depression and the election of the first black U.S. president" (Tillet 2010). So, the album represents a reaction to the economic conditions of the 2008–2010 period, as well as the hope provided by the election of Barack Obama to the U.S. presidency.

Although the Roots are a band well versed in a range of styles, they are—somewhat unfortunately—sometimes regarded primarily as a live hip-hop band. In other words, the Roots can suggest in their live performances the numerous digital samples that require studio wizardry in the work of other artists, as well as the rhythms of the hip-hop genre. Throughout *Wake Up!*, the band; the track producers; and the album producers Ahmir "?uestlove" Thompson, James Poyser, and Legend, integrate hip-hop rhythms, live versions of the kinds of effects that one would ordinarily hear as samples, with some of the distinctive instrumental figures that were integral parts of the original recordings back in the 1960s and 1970s. The sample-like additions sometimes provide interesting subtext to the songs. For example, the addition of the iconic opening trill from the *Mission Impossible* theme in Curtis Mayfield's "Hard Times" suggests the seemingly impossible nature of overcoming the racial discrimination that his character expresses in the lyrics.

Critical reaction to the album was favorable. For example, *Rolling Stone*'s Jodie Rosen wrote that "Together, they [John Legend and the Roots] have made a brilliantly conceived and executed album, reviving music from the Nixon-era heyday of politically engaged R&B . . . They're not imitators—they're heirs" (Rosen 2010). In addition to providing a thematic and emotional connection to the social and political commentary of earlier soul music while incorporating 21st-century musical styles, the entire album highlights John Legend's singing. Although the influence of the great soul singers of the past can be heard in Legend's style, he brings an individual expression to the songs that give them a timeless quality. To put it another way, Legend's voice allows the songs to live in the present and the past. They also live in the future, as the performances still sound musically and thematically relevant approximately a decade after the release of *Wake Up!*

Writing in *The New York Times*, critic Jon Pareles stated that, unlike the light nature of some of the love songs that Legend has sent to the top of the charts in the past, the album *Darkness and Light* "treats love as something far more complex than a panacea and a fount of perpetual reassurance, with music to match," making the album a richer and deeper experience than some of Legend's previous efforts (Pareles 2016).

The opening song on *Darkness and Light*, "I Know Better," is one of the singer-songwriter's most personal-sounding pieces. Written in collaboration with album and track producer Blake Mills, who also provides guitar, bass, and "keys," and Will Oldham, the texture focuses on Legend's voice and Larry Goldings's piano and Hammond organ. The organ and the introspective lyrics suggest a clear tie to gospel music, something not frequently heard in 21st-century soul. Because Legend sings of his successes, failures, and his acknowledgment that "Legend is just a name," the song provides the listener both a sense of identity of Legend and sets up the context for the album's title.

One could argue that other songs, with fuller production, contributions by rappers and other singers, and a greater emphasis on percussion, are less personal sounding; however, throughout the album, Legend's voice is at the fore, and he sings with a sense of passion. One thing that has become increasingly true of John Legend's recordings over the years that is certainly true on *Darkness and Light* is that the man who started out his career as a soul piano player records less frequently on the keyboard.

John Legend continues to be a prolific recording and concert artist. In the 2016 Damien Chazelle movie musical *La La Land*, Legend played the role of Keith, a friend of Ryan Gosling's character, Sebastian. While Sebastian is intent on keeping the jazz genre alive by focusing his piano playing on early- and mid-20th-century styles and thinks of himself as a revolutionary for breaking with contemporary musical trends, Keith breaks away and moves into more modern subgenres of jazz and funk. Keith pointedly asks Sebastian, "How are you going to be a revolutionary, if you're such a traditionalist?" The relationship between Sebastian and Legend's Keith can be interpreted as something of a metaphor for Legend's work over the years. In a sense, Legend succeeds in striking a balance between Keith and Sebastian: he is clearly tied to the great soul vocal tradition of Marvin Gaye and others; however, he tends to include just enough hip-hop era touches that his music represents a distinctly modern version of soul.

CURTIS MAYFIELD: *SUPER FLY*

As *Pitchfork* contributor Mychal Denzel Smith wrote of the place of Curtis Mayfield's soundtrack to the 1972 blaxploitation film *Super Fly*, "The best political music doesn't necessarily announce itself as political because it is concerned first and foremost with the people for whom the politics matter most. That's *Super Fly*. As Mayfield's third studio album as a solo artist, *Super Fly* perfectly encapsulates the post-Civil Rights/early Black Power feel of black America struggling to survive the social and political consequences of the nation's conservative backlash" (Smith 2018). Curiously, at least on the surface, the film and the soundtrack album—taken as two discrete works—seem to deliver fundamentally different political and social messages.

The film has been interpreted widely as glorifying drug-related criminal activity; however, this glorification was not without reason in the context of the time and place. As *Variety*'s Owen Gleiberman wrote of the 1972 movie in a review of its 2018 remake, "If you go back and watch a vintage blaxploitation film like *Super Fly* (1972), it has a time-capsule quality that only enhances the low-rent documentary scuzziness of its atmosphere. The brightly littered Manhattan streets, the cozy squalor of the bars and drug dens, even the cruddiness of the apartments: All fuse into a bombed-out yet strangely liberated mood that lets you know why the hero would choose the life of a cocaine kingpin, because it's the only way he has to leave behind the racist prison of 'a jive job with chump change, day after day'" (Gleiberman 2018).

This suggests a kind of radical defiance, a deliberate turning to crime to—in the vernacular—stick it to "the Man." In contrast, Curtis Mayfield's soundtrack album acknowledges that the criminal activity of the various characters is intricately connected with the poverty, racism, and lack of hope for the future of ghetto life; however, Mayfield offers very little sense that this activity provides real empowerment. I would argue that in large part this is because even in the hard-hitting songs that clearly point to poverty, racism, and so on, Mayfield's falsetto singing lends more of a feeling of sadness to the music than a feeling of open defiance of society.

In "Little Child Runnin' Wild," Mayfield first establishes the theme of the circle of poverty leading to generation after generation having to scrape by to survive. As Mayfield looks at the current generation, though, he ties this poverty and the racism with which the child contends with the child's belief that he needs to make it alone because "he's been had." Absent the film itself, Mayfield's vocal approach suggests a sadness with the situation. The musical setting represents early 1970s' funk, providing a marked contrast with singing that hearkens back to Mayfield's days with the Impressions.

In "Pusherman," Mayfield and Johnny Pate's instrumental arrangement incorporates Afro-Cuban percussion instruments and style, an effect that was in vogue at the time in music that graced both the pop and R&B charts. As had been the case with Mayfield's songs earlier in his career, "Pusherman" contains strong memorable musical hooks. Perhaps most notable, however, is the seductive way he sings the piece's key text, "I'm the pusherman." Mayfield is almost cloying in his seductiveness, almost as if his character is trying too hard to entice his potential clients. Again, this may provide a subtext that suggests that Mayfield's pusher character differs in fundamental ways from the hardened, empowered, politically motivated character of the film.

The *Super Fly* soundtrack album spawned two singles that made it solidly into the Top 10 of both the R&B and pop charts. The first of these, "Freddie's Dead," is the album's next track. The arrangement on "Freddie's Dead" uses orchestral strings like some of the soul recordings that were coming out of cities such as Philadelphia around this time. In fact, some listeners might detect a bit of a connection with "Freddie's Dead" in MFSB's highly popular recording from the following year, "TSOP (The Sound of Philadelphia)." However, more to the point, it even more closely resembles the unison string writing throughout Marvin Gaye's iconic Motown album *What's Going On*. The instrumental accompaniment also makes abundant uses of wah-wah pedal-infused electric guitar to an even greater extent than in the arrangement of "Pusherman."

In this tribute to Fat Freddie, who dies when he is hit by a car while trying to escape from the police, Mayfield tells the listener that Freddie's addiction put him under the control of "the Man"—perhaps a different "Man" than the slumlords and so on that impoverished individuals such as Freddie worked to escape. The song paints Freddie as a sort of pawn in the game of life. This, arguably, is the song that best illustrates the extent to which Curtis Mayfield negated whatever glamour the *Super Fly* film might have implied about the criminal life.

Arguably, the instrumental "Junkie Chase" makes little sense outside the context of the film. The fast pace of the piece conveys the sense of a chase scene; however, because the instrumental voices generally seem to all take accompanying roles (even the piano, which is most prominent, is generally limited to sporadic chords), outside the film, "Junkie Chase" might suggest that backing track for a song, the vocal lines of which were either never written or were exorcised from the final mix of the track.

The instrumental introduction of "Give Me Your Love" is an unusually long minute and a half. Like several of the previous tracks, one of the distinctive aspects of the arrangement is the use of wah-wah pedal electric guitar. Because this effect was so frequently used in the late 1960s and early 1970s, it is something of a double-edged sword with regard to this track and the entire album. On one hand, the effect was very much in vogue at the time. On the other, the effect now sounds dated, similar to how certain 1980s' synthesizer tone colors paint some recordings too fully as being part of the milieu of their decade. To put it another way, the wah-wah effect is too prominent for "Give Me Your Love" to have the kind of timeless feel of, say, Mayfield's earlier hit "People Get Ready."

The next track, "Eddie, You Should Know Better," is a warning to drug dealer Youngblood Priest's partner, Eddie, not to pursue his life of dealing. The lyrics tell Eddie to think of his family and true friends and not to continue to attach himself to Priest. Musically, Mayfield's setting suggests a soul ballad. Perhaps the most interesting part of the piece is the final unresolved dominant (V7 #9) chord that follows the text "I don't think he's gonna make it this time." The unresolved nature of the harmony and the dissonance of the chord create a sense of foreboding.

"No Thing on Me (Cocaine Song)" is Mayfield's warning against drugs and addiction to them. Once again, he portrays those who hook young people on addictive drugs as "the Man." This equate them—even if they are part of the neighborhood, part of the black community—as being on the same level as slumlords and others who take advantage of and discriminate against impoverished urban blacks. One aspect of "No Thing on Me" as a message song is that unlike, say, the message songs on Marvin Gaye's contemporary *What's Going On*, is that the arrangement is busier, with the guitar figures, the orchestral strings, the saxophone obligato, and so on, taking some of the focus away from the lyrics.

The instrumental, "Think," is ballad-like in its style and tempo. The numerous texture changes and the fact that there is no clear melody that goes through these changes gives the piece a backing-track quality. In short, like the album's earlier instrumental, it requires the context of the film to be completely successful.

Although digital reissues of *Super Fly* include the single mix of "Freddie's Dead (Theme from *Super Fly*)" and "Superfly," the two Top 10 pop and R&B singles from the collection, the original album concludes with "Superfly." This is an engaging funk piece in which Mayfield turns the "super fly" of the movie's title—basically, an adjective that in various generations might translate into "super cool," "super hip," "super phat," and so on—and turns into a noun. As Mayfield address Superfly, the flashy individual who flaunts his material success, he delivers the overarching message of the album: that although one has huge obstacles to overcome in the urban ghetto and although one has to do what one can to survive, one must do so with without destroying others like the pimp, the drug dealer, and others who become "the Man." The importance of the message in "Superfly" is clearly brought out in the funk arrangement in which nothing in the accompaniment gets in the way of the lyrics or of Mayfield's message.

It is unusual for a film soundtrack album to add a layer of meaning and significance to the movie that generated it; however, in the case of *Super Fly*, Curtis Mayfield rounded out the meaning of the film in songs that deliver a clear moral message, one that reflects back to his early work in gospel and soul. In doing so, Mayfield's songs call into question the forms of empowerment that some of the film's main characters seem to glorify.

WILSON PICKETT: *LAND OF 1000 DANCES: THE COMPLETE ATLANTIC SINGLES, VOL. 1*

With a few notable exceptions, the most commercially successful and the most impactful part of Wilson Pickett's career was 1965 to 1967. During this period, Pickett was a fixture on the R&B singles charts. and several of his recordings crossed over onto the pop charts. After singing with the gospel group the Violinaires and with the secular vocal group the Falcons, Wilson Pickett undertook a solo career. It was not until he secured a contract with Atlantic Records, however, that his career really took off. *Land of 1000 Dances: The Complete Atlantic Singles, Vol. 1* includes Pickett's early recordings on the label, as well as his most iconic recordings, including "In the Midnight Hour," "634-5789 (Soulsville, U.S.A.)," "Land of 1000 Dances," "Funky Broadway," and "Mustang Sally."

Although Pickett's first single on Atlantic, "I'm Gonna Cry (Cry Baby)," backed with "For Better or Worse" did not chart, the two songs make for interesting study in terms of what they show about how he was initially presented to the public on Atlantic and the extent to which they anticipated aspects of his style that would resonate with the record-buying public within approximately a year.

Pickett cowrote "I'm Gonna Cry (Cry Baby)" with Don Covay. In this up-tempo piece, Pickett portrays a man whose woman has done him wrong. As a result of this mistreatment, he is "gonna cry, cry baby." Like "For Better or Worse," the arrangement is somewhat over-the-top, both instrumentally and vocally. It is easy to think that the song could have been more successful had the horn section and the backing vocals been at least a bit more subdued. What "I'm Gonna Cry (Cry Baby)" does illustrate, though, is Wilson Pickett's power on up-tempo danceable songs, something that drove several of his later hits.

"For Better or Worse," a collaborative effort of Pickett and Don Juan Mancha, includes rhythmic, harmonic, and arrangement cues that suggest the influence of James Brown's earlier hit "I Don't Mind." In fact, part of the reason for the song's relative lack of success might be that it sounds too derivative of the James Brown song, which was already a few years old. In "For Better or Worse," Pickett's character addresses his wife, who apparently has done him wrong on more than one occasion (he has walked out on her in the past) and concludes that he will give her another chance in keeping with their marital vows. As mentioned earlier, the backing vocal and horn section arrangements are somewhat over the top, especially when compared with the backing Wilson Pickett received on "In the Midnight Hour" and his other hits of the 1965 to 1967 period. However, and it is a significant "however," the vocal and instrumental arrangements, particularly on "For Better or Worse" suggest a tie to gospel music and a full backing gospel choir and instrumental ensemble, a stronger tie to gospel than on many of Pickett's later hit singles.

Although Pickett's cowriter on "In the Midnight Hour," Atlantic Records' session guitarist, songwriter, and producer Steve Cropper, later stated that the inspiration for the title and some of the lyrics of the song came from an old gospel recording on which Pickett had sung (Marchese 2016), it appears that Cropper had actually heard an early secular recording on which Pickett performed. In any case, "In the Midnight Hour," which was Pickett's third Atlantic single release, became arguably his most significant hit. The single topped the R&B charts and reached the midway mark on the Top 40 pop charts after its 1965 release. As Pickett had already demonstrated on his earlier singles, he was a powerful highly expressive singer, a soul artist who delivered raw emotion more than most. What sets "In the Midnight Hour" apart from those earlier unsuccessful singles is that "In the Midnight Hour" contains particularly strong and instantly memorable lyrical and melodic hooks. For another thing, the arrangement is more in keeping with the standards in Memphis soul recordings on Atlantic and the related Stax labels, as opposed to the fuller arrangements on Pickett's early Atlantic recordings. The song's importance has been widely recognized. For example, in 2017, the National Recording Preservation Board of the Library of Congress added "In the Midnight Hour" to the National Recording Registry (National Recording Preservation Board of the Library of Congress n.d.), and, in its

2011 listing of the "500 Greatest Songs of All Time," *Rolling Stone* magazine ranked "In the Midnight Hour" at No. 135 (*Rolling Stone* 2011).

Even on the lesser-known songs that Pickett coauthored with other collaborators, such as "I Found a Love, Pt. 1" (the lengthy song was split between the two sides of the 45-rpm single release) Pickett's highly emotional soulfulness shines through. "I Found a Love" was written by Pickett, Willie Schofield, and Bob West and was originally recorded by the Falcons, the soul vocal group with which Pickett performed before he began his solo career. The song opens with a spoken introduction that sets up the premise of the need for love. Pickett's introduction resembles a preacher delivering a sermon, and the stylistic ties to the gospel tradition are confirmed by the texture created by the interaction of his lead sung vocal and the backing singers.

Wilson Pickett continued to record and enjoy success with self-written and cowritten songs; however, especially during the period represented on this compilation album, he also recorded several iconic covers, most notably "Land of 1000 Dances" and "Mustang Sally," and other songs that came from the pens of other writers, such as "Funky Broadway." Although these R&B chart hits crossed over to and did well on the pop charts, they are not the best examples of pure soul in Wilson Pickett's output. What songs such as these did was integrate Pickett's overtly emotional soul style into the dance music styles and rock and roll of the day. In fact, Pickett's versions of some of these covers were more commercially successful at the time and remain better remembered than the originals. For example, Mack Rice's original version of "Mustang Sally" did not make the pop charts and only ascended to No. 15 on the R&B charts. By contrast, Wilson Pickett's recording made it to No. 6 on the R&B charts and to approximately the middle of the Top 40 on the pop charts. Today, when one hears "Mustang Sally" from a DJ playing oldies material or on oldies radio, it is generally the Pickett recording. Likewise, Pickett's recording of "Land of 1000 Dances" eclipsed the chart success of any of the previous versions of the song, despite the fact that by the time his version was released in 1966, the dance steps that are name checked in Chris Kenner's composition were somewhat old and, in some cases, obsolete, such is the pace at which popular culture evolves.

As a soul singer, Wilson Pickett was one of a kind, and his importance as an influence and as an artist ultimately exceeded his impact on the charts, even as considerable as it was in the mid-1960s. And because Pickett's hit singles are his best-remembered work today, this, or any other greatest-hits collection provides an excellent representation of Wilson Pickett's must-hear music.

ELVIS PRESLEY

Elvis Presley's ties to African American music were strong from the beginning of his recording and live-performing career. In fact, Presley's first few single releases caused confusion among radio disc jockeys on both white country stations and black R&B stations, as well as among listeners who wondered if the singer was black or white. Presley covered numerous R&B, blues, and soul songs throughout his career, and his gospel recordings included both songs penned by white and black songwriters. For example, Presley recorded "Peace in the Valley" and "Take My Hand, Precious Lord," both written by the father of black gospel music, Thomas A. Dorsey.

Two of Ray Charles's seminal soul classics were included among Presley's recordings back in the 1950s: "I Got a Woman" and "What'd I Say." In so far as these songs can also be considered early rock-and-roll standards, numerous white rock-and-roll musicians included them in their repertoires in the late 1950s and early 1960s. For example, there are recordings from the early 1960s of Liverpool rock bands such as the Big Three and the Beatles performing these Ray Charles classics. So, although these songs might have established Ray Charles as the leading soul singer of the time, they became somewhat mixed in with songs by Little Richard, Chuck Berry, Gene Vincent, Eddie Cochran, Buddy Holly, and other writers and performers as part of the general 1950s' rock-and-roll repertoire.

Where Elvis Presley showed himself to be part of the world of soul music really came in the late 1960s, with 1969 sessions that were recorded in Memphis, Tennessee—where Presley had not recorded since he left Sun Records for RCA in 1955—and were released as the albums *From Elvis in Memphis* and *Back in Memphis*, and in Presley's chart-topping single of the same period, "Suspicious Minds."

Chips Moman, one of the cowriters of "Do Right Woman, Do Right Man" for Aretha Franklin's *I Never Loved a Man the Way I Love You* album, produced Presley's Memphis sessions. Moman was long associated with Stax Records, the leading Memphis soul label, where he had produced and written for black soul and white country artists alike. Likewise, the backing instrumentalists and singers on Presley's Memphis session had performed on Stax soul records and country records. Author Matt Dobkin discusses the often-unacknowledged close ties between Southern soul and country music throughout *I Never Loved a Man the Way I Loved You*, his study of Franklin's first record on Atlantic. Even more than the Franklin disc, Elvis Presley's Memphis sessions of 1969 closely connect soul, country, and gospel in the choice of material, the arrangements, and in Presley's expressive approach to the songs. As *Rolling Stone*'s Mark Kemp put it 40 years after the albums' initial releases, when Legacy reissued a two-album package of *From Elvis in Memphis* and *Back in Memphis*, "what makes these sessions remarkable: the new-found maturity and soulfulness in Elvis' vocals, and producer Chips Moman's warm, distinctly Southern musical backing" (Kemp 2009).

Several of these tracks demonstrate Presley's soulful approach, with the cover of Clyde McPhatter's "Without Love" on *Back in Memphis* being one of the stronger examples. The lead vocals, the piano-based opening, the backing vocals, and the largeness of the arrangement, all fall within the soul tradition, and the song itself is one of those authentic soul compositions that structurally, harmonically, and melodically draws heavily on the gospel tradition.

One of the sessions' most unusual tracks on *From Elvis in Memphis*, "I'll Hold You in My Heart," opens spontaneously, with Presley playing the piano and starting to sing the first verse, apparently before the rest of the musicians realize that he is ready to begin a take. Perhaps in part because of the sparseness of the arrangement, this is one of the least-commercial soul-sounding tracks; however, as such, it is perhaps the best example from the sessions of the closeness of country and soul.

The Mac Davis song "In the Ghetto" was the big Top-10 pop single on the *From Elvis in Memphis* album. With its subject of the cycle of poverty in urban ghettos and the violence and crime that is linked to poverty, "In the Ghetto" dealt with the same subject matter at approximately the same time as releases from artists including Sly and the Family Stone, James Brown, and others. The theme would be explored in more depth in a few years on Marvin Gaye's *What's Going On* and Stevie Wonder's *Innervisions*, but "In the Ghetto" is definitely a song focused on social issues that disproportionately affected the urban black community, issues that were part of the world of contemporary soul, R&B, and electric blues songs.

It seems reasonable to believe that some listeners might hear the song as patronizing, given that a highly successful white performer took it to the upper reaches of the pop charts. However, the song can also be understood as one that reflects on Elvis Presley's working-class roots and the affinity that he had for African American music going back to his first recordings, before he was rich and famous.

Some of the other songs on *From Elvis in Memphis* and *Back in Memphis* steer more in the direction of county or country pop (e.g., "Gentle on My Mind" and "I'm Moving On") or blues (e.g., Percy Mayfield's "Stranger in My Own Home Town"), but throughout his Memphis sessions, Presley sings with the expression of a soul singer, and the arrangements generally maintain at least a degree of connection to Memphis soul. Perhaps the best example of a pure soul recording by Presley, however, was of Mark James's "Suspicious Minds." When it was released as a single in 1969, it became Presley's last release to top the pop charts. Although one of the most unusual aspects of the recording—and one that is likely to immediately attract the attention of listeners, is the double-fade out. There is much more to consider, particularly when looking at "Suspicious Minds" as the "deep-soul hit" (*Rolling Stone* 2011) that it is. The abrupt change from a moderately fast-paced 4/4 meter to a slower 12/8 meter for the "Oh, let our love survive" section is particularly notable. In this section, Presley fully becomes a blue-eyed soul singer. The recording also features the Memphis Horns, the house brass section that graced numerous soul recordings of the 1960s released on Stax Records, which also helps lend "Suspicious Minds" a genuine soul feel. In the magazine's listing of "500 Greatest Songs of All Time," *Rolling Stone* ranked "Suspicious Minds" at No. 91 (*Rolling Stone* 2011).

OTIS REDDING: *OTIS BLUE/OTIS REDDING SINGS SOUL*

Otis Redding's 1965 album *Otis Blue/Otis Redding Sings Soul* (hereafter referred to as *Otis Blue*) is described by Rob Bowman, author of the extensive liner notes for the Rhino Records CD reissue of the album, as such: "the disc has stood the test of time and is considered by most soul music aficionados to be one of the greatest soul albums ever recorded" (Bowman 2008, 2). The author's assessment comes in the context that in soul music in 1965, albums tended to be collections of a few A-sides and B-sides of hit singles, supplemented with what was sometimes filler material. Because of the arrangements, Redding's singing, and especially the choice of material, in retrospect, *Otis Blue* can be seen as a sort of 11-song compendium of what soul music was all about right in the middle of the 1960s. What makes for particularly interesting listening is how Redding and his Stax/Volt compatriots put their stamps on songs originally associated with Sam Cooke, Solomon Burke, B. B. King, the Rolling Stones, the Temptations, and others.

The album opens with "Ole Man Trouble," one of three songs written or cowritten by Redding. In this piece, Redding begs "Ole Man Trouble" to "stay away" from him. Redding's request for "faith to pick me up" and his invocation of God's name ties the "Ole Man Trouble" to the spiritual and gospel traditions. This is not Otis Redding's most memorable melody—that title would probably have to go to his posthumously released "(Sittin' on the) Dock of the Bay"—but the passion with which Redding sings on the track makes his apparently down-and-out-yet-again character sound believable: he clearly has had all he can take and is now only able to beg in desperation. The instrumental accompaniment on "Ole Man Trouble" is particularly interesting and unusual because of the cross rhythms from the triplet figures in the drums that Al Jackson plays in the second half of the recording.

Because I have examined some of the rhetorical differences between Redding's version of "Respect" and the subtexts associated with the even-better-known Aretha Franklin recording of a couple of years later, suffice it to say that the two versions of the song also differ musically in fundamental ways. The *Otis Blue* version of "Respect"—particularly the single version, which was included on the monophonic version of the album—is more immediately in-your-face impactful, largely because of the rock-like drumming and the horn arrangement, which is in the same ballpark as some of the big-sounding horn arrangements heard in Sam & Dave recordings of the era.

Sam Cooke's "Change Gonna Come" (often given in other recordings as "A Change is Gonna Come") is given an interesting arrangement. The track opens with a mournful trumpet solo that leads into the song proper. The trumpet sets the stage for the text's focus on racial discrimination. However, at the ends of the stanzas, Cooke's lyrics express the hope that "a change is gonna come." One might hear the arrangement and Redding's performance on *Otis Blue* as a suggestion that he is less than fully convinced of the inevitability of this positive social change. There is an underlying sorrow that might be interpreted as suggesting that the civil rights movement of the day—and "A Change Is Gonna Come" was one of the major soul songs of the movement—might well not be the final nail in the proverbial coffin of racism and injustice. In this recording, the song seems to become more like the sorrow songs of the era of slavery. The song's ties to the movement are suggested by the slow triplet chords in the brass and the occasional march-like figures in the drums that call to mind a slow funeral procession or a slow protest march. Another aspect of the arrangement that is worth noting is Steve Cropper's use of tremolo in his electric guitar chording, a practice that creates a sonic tie between this recording and the guitar work of "Pops" Staples in the recordings of the Staple Singers.

"Down in the Valley," credited to Solomon Burke, Bert Berns, Babe Chivian, and Joseph Martin, is a lyrical and musical adaptation of the traditional American folk song of the same name. Recorded earlier by the important but often-overlooked singer Burke, the lyrics concern the singer's sadness, which is heightened by the train he hears in the night that will soon bear his beloved away. Although this is not the most substantial or important song on *Otis Blue*, it does provide the listener an opportunity to experience Redding exhorting the instrumentalists during instrumental breaks, as well as Redding's improvisation on the basic tune. Generally, however, adaptations of familiar songs such as this typically have not aged well, unless there is something fundamentally distinctive about the arrangement or performance.

"I've Been Loving You Too Long," credited to Redding and Jerry Butler, is an interesting ballad. The arrangement focuses on Steve Cropper's accompaniment on electric guitar and includes sudden dynamic changes, particularly when the rhythm section quickly crescendos and the horn section enters the soundscape. Redding and Butler's harmonic vocabulary is also noteworthy, as it includes several unexpected harmonies. Most unexpected is the use of the bVI chord (an F-major chord in the key of A major in this case) in the verses. This chord makes its first appearance during the text, "as you become a habit to me." So, although the lyrics might not stand out dramatically from those of the numerous other love ballads, the musical setting holds the listener's attention to a greater extent than in many of those other ballads of the day.

To the extent that one interprets *Otis Blue* as a sort of 1965 soul compendium, a collection of all that was going on in soul music, then his recording of Sam Cooke's "Shake" ticks one more box on the list. The first half of the 1960s saw any number of dance crazes and dance songs come and go. Cooke's song distills all these down to perhaps one of the simplest dance moves of all: shaking. Redding and the Stax/Volt house band and the Memphis Horns take what in Cooke's version had been pretty much a straight-eighth-note feel and turn into a fast shuffle beat. The recording is particularly notable for its Al Jackson drum fills.

In retrospect, Temptations' recording of Smokey Robinson and Ronald White's "My Girl" would seem to be so iconic that attempting a cover version could be dangerous. Except for one brief passage, the harmony vocals of the Temptations' Motown hit version are absent in the Otis Redding rendition of "My Girl"; however, some of the answer figures that the Temptations sand in their recording are played by the horn section that backs up Redding. Still, the thinner texture, particularly in the vocals, provides a greater level of intimacy in Redding's version of the song. And, in the context of an album that can be viewed as a compendium of what was going on in soul music right in the middle of the 1960s, "My Girl" serves an important function in balancing the album.

The next track, Lou Adler, Herb Alpert, and Sam Cooke's "Wonderful World," was originally recorded by Cooke back in 1960. In the months just before the release of *Otis Blue*, however, the song was making a comeback as a pop-rock hit for Herman's Hermits. In a sense, then, Redding's recording reclaims the song's original soul roots.

Redding incorporates soul's ties to electric blues in the B. B. King and Joe Josea composition "Rock Me Baby." The track demonstrates just how well-suited Redding's gravelly vocal approach is for electric blues. The inclusion of the B. B. King song also reinforces the often-tenuous and contentious connections between blues and soul—the contention coming between gospel and blues, the sacred and the secular. The track features Steve Cropper, who contributes a virtuosic electric guitar solo—somewhat different in tone and style than that associated with B. B. King—but powerful and technically impressive in its own way.

Perhaps the most unusual track on *Otis Blue*, "Satisfaction" is the 1965 hit song by the Rolling Stones. In retrospect, this up-tempo R&B version of the Mick Jagger and Keith Richards composition can be heard almost as a blueprint for the later famous Ike and Tina Turner rave-up treatment of John Fogerty's "Proud Mary." The arrangement and performance are largely successful, perhaps suggesting, among other things, the extent to which the Rolling Stones—originally a British electric blues band—incorporated elements of African American music in some of their original compositions and performances. Arguably, the one aspect of the arrangement that does not work as well as other songs on the album is the scoring of the horn section. It seems to lose some power because of the extremely high pitch range of the trumpet parts in the introduction. The fact that some gospel and soul songs were notable for extended groove sections—more so in live performances than on studio recordings—is illuminated in this recording by Redding's exhortations to the musicians to "keep on a-groovin'" during the instrumental break.

Otis Blue concludes with William Bell's "You Don't Miss Your Water." This soulful ballad of loss in love rounds out the album's rhetorical look at the themes and musical styles, tempos, and so on, associated with soul. This song comes from the viewpoint of "a playboy" who cheated on his lover. Now that she has left him, he realizes just how much he has lost. Not only is the premise a change of pace from the rest of the album's songs, the quietness of the arrangement and performance also offers an intimacy beyond that of the other, bigger, more fully arranged, and more forcefully sung pieces.

The 2006 Rhino CD reissue of *Otis Blue* is on two discs, one of which contains the original stereophonic version of the album, along with bonus material, and one of which contains the original monophonic version of the album. This is important because monophonic singles and albums were real players in the first half of the 1960s, and, in some cases, the monophonic mixes provide very different listening experiences than what today is the more familiar stereo soundscape. In the case of songs that were intended to be released as singles, it is also important to note that throughout the popular music industry of the day, the mixes were designed to sound good on automobile radios and small transistor radios. Interestingly—and this was not necessarily a standard throughout the record industry—on *Otis Blue*, several of the songs on the stereo and mono versions of the album were different recordings. "Respect," for example, was recorded for single release and was rerecorded for the stereo version of the original LP. So, a digital reissue, such as the 2008 double-disc Rhino one, also provides the opportunity to hear differences between the two recordings of "Respect," as well as the two different versions (and different lengths) of "I've Been Loving You Too Long."

Otis Redding was a headliner at the June 1967 Monterey Pop Festival, the first iconic popular music festival of the 1960s, followed two years later by Woodstock. Redding did not perform at Woodstock, however, because he perished in a plane crash six months after his Monterey Pop performance. "(Sittin' on) The Dock of the Bay," a song he recorded just days before the plane crash, topped both the R&B and pop charts, cementing Redding's legacy. Although "(Sittin' on) The Dock of the Bay" does not necessarily reflect the style of the bulk of Redding's work, it remains his most popular and often-heard recording and one of Redding's most expressive, yet understated, vocal performances. The laid-back feel of Redding's posthumous hit also anticipated the direction that soul would head in the early 1970s, with the emergence of singer-songwriters such as Al Green and Bill Withers.

"RESPECT": FROM OTIS REDDING TO ARETHA FRANKLIN[5]

When one mentions the 1960s soul song "Respect," perhaps most people who are familiar with it immediately think of Aretha Franklin's 1967 hit recording. Singer-songwriter Otis Redding wrote the song and was the first to record it. In fact, it was the songwriter himself who took "Respect" to No. 4 on the R&B charts and into the pop Top 40 in 1965. Two years late, however, Franklin's version far outsold Redding's recording and, in the process, became one of the most enduring hits from the 1960s.

Otis Redding was born in Dawson, Georgia, but grew up primarily in Macon, Georgia. During his school years, Redding sang in his church choir and won a series of community talent contests. Redding joined Johnny Jenkins and the Pinetoppers as a singer in 1960. When a 1962 Jenkins recording session ended with time to spare, the producer allowed Redding to cut a couple of songs. This proved to be pivotal in helping establish Redding as a solo recording artist. Redding became one of the leading figures in soul music; however, his life was cut tragically short when he perished in a plane crash in December 1967.

Redding's "Respect" is built around the oscillation of pairs of chords. The melody is not among the most immediately singable of the era; however, the song does exhibit one of the most memorable and strongest hooks of in popular music, the spelling out of the word "respect" in the Aretha Franklin recording. From a musical standpoint, the song is more about its rhythmic feel and danceability and the way in which it is performed than anything else. The arrangement on the 1965 Redding recording differs fundamentally from that on the Franklin recording. One could argue that the arrangement on the Franklin recording is more distinctive; however, it should be noted that the instrumental arrangement on Sam & Dave's 1967 hit "Soul Man" sounds as though it must have, at least in part, been inspired by the arrangement on the Redding recording of "Respect" from two years before. In addition to differences in the instrumental arrangements, it was in the way in which "Respect" was performed by Aretha Franklin and the backing vocal contributions of Franklin's sisters Erma and Carolyn that ensured that her version would become the definitive version of the song.

When one considers "Respect," it is important to focus on several aspects of the song, including the meaning that the listener might derive from Redding's original version, the way in which the meaning seems to shift with Franklin's recording, and the entire social context with which Franklin's recording resonated. Given the times in which it appeared and given the shift from a male singer to a female singer, "Respect" can be interpreted as raising issues such as gender roles, the civil rights movement, the family structure, and so on.

Coming from the voice of its composer, "Respect" seems simply to represent a request from a husband to a wife to give him his "proper respect" when he comes home after a hard day laboring for his family. As such, it seems to reinforce the gender-role stereotype of the male breadwinner and the female homemaker. Franklin's performance from the female perspective brings an entirely different dynamic to the characters' relationship and to the question of gender roles. For example, it is Franklin's character who is the family's breadwinner and who demands respect from her male counterpart. Does this necessarily cast the male character as a so-called househusband? Not necessarily; however, clearly the female character is in control of the couple's finances and is the principal—if not the sole—breadwinner.

It is important to note that Franklin's recording was initially popular just before the women's movement began in earnest at the start of the 1970s. Insofar as Franklin's recording quickly established itself as one of the best-loved and most iconic singles of the late 1960s, it was certainly still part of public consciousness, even as Carole King recorded *Tapestry* and more ephemeral hits such as Helen Reddy's "I Am Woman" became part of the women's movement's presence in popular culture. In this environment, the Aretha Franklin recording of "Respect" can be understood as not only one woman's demand for respect from one man but also as a more generalized call from women for respect from men.

Another interesting aspect of U.S. society of the time that "Respect" raises is its ties to the civil rights movement that some listeners hear in the song. There is little from either Otis Redding's recording or Aretha Franklin's recording—aside from the singers themselves—that clearly defines the race of the characters. Because the song is so closely associated with these two black performers, and because it is the singer's character who does the hardest—read, most labor-intensive—work in the relationship, it does not seem to be entirely out of the question to interpret "Respect" as a call from blacks for respect from whites.

In at least some sense, regardless of whether Otis Redding ever considered "Respect" to be anything more than a song about a male breadwinner who demands his "proper respect" "when [he] gets home" is, in some respects, immaterial. This is because the context of the song's popularity during the counterculture era makes it understandable as much, much more of a cultural metaphor than as a surface-level song.

Aretha Franklin's recording of "Respect" remains one of the most iconic single releases in history. As evidence, *Rolling Stone* ranked the recording at No. 5 in the magazine's "500 Greatest Songs of All Time" (*Rolling Stone* 2011). On the strength of the Franklin recording, "Respect" was inducted into the Grammy Hall of Fame in 1998 (The Recording Academy n.d.), and the National Recording Preservation Board of the Library of Congress added the Franklin recording to the National Recording Registry in 2002 (National Recording Preservation Board of the Library of Congress n.d.). The iconic nature of Aretha Franklin's reworking of "Respect" was acknowledged by Otis Redding himself, who has been widely quoted as having said numerous times something on the order of, "That little girl stole my song." This line, or variations on it, still routinely appear in descriptions of the song and its importance in the body of work that Redding wrote (see, for example, Ross 2017). The song, and particularly Aretha Franklin's recording, continues to live on in countless television and film soundtracks, oldies radio broadcasts, collections of iconic soul and pop hits of the 1960s, and television commercials.

MINNIE RIPERTON: *PERFECT ANGEL*

Minnie Riperton's 1974 album *Perfect Angel* is not necessarily always on music fans' soul radar. However, this album, produced by soul superstar Stevie Wonder under an assumed name for contractual reasons, featured Riperton's unique vocal and songwriting talents, Wonder's talents as producer and keyboardist, and vocal and instrumental contributions from the same musicians with whom Wonder worked on his acclaimed album *Fullfillingness' First Finale*. The songs, most of which were written by Riperton and her husband, songwriter and producer Richard Rudolph, run the gamut from funk, to easy listening, to more traditional soul, to rock, and all the tracks include at least elements of Riperton's ultra-high-pitched coloratura soprano and so-called "whistle register" singing. The album also contained Riperton's biggest commercial success, "Lovin' You."

The album opens with the funk-rock song "Reasons," the basic premise of which is that "the reasons for my life" are numerous, vast, and ever expanding. Riperton expresses the philosophy that life's meaning is basically defined through personal encounters, relationships, and the myriad of things—good and bad—that one experiences from day to day and hour to hour. The sad irony of this song—and similarly themed songs on *Perfect Angel*—is that within approximately a year and a half of the release of the album, Riperton was diagnosed with breast cancer, underwent a radical mastectomy, and was told that the cancer had metastasized. Riperton became a spokesperson for the American Cancer Society, received the Society's Courage Award, and ultimately succumbed to the disease in 1979.

Part of the strength of *Perfect Angel* came from the fact that Wonderlove, Stevie Wonder's backing band, supported Riperton. And in addition to the backing band, El Toro Negro (the Black Taurus), the pseudonym Wonder used because of his contractual ties to Motown (the competitor label Epic released *Perfect Angel*), produced, added his own instrumental contributions, and wrote two of the album's songs. "Reasons" is a showpiece for Wonderlove's instrumentalists, particularly lead guitarist Michael Sembello.

The lyrical theme of "It's So Nice (To See Old Friends)" is encapsulated by the song's title. The track is notable for being built on a brief repetitive chord progression, suggesting late 1960s and early 1970s pieces such as Bob Dylan's "Lay Lady Lay" and John Lennon's "Imagine." Lennon's more complex "Mind Games" is also somewhat similar in harmonic effect. That I mention artists such as Dylan and Lennon in connection with Riperton's work is intentional. Her early work—back in the late 1960s—with the experimental band Rotary Connection, broke down barriers between psychedelic rock and soul, and *Perfect Angel* brings together soul, rock, jazz, and easy listening in a wide-ranging package.

The third track, Stevie Wonder's "Take a Little Trip," invites the listener to "take a little trip through your mind" and to explore the world of one's imagination. Musically and lyrically, the song is consistent with some of Wonder's contemporary songs that he wrote for himself, particularly some of those on *Innervisions*. In fact, the lyrics seem to be connected to the world of inner visions that Wonder also explored in the song "Visions." And like some of Wonder's non-funk work of his *Talking Book* and *Innervisions* period, the melodic and harmonic materials of "Take a Little Trip" reflect the influence of jazz. Riperton's textless vocalizations at the end of the track closely resemble Wonder's work of the period; however, as is the case throughout the album, Riperton includes some of her trademark coloratura and whistle-tone work, which puts a distinctive Minnie Riperton stamp on the track.

Clocking in at less than three minutes, "Seeing You This Way" sounds like something of a trifle on an album that, for the most part, features longer songs. The line, "Seeing you this way makes me feel so happy," sums up the minimalistic lyrics. The musical setting is appropriately upbeat, and the song fits in with the general theme established in the album's opener: that relationships, friendships, and the multitude of things—significant and mundane—that one encounters each day define life's meaning.

The largely piano-based song "The Edge of a Dream" is a somewhat Latin-influenced easygoing exploration of the vision of a world of peace, love, racial equality, freedom, and economic opportunity for all the world's children. Put another way, this song can be understood as a musical exploration of the vision of Rev. Dr. Martin Luther King Jr.'s "I Have a Dream" speech or a secular exploration of the vision expressed in the biblical Book of Isaiah 11:6–8, the so-called peaceable kingdom passage. In retrospect, the jazzy musical setting of this song puts it in the same early 1970s' pop music realm as, for example, Maria Muldaur's recording of "Midnight at the Oasis" or some of the tracks on Carole King's *Rhymes & Reasons* album.

Stevie Wonder provided the album's title track, which is an exploration of simple romantic love. Although this is not the most melodically interesting song on the album, nor one of Stevie Wonder's greatest compositions from this prolific part of his career, Riperton's singing and the shimmering keyboards and Latin percussion make the track engaging.

In the next song, "Every Time He Comes Around," cowriters Riperton and Rudolph, producer Wonder, and lead electric guitarist Michael Sembello create a hard-hitting rock song about sexual desire ("Every time he comes around I feel like I'm on fire"); however, this is tempered with Riperton's hope that this desire is just part of an entire package of true, lasting love. A song such as this is important in helping define Minnie Riperton, if for nothing else than the fact that it tempers "Lovin' You," the song for which she is best remembered.

Paul McCartney wrote and sang that "some people want to fill the world with silly love songs," and artists such as McCartney and Stevie Wonder (e.g., "I Just Called to Say I Love You") enjoyed some of their most commercially successful hits with songs that might have been perceived as lightweight by critics but that resonated favorably with the record-buying public. In its simple harmony and tune and in its acoustic guitar and electric piano-based arrangement, "Lovin' You," which became a No. 1 pop hit for Riperton, might seem, on the surface, to at least be in the same playing field as "Silly Love Songs" and "I Just Called to Say I Love You." Although the song was apparently written as a lullaby-type diversion for Riperton and Rudolph's young daughter, there is a decided element of sexuality to the lyrics. As Riperton sings, "Every time we . . . ooh, I'm more in love with you," the song practically invites the listener to fill in the blanks. The recording of a singing bird that runs throughout the track enhances the implication of early morning lovemaking. The fact that the musical setting is so simple and the music suggests a state of being, a constancy, enhance the lyrics.

Perfect Angel concludes with "Our Lives." Here, Riperton and Rudolph explore the theme of reunion, presumably of a husband and wife. The nature of the cowriters' relationship and the fact that the song mentions that the song's characters have children—which Riperton and Rudolph did—makes this another autobiographical-sounding track.

Perfect Angel is an album filled with desire for continuing love, expressions of deep love, hope for a more agape-type love to run through humanity, and expressions of the importance and the satisfaction of friendships. It is entirely optimistic, accessible, and easy to listen to. It is absent the sense of heartfelt loss that is at the core of many soul recordings; however,

Riperton expresses the optimism and hope of the songs with a style that is clearly part of the world of soul.

As mentioned earlier, Minnie Riperton was diagnosed with breast cancer shortly after the release of *Perfect Angel* and died of the disease at age 31, approximately five years after this, the biggest hit of her career. Although she started her career in the record industry as a secretary at Chess Records before joining the band Rotary Connection and enjoyed a brief recording career as a solo artist, Riperton—particularly on *Perfect Angel*—not only captured the ears of music fans (the album was solidly in the Top 10 of the pop charts and topped the R&B charts, and the single release of "Lovin' You" topped the pop charts and came within a couple of places of topping the R&B charts) brought a vocal approach into the world of R&B and soul that continues to exert an influence. Later whistle-tone and coloratura soprano singers such as Georgia Brown, Jennifer Hudson, Mariah Carey, and others clearly follow in the vocal footsteps of Minnie Riperton. Although the rock style that was integrated into several tracks might not have aged as well as the sound of the rest of the album, *Perfect Angel* remains much more than just an example of a vocal technique that became increasingly mainstream in the 1990s; it remains a vibrant statement of optimism, love, and friendship.

SMOKEY ROBINSON AND THE MIRACLES

Much of the history of the Motown empire, from its beginning through the 1980s, involves Smokey Robinson, either for his work with the Miracles, his solo recordings, songs he wrote or cowrote for other artists, or his role in Motown as an executive. Berry Gordy Jr. may have founded the company, but Smokey Robinson was also at the core of the Motown until MCA bought the enterprise in 1988. Although Robinson has enjoyed considerable success in his decades-long solo career as a singer-songwriter, arguably it was his work with the Miracles that had the biggest impact on soul.

Known variously as the Five Chimes and Matadors, the group led by lead singer William "Smokey" Robinson eventually settled on the name the Miracles by 1958. Beginning in 1965, because lead singer and principal songwriter Robinson was the best-known member of the group, they became known as Smokey Robinson and the Miracles, before reverting to the Miracles upon Robinson's departure in 1972. In addition to Robinson, the group during its heyday included Warren "Pete" Moore, Bobby Rogers, Ronnie White, and Emerson "Sonny" Rogers. Claudette

Rogers, Bobby Rogers's sister and eventually Smokey Robinson's wife, also sang in the group during its early years. Although rarely pictured with the group in its publicity photos, guitarist Marv Tarplin was also an important member of the Miracles over the years and cowrote the hit "The Tracks of My Tears" with Smokey Robinson.

The Miracles' first successful single was "Got a Job," which was an answer to the 1957 No. 1 pop and R&B hit by the Silhouettes, "Get a Job." This 1958 song, cowritten by Berry Gordy, Tyran Carlo (a pseudonym for Billy Davis), and Smokey Robinson, obvious owes several debts to the Silhouettes' hit, including the lyrical premise and the distinctive bass voice part. Based on the 12-bar blues chord progression, "Got a Job" still sounds like a bona fide stand-alone song and not just a parody of and response to "Get a Job." Like "Got a Job," Gordy and Robinson's 1959 composition "Bad Girl" was not an unqualified, defining megahit for the Miracles. Also, like its predecessor, "Bad Girl" was based on a well-established chord progression. In this case, it was the familiar I-vi-IV-V, so-called "oldies progression," a staple of late 1950s and early 1960s pop, doo-wop, and R&B songs, from James Brown's "Try Me" and Jackie Wilson's "Lonely Teardrops," to Ben E. King's "Stand by Me," and dozens of others.

By 1960 and the release of Gordy and Robinson's "Way over There," the Miracles were taking on the popular sound of the Drifters. In particular, the string scoring and Latin-inspired rhythmic feel of the song call to mind the standard sound of arrangements on the hit singles by the Drifters of the late 1950s and early 1960s. Although, like its predecessors, this was not the Miracles' breakthrough hit, Smokey Robinson's lead vocals seem more self-assured on "Way over There." The recording, then, represents a step along the way in defining the group and the natural, easygoing flow that marked Robinson's best lead vocals of the Miracles' subsequent hits.

The Miracles' future hits were built around stronger melodic and lyrical hooks. The group's true breakthrough came with "Shop Around," another piece cowritten by Gordy and Robinson. This song has an instantly identifiable chorus melodic hook, particularly the rhythmic break between the words "mama told me" and "you better shop around." The song is also more powerful rhythmically than the earlier Miracles singles. In "Shop Around," Smokey Robinson sings with a blues inflection and extemporizes on the melody in a manner reminiscent of a descant singer in a gospel choir. In this, and in the best of Robinson's lead vocals, the basic melodic shape is always preserved; however, Robinson's subtle improvisation on the tune gives the piece a feeling of spontaneity.

Not only did the Miracles' 1960 release of "Shop Around" resonate with the record-buying public—it topped the R&B charts and came within one spot of doing the same on the pop charts—it is one of the Miracles' most persistent songs. As evidence that the song maintained its appeal over a decade and a half after the Miracles first recorded it, Captain & Tennille produced a hit pop single version of the song in 1976.

Smokey Robinson was the sole writer of the Miracles' 1962 No. 1 R&B and Top 10 pop hit "You've Really Got a Hold on Me." This song of love when one is least expecting it or looking for it is notable for several strong musical hooks. The understated melody was the most soulful to date of the Miracles' singles releases and suggests the almost resigned and somewhat perplexed feelings Robinson's character expresses in the lyrics. The opening guitar lead line is instantly identifiable; the two-part vocal harmony on the verses is also an important defining point of the song. In fact, the Beatles' 1963 cover of the song focuses on the guitar line and the vocal harmony arrangement of the original.

Without question, the most memorable songs recorded by the Miracles were about love. Interestingly, the songs of happiness and joy tended to be tempered. For example, as already mentioned, in "You've Really Got a Hold on Me," Smokey Robinson's character seems almost to be reluctantly in love. Somewhat similarly, in the 1967 Robinson and Al Cleveland composition "I Second That Emotion," Robinson's character is interested in pursuing a relationship, but only if the woman to whom he sings is willing to commit to "a lifetime of devotion." It seems that Robinson's character has had his heart broken too many times in the past and will not settle for anything less than the guarantee of a future.

There is a vulnerability implied or outwardly expressed in many of these Miracles hits that contrasts with the gender-role stereotypes that might have been more closely associated with decades before the 1960s but that still lingered. Two of the Miracles' other significant hits of the second half of the 1960s, "The Tracks of My Tears" and "The Tears of a Clown," moved even more deeply into the realm of male vulnerability.

The latter song, which Robinson and Motown singer-songwriter Henry Cosby based on an instrumental track by Stevie Wonder, was first recorded by the Miracles in 1967 but was released as a single in 1970, when it topped both the R&B and pop charts. "The Tears of a Clown" is probably the Smokey Robinson and the Miracles song most likely to be heard on oldies radio today. "The Tears of a Clown" takes the well-known image of the heartbroken clown who puts on a smile for his audience while he is dying inside and moves it from the world of Italian composer and librettist Ruggero Leoncavallo's 1892 opera, *Pagliacci*, and into the world of 1960s' soul. Like "I Second That Emotion," "The Tracks of My Tears," and other mid-1960s' Miracles' hits, "The Tears of a Clown" is filled with lyrical and melodic hooks. It is also notable for its unusual orchestration, which includes prominent piccolo and bassoon parts, instruments rarely heard in soul music. The arrangement suggests, though, the atmosphere in which the circus clown might be plying his trade while secretly suffering inside.

With music and/or words to songs such as "Shop Around," "You've Really Got a Hold on Me," "Going to a Go-Go," "The Tracks of My Tears," "The Tears of a Clown," and "Ooo Baby Baby" Smokey Robinson was not only notable as a lead singer, but also as a leading Motown songwriter. Interestingly, one of his most commercially successful collaborative works, written with his fellow Miracles member Ronnie White, was "My Girl," a No. 1 pop and R&B hit for the Temptations. Of all of Robinson's songs, this might be the best remembered, as it seems to periodically find its way into television and motion picture soundtracks. The song's place in 21st-century popular cultural has also been solidified by "My Girl" having been used in television commercials for McKee Foods' Little Debbie Snacks.

After leaving the Miracles, Smokey Robinson embarked on a successful solo career, although he eventually focused his efforts in the music industry as an executive. One of Robinson's most important contributions as a solo artist, however, is probably his 1975 album, *A Quiet Storm*, and the song of the same name. The title and the style of romantic ballads on which Robinson and other singers including Anita Baker and Luther Vandross focused from the mid-1970s onward gave rise to the quiet-storm subgenre of soul music. Quiet storm eventually became a popular radio format. In fact, a report from *The New York Times* News Service stated that by 1987, quiet storm, which includes elements of soul, jazz, and jazz-fusion and consists predominantly of romantic ballads from a span of several decades, was a particularly successful format at attracting advertisers and was found on approximately 40 percent of the urban contemporary radio stations in the largest U.S. radio markets. *The New York Times* report quoted Melvin Lindsey, "a former radio personality at WHUR in Washington who is widely acknowledged as the originator of the [radio] format" as saying, "It's a beautiful black music—it's the counterpart of the easy-listening stations" (*The New York Times* News Service 1987).

In 1987, the Rock and Roll Hall of Fame inducted Smokey Robinson as a member. Because so much of Robinson's iconic work was as part of the Miracles, the fact that the Miracles were not inducted at the same time created controversy. It was not until 25 years later that the rest of the group joined Robinson in the Hall. The entire ensemble's significance was confirmed by the induction of Smokey Robinson and the Miracles into the Vocal Group Hall of Fame in 2001 (The Vocal Group Hall of Fame n.d.). The Miracles were also inducted into the Grammy Hall of Fame for their recordings of "You've Really Got a Hold on Me," "The Tracks of My Tears," "Shop Around," and "The Tears of a Clown" (The Recording Academy n.d.), and the National Recording Preservation Board of the Library of Congress added the group's recording of "The Tracks of My Tears" to the National Recording Registry (National Recording Preservation Board of the Library of Congress n.d.).

SAM & DAVE

From the second half of the 1950s through at least the 1980s, the world of American popular music included notable and, indeed, iconic male duos. The Everly Brothers, the Righteous Brothers, Simon & Garfunkel, Hall & Oates, Jan & Dean, all enjoyed hits; however, arguably the most exciting male duo of the era was Sam & Dave, consisting of Sam Moore and Dave Prater. Although the duo is perhaps best remembered for "Soul Man," particularly in that the song was revived by the Blues Brothers in a virtual copycat version for John Belushi and Dan Aykroyd's *Saturday Night Live* skits, for the 1978 album *Briefcase Full of Blues*, and for the 1980 film *The Blues Brothers*, Sam & Dave enjoyed several other significant hits, including "I Thank You," "Hold On! I'm Comin'," and "You Don't Know Like I Know." Another interesting must-hear Sam & Dave track is "You Don't Know What You Mean to Me."

In his oral recollections of his life and career, Sam Moore said that although his showmanship and stage clothing style influences were Jackie Wilson and Otis Redding, "my musical inspirations were still the great gospel singers. Sam Cooke and R. H. Harris, who was in the Soul Stirrers before Sam. I would visualize how I could break it down: To be so rough, and the gospelly and floating, and moan, and all those things . . . I saw all those gospel singers, and I saw how they could *sell*" (Moore and Marsh 1997, 87).

Sam & Dave had the reputation of being one of the great live acts of the 1960s, in no small part because of the showmanship that came out of these influences. This can easily be seen in any of the numerous filmed live concert and television appearances by the duo available at the time of this writing on YouTube (see, for example, their lengthy performance of "Hold On! I'm Comin'," from the 1966 Stax/Volt concert tour, at https://www.youtube.com/watch?v=Fowldx4hRtI, accessed January 20, 2020). Arguably, Sam Moore's impassioned approach to the verses of many of the duo's songs, both live and on record, calls to mind great black preachers. Perhaps the best example, however, of a direct connection between Sam & Dave's style and gospel music and the black church can be found in "You Don't Know What You Mean to Me." The song opens with a spoken dialogue between Moore and Prater in which Moore introduces his character's level of feeling for his lover with an intensity that suggests the exhortations of a preacher. Although perhaps not one of the duo's must-hear songs, "Sweet Home" also contains highly emotional spoken sections at the beginning and end of the recording, as well as melismatic sung lines that also exhibit a connection to gospel music and the church.

According to Sam Moore, the fact that he tended to sing lead on Sam & Dave recordings and the call-and-response style that marked some their recordings and live performances was born out of necessity. Moore also attributed the duo's vocal texture of featuring one singer (usually Moore) on the verses and harmony in the choruses—as opposed to the standard harmony of early-1960s' vocal groups—in part to the fact that, early in their career, Moore and Prater did not have sufficient time to rehearse together because of Prater's bakery job (Moore and Marsh 1997, 45). Moore also asserted that because "Dave couldn't read [English] well," it was difficult for Prater to work from lyrics sheets. As a result, the duo's standard studio operating procedure was for Moore to record a guide vocal track for Prater so that Prater could learn the words and his harmony part (Moore and Marsh 1997, 69).

Recordings such as "You Don't Know Like I Know," "I Thank You," "You Don't Know What You Mean to Me," "Hold On! I'm Comin'," and "Soul Man" all include chorus sections in which Prater and Moore harmonize. What is certainly true of these songs—not to mention numerous other Sam & Dave recordings—however, is that Moore generally sings the verses either solo or with brief interjections from Prater. Despite Moore's assertion that the duo's texture was all about call-and-response, generally, vocal interplay is limited in many of the hits. There is interplay during the bridge of "Soul Man," both in the studio recording and in Sam & Dave performances that were filmed back during the 1960s. Perhaps the best example of interplay—although it is not traditional call and response—can be heard in the studio version of "Hold On! I'm Comin'."

Part of the story of the success of Sam & Dave revolves around the duo's writers and producers. Jim Stewart produced Sam and Dave's early recordings, including "Hold On! I'm Comin'," "Soul Man," and "You Don't Know Like I Know." After the severing of Stax Records' distribution agreement with Atlantic Records, Isaac Hayes and David Porter became Sam & Dave's producers, assuming responsibility for songs such as "I Thank You" and "You Don't Know What You Mean to Me." The Stax/Volt and Atlantic studio musicians who backed up the labels' other various singing groups and soloists also perform on Sam & Dave's recordings. That is not to say that these recordings necessarily bear a deep resemblance to the work of Otis Redding or other Stax, Volt, or Atlantic artists. The production on the Sam & Dave records, which is particularly easy to appreciate in the digital remasters of the original recordings, regardless of whether the originals were produced by Jim Stewart or Hayes and Porter, is notable for the punchiness and rhythmic impact of the instruments. In this regard, the bulk of Sam & Dave's work is perhaps more immediately danceable than some of the contemporary soul hits by other artists. To put it another way, there was a Sam & Dave sound that was fundamentally different than that of any of their labelmates.

It is important to note that Isaac Hayes and David Porter played a crucial role as Sam & Dave's principal songwriters, well before they took over the production of Sam & Dave's recordings after the distribution agreement ended between Stax and Atlantic and Sam & Dave moved from the former to the latter. In fact, Hayes and Porter were responsible for "Soul Man," "Hold On! I'm Comin'," "I Thank You," "You Don't Know Like I Know," and "When Something Is Wrong with My Baby," the latter a rare song in which Dave Prater sings the opening solo. Porter also wrote "A Place Nobody Can Find" as a solo composition and cowrote "Goodnight Baby" with Booker T. and the M.G.'s' guitarist Steve Cropper. Even some of the Sam & Dave songs written by others, including "You Don't Know What You Mean to Me," a song from the pens of Steve Cropper and Eddie Floyd, are squarely in the same stylistic ballpark as the Hayes and Porter works. The duo's hits, too, generally were medium to up-tempo pieces with memorable melodic and instrumental hooks. This differentiates Sam & Dave from other Stax and Atlantic artists who performed songs by a wider variety of songwriters and in a wider variety of styles, such as Aretha Franklin and Otis Redding, especially in Franklin's inclusion of pop songs in her repertoire and in the ballads that were part of Redding's recorded repertoire.

The vocal textures in the Sam & Dave arrangements are also clearly duet in nature, as opposed to the texture of a soloist with backing harmony singers, which was much more the norm in the soul music of the day. And, the duet style and texture generally were consistent on Sam &

Dave recordings; they varied little from song to song and usually consisted of Sam Moore taking the solo lead during the verses with two-part vocal harmony in the chorus sections.

Although the Sam & Dave sound largely was unique during their heyday of 1965 to 1972, the vocal arrangements of the Righteous Brothers' recordings of the period exhibit at least a degree of the influence of Sam & Dave. Likewise, numerous subsequent soul and rock musicians have named the duo as a musical influence. In addition, the instrumental and vocal arrangement of the Grammy Award-winning single "Soul Man" that Sam & Dave recorded in 1967 was copied for the Blues Brothers' version that comedian/actors John Belushi and Dan Aykroyd performed in November 1978 on NBC's *Saturday Night Live* and recorded as a single and album track the following year, right down to Belushi's exhortation to lead guitarist Steve Cropper (who appeared on both the Sam & Dave and the Blues Brothers' recordings of the song) to "play it, Steve." Sam & Dave's recording of "Soul Man" was inducted by the Recording Academy into the Grammy Hall of Fame in 1999 (The Recording Academy n.d.); in 2018, the National Recording Preservation Board of the Library of Congress added the Righteous Brothers' Sam & Dave-like "You've Lost That Lovin' Feeling" to the National Recording Registry (National Recording Preservation Board of the Library of Congress n.d.); and, in 1992, Sam & Dave were inducted into the Rock and Roll Hall of Fame. In addition, some of Sam & Dave's recordings from the 1960s continue to find their way into film and television soundtracks, even well over a half century after they were initially hits. For example, a brief excerpt from the duo's recording of "Hold On, I'm Coming" was included in the soundtrack of a December 19, 2019, episode of the Amazon Prime program *The Grand Tour*.

NINA SIMONE: *FEELING GOOD: THE VERY BEST OF NINA SIMONE*

Pianist and singer Eunice Waymon changed her name to Nina Simone when she took on a career in jazz to earn enough money to pay for private classical piano lessons. Throughout her career as a pianist and singer, Simone exhibited a unique style that integrated gospel, jazz, classical, blues, and soul music. Simone also played a significant role in the civil rights movement, writing and recording the song "Mississippi Goddam" after the murder of Medgar Evers and the infamous September 1963 church bombing in Alabama that cost four African American girls their lives. Many of the songs in Simone's repertoire were powerful statements about racial equality and formed part of her contribution to the civil rights movement. As author Mark Anthony Neal wrote, "many within the movement viewed her music as an aural counterpart to sit-ins, non-violent demonstrations, and prayer meetings that dominated the movement" (Neal 1999, 48). In addition to her activism on that front, she was also active in the antiwar movement of the 1960s and 1970s.

As a collection of Simone's best-known and most important work, Universal Music Group's (UMG) 2019 album *Feeling Good: The Very Best of Nina Simone* is perhaps the best greatest-hits-type package ever assembled for Simone. The album contains 20 songs, including the must-hear tracks "Feeling Good," "Don't Let Me Be Misunderstood," "Take Me to the Water," "I Put a Spell on You," "Mississippi Goddam," "I Loves You, Porgy," "Nobody Knows You When You're Down and Out," "I'm Going Back Home," and "Strange Fruit." The album's other tracks fill out the listener's experience with Simone but are not necessarily as memorable as those I have listed, although the old jazz standard "My Baby Just Cares for Me" is interesting for how Simone's jazz piano style clearly integrates classical piano technique into the stylistic mix. In addition to the songs included in this collection, Simone's version of Langston Hughes's anti-discrimination and antiwar song "Backlash Blues"; her late 1960s' song "To Be Young, Gifted and Black"; and her cover of the 1950s' film song "Wild Is the Wind" are also worth seeking out. These and some of Simone's more obscure recordings, though, can be difficult to find, except though sources such as YouTube, as some of Simone's albums are out of print.

Feeling Good: The Very Best of Nina Simone opens with "Feeling Good." This song, written by Anthony Newley and Leslie Bricusse for their musical *The Roar of the Greasepaint—The Smell of the Crowd*, is performed by an unnamed black character in the show. Simone's recording dates from 1965, at approximately the same time the musical was running. The track opens with Simone singing the first verse a cappella. In part because of the minor-key tonality, short blues-like phrases, and imagery drawn from nature (e.g., fish, dragonflies, butterflies, etc.) to represent freedom, the piece resembles a 19th-century spiritual, particularly in Simone's a cappella rendition of the opening.

When the instrumental accompaniment enters, it is easy to appreciate one of the important factors that distinguished Nina Simone's studio recordings—the instrumentation and the horn section lines reflect the style and aesthetics of big band jazz. At the same time, the writing for the orchestral strings and the repeated triplet figures in the piano reflect back to the 1950s: the incorporation of strings reminiscent of some of the recordings of that decade by jazz vocalists such as Ella Fitzgerald and Frank Sinatra, and the piano figure reminiscent of late-1950s rock and roll ballads. Simone's recording of "Feeling Good" is definitive—although numerous other artists recorded the show tune—the legacy of the Simone version has been kept alive through the recording's inclusion in television program and film soundtracks and in television commercials.

The song "Don't Let Me Be Misunderstood" might have been one of the major British Invasion hit recordings by the Animals, but it first appeared on Nina Simone's album *Broadway—Blues—Ballads* and, in fact, was one of the songs specifically written for the album. The album was not particularly well received by reviewers, including *AllMusic*'s Richie Unterberger; however, Unterberger calls "Don't Let Me Be Misunderstood" a "first-rate" track (Unterberger n.d.). In some respects, this is one of the most conventional soul recordings in the collection, particularly with the backing female chorus and the chunky guitar chords. Simone's singing, too, is filled with a sorrowful expression.

Although on a literal level, the lyrics of "Don't Let Me Be Misunderstood" seem to come from a character who unintentionally creates relationship problems with her lover, it is easy to understand why some listeners detect a deeper subtext. Given Simone's activity and visibility in the civil rights movement, one can interpret this song as an apology of sorts for offending some listeners with the rhetoric of some of her earlier recordings and public stances. Hearing the song in this way is a disservice to Simone and the causes she championed. It is also an interpretation that receives no real lyrical support, in contrast to other multilevel songs of the period, such as Curtis Mayfield's "People Get Ready." Still, it is interesting to consider "Don't Let Me Be Misunderstood" as a minor retreat from songs such as "Mississippi Goddam," particularly as Simone later stated in an interview that "Mississippi Goddam," a potent protest of racial discrimination and inequality, was the song that most hurt her career (*Jet* 1986).

"Take Me to the Water" is a reinterpretation of the old spiritual of the same name. Although Simone's arrangement did not contain all of the text found in some publications of the song, it preserves the theme of baptism that is at the core of many versions. Simone's lyrical vocal style and the inclusion of a backing chorus suggest strong ties to the gospel music tradition. Interestingly, however, Simone's piano playing late in the song is perhaps more reflective of the style of 19th-century European virtuoso piano composers (e.g., Frédéric Chopin) than of a purely 20th-century gospel style.

Simone's cover of Screamin' Jay Hawkins's rock-and-roll classic "I Put a Spell on You" transforms the song from its original context—and differentiates it from later well-known versions by the likes of Creedence Clearwater Revival and others—by turning it into a soul ballad. In fact, the overall feel is not in an entirely different ballpark as the famous Etta James recording of "At Last," detailed elsewhere in this chapter. Despite how well known the more heavily R&B and rock versions of the song are, Simone's performance is effective.

The album includes a live recording of "Mississippi Goddam," one of Nina Simone's best-known compositions. In the song, Simone focuses on the lynchings and church bombings in Mississippi and Alabama of the early 1960s, as well as on economic, employment, and other inequities based on race. This subject matter alone is not what makes the song stand out, as other protest singer-songwriters—black (e.g., Josh White) and white (e.g., Phil Ochs)—had dealt with or would shortly deal with similar issues in their music. Simone puts a highly personal stamp on the issues, so that they are anything but abstractions. What makes this piece stand out from other protest material of the time is that this performance is in a fast-paced style that some listeners might connect more with musical theater or a cabaret than with civil rights–era protest music. In fact, it is the musical style that heightens the sense of irony and the bite of the social observation and commentary that runs through Simone's lyrics. The importance of "Mississippi Goddam" was recognized by the National Recording Preservation Board of the Library of Congress, which inducted the song into the National Recording Registry in 2018 (National Recording Preservation Board of the Library of Congress n.d.).

Although it is not necessarily Nina Simone's most important recording, "I Loves You, Porgy," a song originally from George Gershwin's "folk opera" (Gershwin's term for the work) *Porgy and Bess*, was Simone's biggest commercial success on the singles charts. Because of the context of this discussion (a book on soul music), it is important to note that the recording reflects the spirit and style of a small jazz combo in a club more than what one might typically consider to be soul music. It is mentioned as a must-hear selection because it helps demonstrate just how difficult it is to define Nina Simone's style. "I Loves You, Porgy" illustrates that not only did Simone integrate jazz, soul, musical theater, and classical influences, she was also adept at shifting fully and convincingly into any of these styles. The importance of "I Loves You, Porgy" in the Nina Simone catalog is confirmed by The Recording Academy, which inducted the song into the Grammy Hall of Fame in 2000 (The Recording Academy n.d.).

Bessie Smith original popularized the old blues standard "Nobody Knows You When You're Down and Out" in the 1920s. Simone's recording straddles the lines between blues, jazz, and soul music. Although Jimmy Cox's lyrics find a former millionaire reflecting on the extent of old friends' rejection after the loss of fortune, Simone's performance might be heard by some listeners as adding a racial subtext, particularly given her activism in the civil rights movement of the time. Specifically, her character can be understood as a projection of the economic and broader social plight of American blacks.

Although perhaps not the most essential Nina Simone performance, another album cut, Rudy Stevenson's "I'm Going Back Home," is the song in this collection most reflective of the classic soul of the late 1950s, the time period in which Ray Charles was marrying the musical style of upbeat gospel music with secular lyrics. This, despite the fact that the song's appearance on Simone's 1967 album, *The High Priestess of Soul* came approximately a decade after the pioneering work of Charles.

Billie Holiday is the singer most closely associated with the Abel Meeropol (writing under the pseudonym Lewis Allan) 1937 anti-lynching song "Strange Fruit." In fact, as her signature song, there are countless audio recorded and filmed Holiday performances of the piece. Simone's 1965 recording owes a debt of gratitude to Holiday's style. In some respects, particularly in Simone's piano work, the song is even more stark and haunting than some of Holiday's performances. One of interesting aspects of the song's placement on this greatest hits album (immediately before "Nobody Knows You When You're Down and Out") is that the two songs can be heard as a miniature tribute to black women singers of the past who recorded songs of social commentary: Holiday and Bessie Smith. Despite the close association of "Strange Fruit" with Billie Holiday, it was Simone's recording of the song that rap artist and music producer Kanye West sampled for his *Yeezus* track "Blood on the Leaves."

The songs that Nina Simone wrote, and some of those of other songwriters, were politically and socially charged. Although that might have limited record sales and radio airplay in her heyday of the late 1950s through the 1960s, Simone has more recently been praised for her efforts toward social justice. The Rock and Roll Hall of Fame inducted Simone in 2018, and Simone's social activism is at the center of the Hall's biography of her (The Rock and Roll Hall of Fame 2018). Simone's continuing recognition is also confirmed by preservation efforts that concluded in 2019 on her childhood home in Tryon, North Carolina. This preservation was covered in *Preservation*, the magazine of the National Trust for Historic Preservation (see Som 2019).

By integrating elements of classical piano music, musical theater and cabaret style, big band jazz, and a cappella solo-voice spirituals, the recordings and live performances of Nina Simone broadened and deepened the definition of soul music. The songs in her repertoire that confronted racism and that protested U.S. participation in the Vietnam Conflict also stand as some of the strongest statements on these social issues to come out of the era's soul-related performers.

PERCY SLEDGE: "WHEN A MAN LOVES A WOMAN"

Percy Sledge's recording of "When a Man Loves a Woman" is perhaps one of the most curious examples of must-hear soul. The song itself is attributed to Calvin Lewis and Andrew Wright, members of the Esquires, a group in which Percy Sledge was the lead singer. Sledge has stated in interviews that it was he who improvised the original version of the song after asking his bandmates to provide him with a slow blues backing (Roberts 2015). Because of the nature of the musical setting, particularly the harmonic scheme of the song, it is important to note that Sledge's recollections appear not to be entirely accurate, as "When a Man Loves a Woman" has little to do with blues music in form, phrase structure, or harmonic vocabulary.

The ties between this song and sacred music are strong, but some of the musical materials differ fundamentally from most of the pieces associated with the soul genre. Notably, the stepwise descending bass line is like that in another well-known 1960s' classic hit, Procol Harum's "A Whiter Shade of Pale," which was released approximately a year after "When a Man Loves a Woman." However, looking backward in musical history, the stepwise bass line of both songs resembles the well-known "Air" from Johann Sebastian Bach's *Orchestral Suite No. 3*, BMW 1068 (the Bach catalog designation of the composition), widely known as the "Air on the G String," because the composition's melody can be played entirely on the G string of the violin.

A more harmonically conventional bridge balances this unusual harmonic structure and bass line in the verses. In fact, the composers' use of two principal sections in the song calls to mind the familiar AABA structure that was frequently the basis of early and mid-20th century American popular songs. In the classic American songbook of that period, the A and B sections generally had clearly defined contrasting melodic material and harmonic schemes. Such is the case with "When a Man Loves a Woman," although the overall structure of the song is AABAA. In this song, the title line, which opens each verse (A section) soars high into Percy Sledge's range. This seems to drive home the intent of the song: to show the strain and pain love puts his character through. In fact, one might describe

Sledge's character as obsessive, as did *Los Angeles Times* report Randall Roberts, who wrote in his obituary of Sledge, "A ballad about a devotion bordering on obsession, the song features Sledge embodying a soul who's desperate, lost and so bent on pleasing his woman that he's willing to turn his back on his friends, spend all his money on her, 'give up all his comforts and sleep out in the rain'" (Roberts 2015). The soaring melody on the title line, then, exemplifies the character's obsession and desperation.

Several aspects of the song tie "When a Man Loves a Woman" to the world of gospel music. For one thing, the eight-measure-long A sections of the song each consist of two musically identical four-measure phrases with different lyrics. The resulting degree of musical repetition in the song is reminiscent of the way in which gospel choruses are repeated many times in some Christian churches. The largeness and the spaciousness of the arrangement and production but, especially, Sledge's highly emotional singing style also connect "When a Man Loves a Woman" to the gospel tradition. And this is true not only of the title line but also Sledge's singing in his upper register near the end of the bridge section. The slow compound quadruple (12/8) meter of the song also suggests ties to the gospel tradition.

The final statement of the A section and the recording's fade-out add a prominent horn section to the texture. David Hood, a one-time bass player at FAME Studios and with the Muscle Shoals Rhythm Section, was quoted as saying that Atlantic Records' producer Jerry Wexler insisted that the horn section overdubs be rerecorded with different players because of the out-of-tune nature of the original recording. According to Hood, the horn tracks were re-recorded, but the original version was released anyway (*Songfacts.com* n.d.). Years later, Rhino Records released a Percy Sledge collection that included both versions of the song. Interestingly. the version with the alternative overdubs includes not just a more controlled and in-tune horn section but also a backing chorus. This vocal backup to Sledge connects the song even more strongly to more conventional soul music, as well as to its gospel cousin.

The original recording has a rawer quality to it than some of the significantly slicker soul recordings of the day and of the years before "When a Man Loves a Woman" was recorded. The nature of the brass section overdubs and the backing vocals in the alternative version smooth out the some of the rawness. Arguably, however, the fact that "When a Man Loves a Woman" is not as slick as many hit soul songs at least in part adds to its believability as an emotional expression of the pain and torment that can be caused by the blindness of an obsessive love. And some listeners who love the recording as originally released will undoubtedly hear the alternate version as having artificially grafted-on components, so iconic is the original.

Percy Sledge's recording of the song topped both the pop and R&B charts of the day. In fact, it can reasonably be argued that "When a Man Loves a Woman" not only defines the way in which love can change someone but is also a recording that defines the middle of the 1960s. It can be understood as one of the quintessential examples of soul music from that time period, despite so many aspects of the song standing in sharp contrast to the era's musical expectations (e.g., the Bach-like bassline and verse harmonic scheme, the out-of-tune brass section, the high degree of melodic repetition, and so on). It is probably no surprise, then, that when that era is portrayed, when love's effects on one's behavior and relationship with friends ("turn his back on his best friend if he puts her down"), and when the desperation that love can cause are part of a film's storyline, Percy Sledge's recording can be a natural fit for the soundtrack. The recording has been used in several such contexts; however, perhaps the most popular movie in which it was included in the soundtrack was the 1983 film *The Big Chill*.

"When a Man Loves a Woman" has been widely recognized as one of the greatest singles in the history of the recording industry. For example, in 1999, the Recording Academy inducted "When a Man Loves a Woman" into the Grammy Hall of Fame (The Recording Academy n.d.), and, in 2011, *Rolling Stone* ranked Percy Sledge's recording of the song at No. 53 in the magazine's list of "500 Greatest Songs of All Time" (*Rolling Stone* 2011). Percy Sledge himself was enshrined in the Rock and Roll Hall of Fame in 2005.

Over the course of the next couple of years, Percy Sledge recorded other songs, often covers of soul songs most closely associated with other singers. In fact, Atlantic Records' 1987 compilation CD *Percy Sledge: The Ultimate Collection* is something of a mixed bag, largely populated by covers as wide ranging as "Love Me Tender" and "You've Really Got a Hold on Me." The disc also contains Sledge's Top 10 R&B singles, "Warm and Tender Love," "It Tears Me Up," and "Take Time to Know Her." Nearly all of Sledge's Atlantic recordings were made in Muscle Shoals, Alabama, at the same FAME Studios where other soul stars of the day also recorded. However, unlike some of his contemporaries, Sledge today is remembered almost entirely for one song, albeit a giant one in the story of 1960s' soul, "When a Man Loves a Woman."

DUSTY SPRINGFIELD: *DUSTY IN MEMPHIS*[6]

When an American thinks of British pop stars of the 1960s, it is far too easy to remember primarily the Beatles, the Rolling Stones, the Who, Herman's Hermits, the Dave Clark Five, the Yardbirds, the Kinks, and all the other male rock, pop, and blues bands that dominated the American charts and radio airwaves during the 1964 to 1966 British Invasion. Unfortunately, these bands were so prominent that it is easy to overlook the 15 U.S. Top 10 singles that Petula Clark recorded between 1964 and 1968. Likewise, Dusty Springfield's contributions, such as the 10 singles that made the *Billboard* Top 40 between 1964 and the end of the decade, can get lost in the shuffle. Even more important than those singles, Springfield made an important mark as perhaps the best British soul singer of the 1960s. Although Springfield's 1969 album *Dusty in Memphis* was not an overwhelming commercial success, in the 21st century, it continues to be viewed as one of the greatest British soul albums ever recorded.

Born Mary O'Brien, Springfield grew up listening to a wide range of musical styles. Her first professional experience came in a female vocal group, the Lana Sisters. From 1960 to 1963, she performed in the Springfields, a folk trio. She took the stage name Dusty Springfield during this time. Springfield left the trio and the folk style for a solo career built on pop and soul material. She was also instrumental in the business arrangements that brought top Motown artists to the United Kingdom in 1965, and she was the only white singer to be on the bill of some of the shows in which she appeared.

Some of Springfield's recordings prior to the 1968 recording of *Dusty in Memphis* include the feel of soul music; however, her work with famed Atlantic Records producers Jerry Wexler, Arif Mardin, and Tom Dowd took her soulful leanings straight to the source. Interestingly, while the instrumental and vocal backing tracks were recorded in Memphis by Atlantic stalwarts (including Aretha Franklin's backing singers, the Sweet Inspirations) in September 1968, Springfield's lead vocals were recorded at separate sessions in New York. Although Springfield's emotional, soulful vocals are certainly a large part of what makes *Dusty in Memphis* continue to stand out as one of the greatest albums of the rock era, what also makes it stand out are the production and the choice of repertoire. Ironically, Dusty Springfield's greatest album as a soul singer is a collection of largely pop material (including four songs written the highly successful Brill Building team of Gerry Goffin and Carole King), arranged and recorded in the soul style, as opposed to a collection of tried-and-true soul songs. Although Wexler, Mardin, Dowd, and Springfield's choice of songs might seem unlikely at first glance—this was, after all, the great soul label Atlantic Records—it is an important part of the reason that the album holds up so well: a collection filled with soul classics of the day probably would have seemed far too derivative. The fact that the album integrates pop, soul, touches of jazz, cabaret song, and the influence of Tin Pan Alley–style torch song means that it stands apart from just about every other album of the late 1960s.

Dusty in Memphis opens with Brill Building writers Barry Mann and Cynthia Weil's "Just a Little Lovin'." This triple-meter song, at just over two minutes, is the shortest track on the album. As such, and taken as a stand-alone song, it can sound underdeveloped; however, in the context of the songs that follow it, "Just a Little Lovin'" functions more like an introduction to the composite work. Mann and Weil establish the theme of love—and indeed physical love—and provide the first reference on *Dusty in Memphis* to early morning lovemaking. The rest of the album continues to explore the theme of love (ecstatic, broken, unrequited, and so on), and the idea of early morning lovemaking returns in more metaphorical form in the album's sixth track, "Breakfast in Bed." "Just a Little Lovin'" includes a string arrangement that anticipates the texture of many of the songs on the album. The jazz-like melody of the song and the jazz-waltz metrical feel call to mind some of the popular recordings of Hal David and Burt Bacharach songs by Dionne Warwick between 1962 and 1971. However, there are also twinges of Aretha Franklin–style soul in the vocal range used by Springfield, as well as in some of the improvised ornamentations she provides. Although the melody has some Bacharach-style, almost sing-song phrases, there are also phrases with a surface sophistication that a composer such as Bacharach seemed to almost consciously avoid in some of his most commercially successful work. As unlikely as it might seem on the surface, this mixture of soul, adult contemporary, jazz, and Brill Building pop makes this song and the rest of *Dusty in Memphis* so intriguing.

Gerry Goffin and Carole King's "So Much Love" moves closer in the direction of Atlantic soul. From the early 1960s forward Goffin and King had somewhat specialized in writing music for female African American singers that sounded authentic, to the extent that some of their compositions for Little Eva, Earl-Jean, the Cookies, and others were sometimes more successful on the R&B charts than on the pop charts. Although the backing singers and Springfield's own singing provide hints of soul, there are some obvious harmonic signifiers (such as the chromatic voice leading that is frequently used in black gospel-based soul) that composer King avoids. The influence of gospel music is there, but only in part. The result is that "So Much Love" hints at middle-of-the-road pop enough that it never sounds like Dusty Springfield is trying to imitate a singer such as Aretha Franklin.

The album's big hit was "Son of a Preacher Man." Written by John Hurley and Ronnie Wilkins, it is the closest song on *Dusty in Memphis* to conventional soul music. In fact, the song had been offered to Atlantic

Records' star Aretha Franklin, who initially turned it down. Eventually Franklin recorded "Son of a Preacher Man," but not until after Springfield had already done so. The lyrics concern Billy Ray, the son of the local preacher, who took Springfield's character out for walks when his father came calling on the girl's family, presumably in the singer's teen years. Eventually, Billy Ray sweet-talks her and steals kisses, and then presumably the two make love. The references to the consummation of the relationship are veiled enough that there is nothing lurid about the song. Since "Son of a Preacher Man" seems to be framed as a reflective piece, looking back at the singer's younger days, it is interesting that this first lover was the only male who "could ever reach [her]." The implied inability to ever fall in love and/or become intimate with another man later in life ties the song to "So Much Love," as well as to some of the material found later on the album.

Although we need not necessarily detail all the songs on *Dusty in Memphis*, two more of the tracks go a long way in demonstrating how, rhetorically and musically, this album fits within the soul genre. In Randy Newman's "I Don't Want to Hear It Anymore," Springfield's character lives in an apartment complex with the proverbial thin walls. She recounts what she learned about her lover's indiscretions from overhearing the neighbors talk. She tells her lover that she is tired of hearing all the talk; however, in Newman's text, the female protagonist never tells her lover exactly what the next step will be. In fact, in Springfield's interpretation of the song, the most pervasive mood is that of resignation—much more so than, say, anger. This interpretation turns "I Don't Want to Hear It Anymore" into what some listeners might understand as an expression of codependency: Springfield's character might be tired of hearing the neighborhood gossip about her lover, but she seems to be so addicted to the relationship that she will continue to put up with her lover's dishonesty.

The album's penultimate track, Goffin and King's "No Easy Way Down," finds Springfield's character singing that when one has scaled the highest heights in life, "there is no easy way down." In other words, Goffin's text tells the listener that the higher one climbs (in life, in love, and so on), the harder one falls. The musical setting represents King's gospel-influenced style of the late 1960s and early 1970s, perhaps best epitomized by her songs with parenthetical titles such as "(You Make Me Feel Like) A Natural Woman" and "Hi-De-Ho (That Old Sweet Roll)," the former a hit for Aretha Franklin and the latter a hit for the jazz-rock band Blood, Sweat & Tears. For her part, Springfield provides an eerie feeling of emotional detachment, suggesting that her character's fall was so devastating that she is now emotionally dead.

Even in the songs on *Dusty in Memphis* that do not conveniently fit into the kinds of rhythmic grooves or instrumental backings of much of the soul music of the era (e.g., "The Windmills of Your Mind"), the songs delve deeply into emotions in the manner of soul music, and Dusty Springfield's vocal style reflects a clear affinity with African American soul music throughout. Add to that the fact that the backing instrumentalists and singers also contributed to the numerous soul singles and albums that came out of Atlantic Records, and *Dusty in Memphis* is arguably one of the best examples of blue-eyed soul ever.

THE STAPLE SINGERS: *BE ALTITUDE: RESPECT YOURSELF*

With their long history in gospel music and a recording career that went back to the early 1950s, the Staple Singers continued to represent the closest gospel ties of any artist(s) commonly identified as "soul" musicians. And through the contacts that Roebuck "Pops" Staples had growing up in the early 20th century, the Staples family had ties to the Delta blues tradition. Arguably, the Staple Singers' most fully successful soul album was the 1972 collection *Be Altitude: Respect Yourself*. All in all, the album's title captures the overarching theme, despite the pun (beatitude/*Be Altitude*). Several songs, even written by disparate composers, stress the importance of one's attitude in making a positive contribution to the world. The theme of self-respect and respect for one's fellow humans also runs through the songs, so there is a consistency to the collection that makes it feel somewhat like a concept album. Despite the strong gospel credibility of the Staple Singers, most of the songs on *Be Altitude: Respect Yourself* are not as much religious as they are inspirational.

The album opens with "This World," a song from the pens of Herb Shapiro and Gary William Friedman. The lyrics revolve around the choices people have between caring for the world and for others or "throw[ing] it away." The focus is on individuals' responsibility for the choices they make and on how their attitude shapes their reactions to negative occurrences in life. The song features a full scoring within the brass and rhythm sections. This brings up one of the aspects of the album that is important to note: although there is a consistency of lyrical message, producer/arranger Al Bell varies the texture of the mixes of the songs, achieving musical variety. "This World," like all the album's songs, features Mavis Staples's gospel-inspired vocal improvisation.

Although "I'll Take You There" was the most successful hit single from the album, Mack Rice and Luther Ingram's "Respect Yourself" also performed well on the pop and soul charts. The foreground message of the song is that one must have self-respect and act responsibly to improve the world. Although it is largely framed around individuals' self-respect and action, the song can also be understood as a more global call for self-respect (and respect from others) for African Americans.

"Respect Yourself" includes prominent vocals by the Staples family's patriarch, Roebuck "Pops" Staples, the father of daughters Cleotha, Mavis, and Yvonne (the four made up the group at the time of this album). However, perhaps the most notable aspect is Mavis Staples's vocal improvisation. As the BBC's Lloyd Bradley wrote of the track, "Mavis [Staples] works herself up into a foot-stomping testifyin' frenzy that manages supremely angry and monumentally uplifting at the same time" (Bradley 2010). Like several of the songs on the album, there is nothing cutting edge about the melody of the song (the interest mostly lies in the extemporaneous vocal material), but it does feature a solid instrumental groove and, like the rest of the songs on the album, is built around a focused, clearly articulated message.

Like several of the other songs on *Be Altitude: Respect Yourself*, "Name the Missing Word," a piece from the pens of Homer Banks, Raymond Jackson, and Bettye Crutcher, suffers from a string arrangement and tone color that has not aged particularly well. The tone color is somewhat otherworldly—perhaps unintentionally—and curiously reminiscent of the string scoring and tone color on Led Zepplin's "Kashmir."

The album's fourth track, "I'll Take You There," was written by producer/arranger Al Bell under his given name, Alvertis Isbell. Certainly, the Staple Singers enjoyed several other hits on the pop and R&B charts; however, for some music fans, this is the song that defines the group. Bell's lyrics speak of a place where there are no worries and where racism does not exist. The language is vague enough that one could attach a purely religious interpretation on the location of this place (e.g., heaven); however, another interpretation is as an expression of hope for a future earthly life in which all human beings are equally valued and respected. In this respect, "I'll Take You There" reflects on the lyrical procedures of some of the 19th-century spirituals, songs that were also open to multiple meanings.

Musically, "I'll Take You There" is notable for its unusual electric bass obbligato, which begins approximately 1:52 into the recording. Notably, this hypnotic song is structured like a gospel or praise chorus. In other words, there are no musically contrasting verses. This structure links "I'll Take You There" firmly with the black gospel tradition, and it made the song highly distinctive within the world of early 1970s' popular music, making it even more noteworthy that the single release of the song topped the pop charts. The single release shaved approximately a minute and a half off the album version. Both versions are must-hear recordings; however, the lengthier album version provides more of the spirit of how a chorus such as this might be experienced in worship.

Also notable of "I'll Take You There" are elements of reggae influence in the rhythms. In fact, comparison of this recording with, say, Johnny Nash's popular hit "I Can See Clearly Now," which was released just after it, demonstrates how the influence of Jamaican music was finding its way into the upper reaches of the R&B and pop charts. The Staple Singers' recording of "I'll Take You There" was inducted into the Recording Academy's Grammy Hall of Fame in 1999 (The Recording Academy n.d.), and their recording has been included in the soundtrack of several films and television shows over the years.

Don Covay, William Stevenson, and Wilson Pickett's "This Old Town (People in This Town)" was recorded by Pickett a couple of years before the Staple Singers included it on *Be Altitude: Respect Yourself*. Lyrically, the song continues the basic theme of "I'll Take You There." In this case, the vision is of a town in which respect and brotherhood and sisterhood abound. Musically, it offers a contrast to its predecessor in that it is a faster tempo and includes contrasting instrumental and vocal textures in some of its sections, as opposed to the more uniform texture of "I'll Take You There."

According to Broadcast Music Incorporated's (BMI) database of songs, composers, and publishers the next song, "We the People," was written by Carl William Smith and Marshall Jones (https://repertoire.bmi.com/ListView.aspx?torow=25&fromrow=1&page=1, accessed August 6, 2019), although some websites misidentify Smith's cowriter as Booker T. Jones, the leader and organist of Booker T. and the M.G.'s. "We the People" is another piece that emphasizes personal responsibility for making the world a better place, both on local and global levels. The song has some of musical feel of "I'll Take You There" as a result of the church-like call and response over a repeating instrumental riff.

Written by Homer Banks and Raymond Jackson, "Are You Sure," poses the basic question, "are you sure there's nothing you can do" to improve the world, to help other people out, and so on. Like "I'll Take You There," "Are You Sure" suggests the influence of Caribbean music in its rhythms. Lloyd Bradley's BBC review of the album points to this track as an example of "country soul" (Bradley 2010), but I hear it as much more reggae influenced. The theme of social change that runs through the lyrics, too, aligns with the reggae music of the period.

With Roebuck Staples's "Who Do You Think You Are (Jesus Christ the Superstar)?" the album increases in its overt religious imagery. Like the album's other songs, the message is clear and, in this case, encapsulated in the title. This is also one of the few songs on the album that provides an extended example of "Pops" Staples's lead singing.

Another Homer Banks and Raymond Jackson song, "I'm Just another Soldier," mentions assassinated individuals "Martin" (Luther King Jr.), "John" (Kennedy), and "Bobby" (Kennedy) as soldiers against hatred. The song paints the singer's character as "just another soldier in the army of love"—in other words, as a person carrying on the work of the Kennedys and King. The song's harmonic progression focuses on the I, IV, and V chords, standard fare for gospel music. The arrangement and singing style of the backing vocal chorus reinforces its tie to traditional gospel music.

The final song, "Who," which came from the pens of John Barry and Bobby Bloom, is the clearest example of a song of faith on the album. The basic message is to turn to belief when one is searching for the answers of life. Unlike the more gospel chorus–like structures on the album, "Who" has clearly defined verses and chorus sections. One aspect of the song that has not aged well is the overdubbed string arrangement, a weakness felt on a few other tracks. Overall, however, *Be Altitude: Respect Yourself* remains one of the classic works that closes whatever gap might exist between gospel and soul.

THE SUPREMES

In a 1974 interview, Martha Reeves, lead singer of Motown's Martha and the Vandellas, said "Martha and the Vandellas had a rowdiness about them . . . Not like the syrupy baby-dolls that didn't get down," adding that "the Supremes were pretty to look at, sure, but you didn't exactly dance in the streets" (Hildebrand 1994, 192). That may have been the case, but on the pop singles charts, the Supremes outshone every artist of the 1960s with one exception: the Beatles. Although the group enjoyed several No. 1 hits on the R&B charts, the Supremes (under that moniker and under the moniker of Diana Ross and the Supremes) hit the top of the U.S. pop charts 13 times between 1964 and 1969.

The first incarnation of the Supremes consisted of Diana Ross, Florence Ballard, and Mary Wilson. In 1967, the group was renamed Diana Ross and the Supremes; Ballard left the group and was replaced by Cindy Birdsong. After Ross left in 1970 to pursue a highly successful solo career, the Supremes continued, with several personnel changes over the years; Mary Wilson was the one constant member up to the group's disbanding in 1977.

As alluded to earlier, the Supremes were the best-charting American act on the singles charts between 1964 and 1969. It is important to keep in mind that the trio's success was predominantly on the pop charts. Although several of their recordings placed high on the R&B charts, only "Back in My Arms Again," "You Can't Hurry Love," "You Keep Me Hangin' On," "Love Is Here and Now You're Gone," "I'm Gonna Make You Love Me" (which also featured the Temptations), and "Someday We'll Be Together" topped both the pop and R&B charts, and only the post-Ross single "Stoned Love" topped the R&B charts without doing the same on the pop charts.

The fact that "Where Did Our Love Go," "Baby Love," "Come See About Me," "Stop! In the Name of Love," "I Hear a Symphony," "The Happening," and "Love Child" fared better on the pop charts than on the R&B charts is telling about the group's audience demographics. The Supremes' releases seemed to resonate with white audiences to an unprecedented degree. Based on their pop chart success, it could be argued that of all the commercially successful Motown acts of the 1960s—and there were more than just a few—the Supremes personified Motown founder Berry Gordy Jr.'s goal of making Motown "the Sound of Young America," as the company billed itself. The Supremes, more than Motown's other artists, helped bring a specific brand of soul music to U.S. audiences that transcended race.

The Supremes' chart-topping singles, particularly between 1964 and 1967, contained several defining factors that did not necessarily run throughout the work of the entire roster of Motown artists of the period, whether their recordings were released on Motown, Tamla, or Gordy, all parts of the Motown family. For example, the singles of one particular year might feature handclaps on beats two and four, while in another year, the tambourine might provide the backbeat. In this respect, the production of the Supremes' singles—generally by Brian Holland and Lamont Dozier who, along with Eddie Holland Jr., also wrote the vast majority of the Supremes' hits—resembled what Berry Gordy might have experienced during his days working on the automotive assembly lines before starting Motown: minor changes to refresh a given automobile model from year to year.

Holland and Dozier also created a distinctive Supremes sound—again, one that did not necessarily carry through the entire Motown catalog. The Supremes' hits feature the use of reverberation on the lead and backing vocals, which gives the singing a warm sound. Compare, for example, Holland and Dozier's production on "Stop! In the Name of Love" with their production on Martha and the Vandellas' "Heat Wave" or Mickey Stevenson's production on Martha and the Vandellas' "Dancing in the Streets," noting that Martha and the Vandellas were also Motown artists; the sonic styles are entirely different.

Similarly, Supremes' recordings, the hit singles and album cuts, tended to include certain instrumental touches, such as tambourine, shimmering vibraphone, orchestral strings, woodwinds and brass, and prominent baritone saxophone that helped define the Supremes' sound, particularly during first several years of their success.

When considering the Supremes' brand of soul, a brand that seemed to bring at least something of the genre to the widest possible spectrum of the U.S. audience, it is also important to note the emphasis that Motown placed on preparing and presenting artists to achieve the widest appeal. Motown artists were trained in deportment and elocution, and the company tried to ensure that they had strong visual appeal. In the case of the Supremes, this translated into live and televised appearances, with elegant matching evening gowns and jewelry and nearly matching hairstyles.

Although the Motown approach might seem like it could zap the soul out of musical artists, the Holland, Dozier, and Holland songs about a range of aspects of love, the appealing production, and the beautiful singing on the Supremes' hits struck an emotional and commercial chord between 1964 and the end of the 1960s. It was a decidedly polished approach to soul, even among Motown artists—as Martha Reeves alluded to in the 1974 interview in which she referred to the Supremes as "syrupy baby-dolls" (Hildebrand 1994, 192)—but it led to this subset of soul selling more records, receiving more radio airplay, receiving more jukebox plays, and being seen on more television programs than any of what some people might call more "authentic" versions of soul music. As such, it undoubtedly shaped many listeners' perception of just what "soul music" was.

Although the Supremes released numerous successful albums, the group's primary impact came by way of the singles. With 14 songs that topped the pop and/or R&B charts, just a collection of their most successful singles gives the music fan a great overview of the work of the most commercially successful all-female vocal group of all time. Motown's 2017 digital release *Diana Ross & the Supremes: Number 1's* includes all of the group's and all of Ross's solo chart-topping hits and represents a must-hear album.

The Supremes were inducted into the Rock and Roll Hall of Fame in 1988 and the Vocal Group Hall of Fame in 1998. Their 1960s' hits remain a staple in oldies radio and oldies satellite radio services.

THE TEMPTATIONS

Over the years, the Temptations underwent numerous personnel changes; however, during the group's heyday of the mid 1960s into the early 1970s, the most significant changes were in the lead-singer position. The best-known lineup of the Temptations, which was responsible for the group's pre-1968 hits, included David Ruffin, Melvin Franklin, Otis Williams, Paul Williams, and Eddie Kendricks. It is important to note that when lead singer David Ruffin left the group in 1968, Motown's writers and producers fundamentally changed the nature of the material that the group recorded, as we will explore in detail later. This dramatic change not only better fit the vocal style of new lead vocalist Dennis Edwards, it also helped keep the Temptations relevant for several years as an R&B and pop chart favorite, even as other successful early to mid-1960s' Motown acts began to fade.

Before considering individual must-hear recordings by the Temptations, it is important to note that the group stood out from other Motown artists in one very important way. The Temptations certainly enjoyed pop-chart success, particularly with the hits that are still heard on oldies radio today; however, they are notable for recording songs that generally performed better on the R&B charts than on the pop charts, suggesting that their work resonated particularly strongly with black audiences.

As seems to have been the case with many such groups in the late 1950s and early 1960s, the Temptations came into being from rival vocal groups that coalesced into the Temptations under the group's original name, the Elgins, by 1961. At that time, and when the group was renamed the Temptations, the group included Melvin Franklin, Otis Williams, Paul Williams, Eddie Kendricks, and Eldridge "Al" Bryant. David Ruffin joined the group after Bryant left and shortly before the Temptations' run of R&B and pop hits. The must-hear music that came out during this segment of the group's career, the part that is sometimes referred to as the David Ruffin era and that some fans think of as the golden era of the Temptations, include "The Way You Do the Things You Do," "My Girl," "Ain't Too Proud to Beg," and "Beauty Is Only Skin Deep."

Consideration of just these five songs illustrates something of the nature of Motown songs of the mid-1960s. All five were written by musicians associated with Motown and its labels Gordy and Tamla. Smokey Robinson and Bobby Rogers of the Miracles wrote "The Way You Do the Things You Do" for the Temptations, with Robinson handling the recording's production. The single release came within one spot of making it into the pop Top 10; however, it topped the R&B charts of the day.

Miracles members Robinson and Ronald White wrote "My Girl" for the Temptations and produced the recording. "My Girl" topped both the pop and the R&B charts and remains a popular classic at the end of the second decade of the 21st century, well over a half century since its release. In fact, "My Girl" continues to be included in television and film soundtracks, and, in the 21st century, a non-Temptations version has been used in television advertising campaigns for Little Debbie snacks.

"Ain't Too Proud to Beg," came from the pens of Motown songwriters Norman Whitfield and Eddie Holland. Whitfield, who continued to be associated with the Temptations' recordings for years, produced the recording. The single release was one of the more extreme examples of the disparity between the Temptations' relative performance on the pop and R&B charts, especially compared to the pop-chart success of Motown's top female group, the Supremes. "Ain't Too Proud to Beg" topped the R&B charts but only rose as high as No. 13 on the pop charts. Another Whitfield and Holland composition, "Beauty Is Only Skin Deep," was also produced by Whitfield and topped out at No. 3 on the pop charts and No. 1 on the R&B charts.

Although some of the Tempatations' hits from the middle of the 1960s are based on the Motown swing rhythmic feel (e.g., the triple subdivision of the beat in "The Way You Do the Things You Do"), and some are based on a straight eighth-note feel (e.g., the duple subdivision of the beat in "My Girl"), all five of these songs share several traits. All include numerous melodic and arrangement hooks. For example, the title lines of the songs tend to stand out melodically from the rest of the material; the finger snaps, harp glissandi, and minimalistic electric guitar lead part in "My Girl" are instantly memorable; and so on.

After David Ruffin left the Temptations in 1968 to pursue a solo career and Dennis Edwards replaced him, producer Norman Whitfield moved the group into a more psychedelic direction. This led to significant hard-hitting, powerful soul hits such as "Cloud Nine," "Ball of Confusion (That's What the World Is Today)," and "Psychedelic Shack." Although these so-called psychedelic soul songs were strong sellers, the Temptations' song from this era that perhaps connected more thoroughly with conventional soul was "I Can't Get Next to You." In fact, other soul artists continued to cover "I Can't Get Next to You" well into the 1970s. For the Temptations, "I Can't Get Next to You" topped the pop and the R&B charts. Another important early 1970s recording was "Just My Imagination (Running Away with Me)." In contrast to the funkier psychedelic soul recordings that preceded it over the past several years, "Just My Imagination (Running Away with Me)" recaptured the spirit of the early and mid-1960s ballad hits of the Temptations.

After "Just My Imagination," Eddie Kendricks and Paul Williams left the Temptations. The group has remained active to the present, although with numerous personnel changes over the years; however, with few exceptions, the departure of Kendricks and Williams marked a fundamental change in the Temptations in terms of commercial success—the group increasingly became an oldies act. The one exception—and a transitional recording because it was made during the period between Kendricks's departure and Williams's departure, was the Temptations' last great hit, "Papa Was a Rolling Stone." Rare for the Temptations, the single release of "Papa Was a Rolling Stone" topped the pop charts but rose only to No. 5 on the R&B charts.

In general, the Temptations' work from the late 1960s and into the early 1970s is not as frequently heard today as are the more classic ballads from the David Ruffin era. Still, one of the important attributes of the Norman Whitfield productions from the late 1960s and early 1970s is the focus on shared and traded lead vocals, in which lines were passed from singer to singer (see, for example, a performance of "I Can't Get Next to You" at https://www.youtube.com/watch?v=B9dde4p6OBU, accessed January 20, 2020). Similarly, the group's last great hit, also a Norman Whitfield production, "Papa Was a Rolling Stone," features lines tossed from singer to singer. In the context of "Papa Was a Rolling Stone," this technique works particularly effectively, as it gives the listener a sense of the members of the group portraying brothers who had to deal with the harsh realities of their father's philandering and unsupportive ways. The shared vocals of these late Temptations hits stood in sharp contrast to the Temptations' recordings and live performances of the early 1960s, which tended to feature one lead singer and the other Temptations playing backing roles. This new vocal arrangement style set the stage for the similar shared lead vocals in later soul groups such as Boyz II Men and pop's so-called boy bands of the 1990s and early 2000s (e.g., the Backstreet Boys).

The Temptations received numerous awards over the years, and the legacy of their music, which included 14 R&B chart-topping albums and over a dozen R&B chart-topping singles, has most recently been advanced by the 2019 Broadway opening of the multiple Tony Award-winning jukebox musical *Ain't Too Proud to Beg: The Life and Times of the Temptations*, which includes all of the group's best-remembered soul hits.

SISTER ROSETTA THARPE

Because of how well known Ray Charles was throughout his career and after the popular 2004 film *Ray* brought his work back into the limelight, some music fans might assume that he originated the breaking down of the barriers between African American sacred and secular music to form soul with the fitting of secular lyrics to sacred melodies. Several notable artists had straddled the lines between the sacred and the secular years before Ray Charles. For example, before he became known as Thomas A. Dorsey, composer of such classic sacred songs as "Take My Hand, Precious Lord" and "Peace in the Valley" and widely acknowledged as the Father of Gospel Music, Dorsey had earlier in life been known as Georgia Tom, the blues piano player on bawdy songs recorded by singer Tampa Red in the 1920s. Perhaps the most notable and most successful pre-Ray Charles musician to straddle the boundary between the sacred and the secular in a manner that influenced countless later soul singers, however, was Sister Rosetta Tharpe.

Born in 1915, Tharpe grew up singing gospel music; however, in the late 1930s, she began singing with Lucky Millinder's jazz orchestra. Tharpe's recordings with Millinder's band included sacred material, such as the gospel songs "That's All," "The Lonesome Road," and others. At the same time, however, in her recordings with Millinder and other jazz bandleaders, Tharpe performed and recorded secular songs, including the double-entendre piece "I Want a Tall Skinny Papa." Because Tharpe had already enjoyed commercial success and public acceptance as a gospel singer, her association with secular and even risqué material caused controversy. As *AllMusic* reviewer Stewart Mason writes, "Though in retrospect the sentiments of songs like 'I Want a Tall Skinny Papa' seem tame, the outcry was similar to when Sam Cooke went pop in the late '50s: how dare the pop market take away our Sister?" (Mason n.d.).

Throughout the rest of her career, Tharpe freely mixed jazz, blues, folk, and gospel music, although when she was free of contractual requirements, her later work avoided material such as "I Want a Tall Skinny Papa." It was not only this successful crossing of genre boundaries that marked Tharpe's importance. She was also a skilled electric guitarist at a time when the instrument was associated almost exclusively with male performers. In fact, in her live appearances, Tharpe was known to share self-deprecating asides with the audience—such as "pretty good for a woman"—after her guitar solos. She does so, for example, in a 1964 performance of the blues standard "Trouble in Mind" in Manchester, England, available at the time of this writing on YouTube (see, https://www.youtube.com/watch

?v=rzRm4K7NZm0, accessed January 21, 2020). That concert in Britain, in fact, provides an example of Tharpe's mixture of repertoire and a late-career example of the soulfulness of her singing. At the same event at which she performed "Trouble in Mind," she also performed a fast-paced gospel version of the spiritual "Didn't It Rain," a song that Tharpe had first recorded back in the 1940s (see, https://www.youtube.com/watch?v=5SoZG4yDaJA, accessed January 21, 2020).

Sister Rosetta Tharpe's 1944 recording of the spiritual "Down by the Riverside" is particularly interesting. Although she is presented in a big-band setting, the arrangement contains a Tharpe guitar solo. Perhaps most notably, Tharpe's rhythmic approach fits in the middle of the gap between the triplet-based swing feel of the rest of the band and the straight eighth-notes that began to mark rock and roll music in the 1950s and beyond. Tharpe's rhythmic approach is all the more noticeable on this recording because her solo occurs just before a saxophone solo, which follows the swing jazz triplet feel significantly more fully.

It is important to note that Tharpe was blurring the lines between the triplet swing feel and the straight eighth-notes that became prevalent in rock and roll in 1944, four years before the release of John Lee Hooker's "Boogie Chillen." This timeline is significant in that some scholars, such as Fernando Benadon and Ted Gioia point to the 1948 Hooker recording as a primary example of the rhythmic transition (Benadon and Gioia 2009).

Also notable is that Tharpe's version of "Down By the Riverside," like other gospel songs Tharpe recorded from the late 1930s well into the 1940s, bridges the gap between gospel and jazz, much like soul would bridge the gap between gospel and R&B in the 1950s. In 2004, the National Recording Preservation Board of the Library of Congress added Rosetta Tharpe's recording of "Down by the Riverside" to the National Recording Registry (National Recording Preservation Board of the Library of Congress n.d.).

Tharpe's 1945 recording of "Strange Things Happening Every Day" nearly topped what would come to be known as the R&B charts (the offensive term "Race Records" was still being used by, among others, the trade publication *Billboard* at the time), the first time that a gospel single had charted so high. This recording features a small instrumental and male vocal chorus, in sharp contrast to the big-band settings of earlier Tharpe recordings. Tharpe provides a guitar solo that is arguably more intricate than those of her other performances mentioned in this entry. Because of the absence of a horn section, "Strange Things Happening Every Day" straddles the line between blues and gospel, much like a recording such as "Down by the Riverside" straddles the line between jazz and gospel.

When considering Sister Rosetta Tharpe purely as a vocalist, it should be noted that as her voice matured, it deepened and, arguably, grew more expressive and perhaps closer in tone quality to what some listeners might associate with soul music. This is one of the reasons that late-1950s and 1960s' performances, such as those captured in Granada Television's film of her 1964 Manchester, England, performance are so important: Tharpe's voice displays a depth and expression not necessarily heard in some of the studio recordings of the late 1930s and into the 1940s.

Although the bulk of Sister Rosetta Tharpe's work might have pre-dated what many listeners might consider the birth of the soul genre, Tharpe's ability to successfully straddle the lines between the sacred and the secular and the lines between genres such as folk, blues, jazz, and gospel, and her incorporation of guitar—and particularly electric guitar—playing into gospel—not to mention her being considered one of the early influences on the development of rock and roll—make her gospel recordings an important building block in the establishment of soul, with the songs, studio and live recordings mentioned above must-hear works.

JACKIE WILSON

Ultimately, Jackie Wilson's biography reads like a great tragedy, particularly as he suffered a massive heart attack while performing on stage in 1975. Wilson never fully recovered from the heart attack and subsequent coma and spent the rest of his life—a little over eight more years—in constant care. To add to the tragedy of his story, the final eight years of his life were marked with legal battles between various family members for control over his affairs. Despite the tragedy, during his singing career, Jackie Wilson, who was known as Mr. Excitement, recorded a song that helped propel Berry Gordy Jr. on his way to founding Motown; helped establish soul as a separate entity from R&B; recorded one of the greatest soul hits of the 1960s; and influenced later musicians, especially with the showmanship that he exhibited in his live performances.

Born in Detroit in 1934, Wilson joined Billy Ward and his Dominoes in 1953 as the replacement for Clyde McPhatter, who had left to form the Drifters. Wilson left the group to start his solo career in 1957. His first single release was "Reet Petite (The Finest Girl You'd Ever Want to Meet)," written by Berry Gordy Jr. Although the recording was not necessarily an unqualified hit, "Reet Petite" suggested that Gordy's work as a songwriter might eventually pay off, which it did within a few years, with his first hits and with his founding of Motown. It is an interesting record, particularly because Wilson is backed by a horn section that resembled that of a jazz big band more than the horn section of a typical R&B band of the time. The recording is also notable for the vibrato of Wilson's singing. It would be highly unfair to call Wilson the Black Elvis, as was done back in the day, or to refer to Elvis Presley as the White Jackie Wilson; however, "Reet Petite" demonstrates that both singers shared a remarkably similar-sounding vibrato and vocal tone color.

The 1958 song "Lonely Teardrops" became Wilson's signature song. In fact, it was this piece that Wilson was performing when he suffered his heart attack 17 years later. The song itself is built around the familiar I-vi-IV-V chord progression commonly known as the oldies progression or the "Heart and Soul" progression—the former designation because it was so pervasive in the popular hits of the late 1950s, and the latter because the progression formed the basis of Hoagy Carmichael's early 20th-century song "Heart and Soul." The arrangement of the Wilson recording is pretty much standard fare for the late 1950s, with the exception of raked guitar arpeggios that sound as though they were meant to mimic the falling teardrops of the song's lyrics—a touch that some listeners might find somewhat corny today.

"Lonely Teardrops," a must-hear example of Wilson's work, was the first of a string of No. 1 R&B chart hits je enjoyed through 1967. Others included "You Better Know It," "A Woman, a Lover, a Friend," "Doggin' Around," "Baby Workout," and "(Your Love Keeps Lifting Me) Higher and Higher." By the time of "A Woman, A Lover, A Friend" and "Doggin' Around" were recorded in 1960, Jackie Wilson's singing could be labeled more soul than rock and roll in nature. In fact, a comparison of either of these two songs with Wilson's 1957 and 1958 hits shows just how much more soulful he had become in a short period of time. "Doggin' Around," in particular, is notable for Wilson's wide dynamic contrasts, reminiscent of how volume changes are used for dramatic effect in gospel music and in the oratory associated with some churches. It is this kind of connection with gospel performance practice that marked Wilson's transition from a rock and roll and R&B singer to a soul singer, at least in the most important and best-remembered part of his repertoire.

In addition to "Lonely Teardrops," perhaps Wilson's best-remembered recording is the 1967 hit, Wilson's last No. 1 single on the R&B charts, "(Your Love Keeps Lifting Me) Higher and Higher." In fact, late in the second decade of the 21st century, this is the Jackie Wilson recording that one is most likely to hear on oldies radio or decade-based internet radio (e.g., I Heart Radio's 1970s channel). Anecdotally, it is the only Jackie Wilson recording that I have heard broadcast on these media in recent years. This Gary Jackson, Raynard Minor, and Carl William Smith song exhibits the connections that between the soul genre and sacred gospel music. Specifically, in a gospel song, the grace of God or faith would likely be that which would lift the singer's character "higher and higher." "(Your Love Keeps Lifting Me) Higher and Higher" secularizes this elevation of the character's state of being while using similar musical resources and a similar singing style as one might hear in gospel music.

Although Jackie Wilson's work in the late 1950s and early 1960s helped define rock and roll, "(Your Love Keeps Lifting Me) Higher and Higher" has been widely recognized as Wilson's best and most important recording. *Rolling Stone* ranked Wilson's recording of the song at No. 248 in the magazine's revised 2011 listing of "500 Greatest Songs of All Time" (*Rolling Stone* 2011). Wilson's recording of "(Your Love Keeps Lifting Me) Higher and Higher" was also inducted by the Recording Academy into the Grammy Hall of Fame in 1999 (The Recording Academy n.d.).

Part of the challenge in assessing the work of Jackie Wilson is that some of the recordings he made pale in comparison to his great hits. In fact, listeners might consider some, such as the 1957 recording of the old Tin Pan Alley song "By the Light of the Silvery Moon," as downright embarrassing. The arrangement on this track, the B-side of "Reet Petite," includes accordion, which suggests the extent to which "By the Light of the Silvery Moon" sounds more like the work of easy-listening bandleader Lawrence Welk than the work of a rock and roll, R&B, or soul singer with backing ensemble.

Recordings such as "By the Light of the Silvery Moon" seem to have been geared toward building a white audience for Jackie Wilson. And several of Wilson's singles, such as "My Empty Arms" and "Alone at Last" performed better on the pop charts than on the R&B charts. Although these songs are not nearly as embarrassing as the B-side of "Reet Petite," the orchestrations represent the world of middle-of-the-road pop music and make them recordings that have not aged nearly as well as Wilson's R&B chart hits.

Interestingly, in the late 1980s, ABC's *20/20* program did an investigation into the financial dealings of Wilson's label, Brunswick Records, in light of the financial challenges that eight years of nursing home care for Wilson created. Songwriting credits, royalty payments, and the like, all came under scrutiny. It is safe to say that the reporters held up Jackie Wilson as a classic example of a victim of unethical record industry practices of the 1950s and 1960s.

The legacy of Jackie Wilson certainly is marred by some of the recordings he made, the financial challenges he faced, and the accusations of massive fraud committed by Brunswick Records and its principals that seemed to have led to the singer's financial challenges years before his devastating heart attack and lengthy stay in a nursing facility. However, listening to his greatest successes on the R&B charts—especially "Lonely Teardrops" and "(Your Love Keeps Lifting Me) Higher and Higher"—and watching videos of his concert, club, and television performances (YouTube offers numerous videos of Wilson in action) provides a considerably more optimistic view of Jackie Wilson's legacy. And, Wilson's legacy was most recently recognized in 2019 with the placement of his posthumous star on the Hollywood Walk of Fame at 7057 Hollywood Boulevard (*Hollywood Walk of Fame* Website 2019).

BILL WITHERS

Primarily known for the hit singles "Ain't No Sunshine" "Lean on Me," and "Just the Two of Us," Bill Withers represents an easygoing approach to soulful expression in singing and songwriting. Withers's primary contributions to the genre steer clear of a focus on sheer vocal technique and the big instrumental and backing arrangements of some other soul artists. His best recordings deliver clear messages through a simple and thoroughly believable vocal style.

Compared with some of the other artists profiled in this chapter, Bill Withers was something of a latecomer to the musical world. After serving in the U.S. Navy for nine years, Withers moved to Los Angeles and worked in manufacturing as a laborer. He continued to keep his proverbial day job even after recording his first album, as he was not entirely certain he would succeed as a recording artist. In fact, Withers was 33 years old when his debut album was released.

His 1971 debut album, *Just as I Am*, consisted of only two covers, with the rest of the songs being Bill Withers originals. The album spawned two singles: "Grandma's Hands" and "Ain't No Sunshine," the latter of which established Withers as a star. "Ain't No Sunshine" reached No. 6 on the R&B charts and No. 3 on the pop charts.

Booker T. Jones—of Booker T. and the M.G.'s fame—produced *Just as I Am*. The album and its principal hit, "Ain't No Sunshine," presented Withers's engaging, heartfelt singing with an almost minimalistic approach to the instrumental arrangements. The gospel-like backing vocals, brass sections, and so on, heard on some soul recordings of the era were absent in Jones's productions. Although "Ain't No Sunshine" incorporates orchestral strings, the string writing focuses on simple figures that answer the vocal lines and rhythmically match the bass line that Withers plays on guitar.

Some commentators have connected Withers's early recordings with folk music. Given that he largely performed and recorded original material, with few overt ties to folk, I prefer to think of him as a soul singer-songwriter who focused on acoustic guitar (his instrument) as accompaniment. Incidentally, Withers's playing on "Ain't No Sunshine" is perhaps best experienced in some of his live performances, which are even clearer in texture than the studio recording (see, for example, https://www.youtube.com/watch?v=CICIOJqEb5c, accessed January 21, 2020; an earlier posting of this performance at https://www.youtube.com/watch?v=tIdIqbv7SPo, which is currently unavailable, had well in excess of 260 million views as of October 20, 2019). As the Rock and Roll Hall of Fame's induction page for Withers quotes the musician, "Not a lot of people got me . . . Here I was, this black guy playing an acoustic guitar, and I wasn't playing the gut-bucket blues. People had a certain slot they expected you to fit in to" (The Rock and Roll Hall of Fame 2015). Lee Hildbrand also hints at the unusual, almost uncategorizable nature of Withers and his music, writing, "If Withers had gotten into the music business as a means of making money—which he did—his warm, scratchy tenor voice and sensitive, highly literate songs betrayed an artist with much more on his mind than simply being commercial" (Hildebrand 1994, 256).

The emphasis on acoustic guitar, the light. relatively thin (for an early 1970s soul recording) texture, and the pointed simply clarity of Withers's tale of feeling lost "every time she goes away" all were attractive and defining aspects of "Ain't No Sunshine" and Withers's unusual space within the world of soul. The simplicity of the string arrangement, too, adds poignancy to the mood that Withers established in his lyrics. The melody of the song is also easy to remember—perhaps one of the reasons that "Ain't No Sunshine" has been widely covered. As if that all were not enough to make this out-of-nowhere song to have made an immediate impact, Withers's recording has one other unusual defining hook: the singer's repetition of the words "I know" over two dozen times in a row.

Withers's 1972 album *Still Bill* consisted solely of originals. Although the Withers sound still filled a part of the soul spectrum that Withers had to himself, *Still Bill* expanded Withers's stylistic range. In fact, *AllMusic* reviewer Stephen Thomas Erlewine went so far as to describe *Still Bill* as "a remarkable summation of a number of contemporary styles" (Erlewine n.d.-a.). Although it is a highly regarded album, today it is probably best remembered for the song "Lean on Me," the artist's biggest hit ever. "Lean on Me" resonated with a wide range of audiences at the time of its release. The single topped both the R&B and pop charts and joined songs such as Paul Simon's composition "Bridge over Troubled Water"

(1970) and Carole King's composition "You've Got a Friend" (1971) as definers of a gentle approach to love and friendship that seemed to fill a need created by the social and political unrest of the late 1960s and the beginning of the 1970s. All three songs, however well they met the needs of the time, were spiritual descendants of Ben E. King's "Stand by Me" from the at least somewhat less turbulent early 1960s.

These three songs contain clear references to gospel music. In part, this comes from the rhythmic and harmonic feel of the piano parts. Connections to the gospel tradition—and even back to African music—are strongest in "Lean on Me," particularly as a result of the double-time feel and change of metrical emphasis that occurs in the "You just call on me, brother . . . " section.

Perhaps one of the most iconic features of "Lean on Me" is how simple the piano part is in the song's introduction. In fact, the song is in the key of C major, arguably the easiest key for piano players of limited experience because only the white keys are used, and the basic chord progression that defines the verses—and which is heard in the introduction—is based on simple triads (three-note chords) moving in parallel motion. Compared with its piano-based spiritual kin of the time, such as Simon and Garfunkel's version of "Bridge over Troubled Water" and Carole King's recording of "You've Got a Friend," "Lean on Me" is far more amenable to the novice pianist, certainly a point in its favor in terms of maintaining a strong legacy for singers and piano players.

Bill Withers continued to record and tour after his early-1970s' success with "Ain't No Sunshine" and "Lean on Me." Although these two songs established Withers as a largely acoustically based (again, some would say "folk-based") soul singer-songwriter, he continued to explore other settings and styles within the genre. His connections with a more jazz-based approach marked a return to near the top of the R&B/Soul and pop charts at the start of the 1980s, when Withers and saxophonist Grover Washington Jr. recorded "Just the Two of Us." The song, cowritten by Withers, Ralph MacDonald, and William Salter, was the best-remembered track on Washington's 1980 album *Winelight*, which topped the jazz charts, nearly topped the soul charts, and made it solidly into the Top 10 of the pop charts. In fact, the album was representative of the subgenre often labeled smooth jazz. Washington, singer-guitarist George Benson, and other members of the smooth jazz cadre enjoyed exceptionally strong record sales (for jazz in the late 1970s and through the 1980s), thereby bringing numerous new fans to jazz, although some later practitioners of the style did not necessarily consistently produce material that resonated well with music critics or with fans of less-commercial and earlier jazz styles.

The *Winelight* version of "Just the Two of Us" was truncated for single release, which placed more of the emphasis on Withers as a vocalist and less on the instrumental work of Washington and his ensemble. The single, which had a decidedly more conventionally commercial and slicker-sounding arrangement and production than Withers's iconic hits from the early 1970s, came within a tick or two of the top of the pop, R&B, and adult contemporary charts in 1981. "Just the Two of Us" earned a Grammy Award for Best Rhythm & Blues Song. It can be argued that "Just the Two of Us" and George Benson's hit recording of "On Broadway" are the two best-remembered and most iconic vocal works to come out of the smooth jazz genre.

Although, on the surface at least, "Just the Two of Us" occupies a different space on the soul spectrum than Withers's earlier hits, "Just the Two of Us," "Lean on Me," "Ain't No Sunshine," and his other compositions and recordings share a clear, thoroughly genuine-sounding expression of emotions associated with a variety of human relationships.

STEVIE WONDER IN THE 1960S

One of the challenges in defining the career of Stevie Wonder is that his hit singles and albums have included soul, funk, jazz, Latin, pop, and even middle-of-the-road pop songs. So, we will not be as concerned with the Stevie Wonder of "For Once in My Life," "My Cherie Amour," and "Sunny," as we will be with the clearer examples of his approach-to-Motown-soul of songs such as "Uptight (Everything's Alright)," "I Was Made to Love Her," and "Signed, Sealed, Delivered I'm Yours." In terms of Stevie Wonder's 1960s' covers of songs from the pens of folk revival and rock writers such as Bob Dylan and John Lennon and Paul McCartney, we will also consider the connection of soul and the political ramifications of Wonder's interpretation of Dylan's "Blowing in the Wind."

After he turned 21, negotiated a new contract with Motown, and took control of his recorded output, Stevie Wonder wrote virtually all the songs he subsequently recorded. Even during the 1960s, however, he had a hand in writing many of his big hits. The first of Wonder's must-hear early songs is the 1965 piece "Uptight (Everything's Alright)." Credited to Sylvia Moy, Wonder, and Henry Cosby, this song reached No. 1 on the R&B charts and made it within a couple of spots of doing the same on the pop charts. Generally, in Wonder's early hits, he was responsible for the music or, at the very least, for the basic musical figures, chord progressions and riffs, on which the songs were based. Certainly, "Uptight (Everything's Alright)" is filled with strong musical hooks, from the melody of the chorus to the horn section figures that accompany Wonder's singing. The tempo and the arrangement are more high-energy and more powerful than in many of the Motown hits of the time. The musical attribute of hits such as this, in part, seems to mark Stevie Wonder as more of an artist marketed to a young audience than, say, the Supremes or some of the other vocal groups associated with Motown and its various labels.

Although by all accounts, Wonder's collaborators in these early songs had more to do directly with the lyrics than Wonder did himself, "Uptight (Everything's Alright)" established a theme Wonder returned to time and time again, whether writing in collaboration or writing his own words and music. Here, he portrays "a poor boy from the wrong side of the tracks" who is in love with a girl from a more affluent background. Although the details varied over the years, it is this general theme of opposites attracting that Wonder continues to return to time to time again.

"Uptight (Everything's Alright)" was the big hit on the album *Uptight*. Arguably, a thorough listening to the entire album suggests that, at the time, Stevie Wonder was a more significant singles artist than an album-oriented artist. That changed once Wonder reached the age of maturity and took control of his material. It is in this light that it is best, then, to experience and to appreciate Stevie Wonder's pre-1972 recordings as a group separate from his later recordings. It is also important to note that Wonder's high-energy original material, such as "Uptight (Everything's Alright)," tended to reach slightly higher on the R&B charts than on the pop charts. This was not necessarily the case with all Motown artists, and it suggests the degree to which Wonder—often later considered a pop star—resonated with black audiences in the 1960s.

"I Was Made to Love Her," a hit 1967 release on Motown's Tamla label, is credited to Lula Mae Hardaway (Wonder's mother), Sylvia Moy, Wonder, and Henry Cosby. A defining feature of Wonder's later recordings was the distinctiveness of some of the instrumental tone colors, particularly his playing of the clavinet and other electronic keyboards. "I Was Made to Love Her" features Wonder playing harmonica in the introduction, another instrument long connected with him. Another particularly distinctive feature of this song is the use of the electric sitar, an instrument that played an even more prominent role on "Signed, Sealed, Delivered I'm Yours" three years later.

"I Was Made to Love Her" is, in essence, a groove piece that uses the same four-measure chord progression repeatedly throughout. Although this structure means that there is little musical distinction between, say, verse and chorus sections, in live concert and televised performances, it gives Wonder ample opportunity to improvise vocal lines. The lyrical theme is related to that of "Uptight (Everything's Alright)." In the earlier song, the challenge posed is that the characters came from decidedly different socioeconomic backgrounds. In this song, Wonder's character contends with his parents disapprove of the subject of his heart's desire. Although Motown had Wonder record ballads and middle-of-the-road pop songs through the end of the first—pre-21—phase of his career, "I Was Made to Love Her" anticipates the brand of funk that came to fruition in 1970s' songs such as "Superstition," "Higher Ground," and "Living for the City." "I Was Made to Love" peaked at No. 1 on the R&B charts and No. 2 on the pop charts.

Although one could argue about when the decade of the 1970s truly started, the 1970 release "Signed, Sealed, Delivered I'm Yours" can be understood as the culmination of Wonder's work in the first phase of his career; therefore, we will consider it part of Stevie Wonder's 1960s' recordings. Lula Mae Hardaway, Wonder, Syreeta Wright, and Lee Garrett wrote the song, which, in typical fashion for the high-energy songs of this part of Stevie Wonder's career topped the R&B charts and just missed hitting No. 1 on the pop charts. As an early example of Wonder's work as a record producer, this song is notable. For one thing, the overall sound is clearer, which gives Wonder's lead vocal and the instrumental and backing vocal lines more clarity. Although not as fully realized as it would be on Wonder's 1973 and 1974 recordings, the clarity of the production allows Wonder's rhythmic inhalations and improvised vocal fills, screams, and melismas to form a more important part of the texture than on some of the murkier non-Wonder-produced recordings of several years earlier. Michael Jackson took up this vocal approach in his solo career, particularly in his recordings of the 1980s.

Although our focus here is on the noteworthy singles that Stevie Wonder cowrote in the first part of his career, there can be more to some of his cover recordings than might first appear on the surface. For that reason, some of them are particularly notable. Such is the case with his 1966 recording of Bob Dylan's "Blowin' in the Wind." The single release topped out at No. 9 on the pop charts. Although not as commercially successful as Peter, Paul and Mary's earlier hit version, the Stevie Wonder rendition is notable for being a rare pre-1970 Motown release of politically motivated material. More importantly, however, is the way in which Wonder's performance heightens part of the message of Dylan's song.

The backing instrumental arrangement incorporates an easygoing version of Motown swing, which is certainly disarming enough. In the stanza where Dylan's original lyrics asked how long it would take for "some people" to be free, Wonder changes the line and asks, "How many years can a man exist before he's allowed to be free?" His delivers extra emphasis on the word "man." By doing this, Wonder rhetorically emphasizes the humanity of blacks and captures the "don't call me 'boy'" spirit of the day. So, while traditionally listeners might have focused on the antiwar references of the early part of the song, Stevie Wonder's change of a couple of words and the added emphasis with which he sings his revised text helps emphasize the theme of racism and racial injustice. Although this is not the most overtly soul-like recording in the Stevie Wonder canon, the emphasis on overcoming racial injustice is fully in keeping with some of the soul music of the era.

When Stevie Wonder turned 21 in 1971, he entered into a new relationship with Motown, one that enabled him to take more direct control of his recordings as a writer, singer, instrumentalist, and producer. In many respects—particularly with regard to Wonder's songs of social justice—his work from 1971 through the middle of the decade outshines and some of his work of the 1960s and is better remembered. Be that as it may, songs such as "Uptight (Everything's Alright)," "I Was Made to Love Her," and "Signed, Sealed, Delivered I'm Yours" are among the catchiest and most energetic examples of Motown soul of the 1960s and remain must-hear tracks.

STEVIE WONDER: *SONGS IN THE KEY OF LIFE*[7]

Given his immense popularity and the longevity of his career as a recording artist, it is curious that only two Stevie Wonder albums ever made it all the way to No. 1 on both the *Billboard* R&B and pop charts. That the 1974 album *Fullfillingness' First Finale* did so might be attributed to the facts that Wonder had developed a huge fan base with his 1972 and 1973 work and that the album marked his return from a near-fatal automobile accident. That *Songs in the Key of Life* was Wonder's second album to hit No. 1 on both charts can be attributed to the strength, breadth, and depth of the material: there literally is something for everyone in this massive package. Indeed, this double album—plus an extended-play bonus disc—is, in many respects. Stevie Wonder's greatest achievement as an artist. As Mark Anthony Neal writes, "The brilliance of *Songs in the Key of Life* within the confines of black concept recordings had been preceded only by Marvin Gaye's *What's Going On* and arguably matched only by Prince's *Sign of the Times* in 1987" (Neal 1999, 110).

If *Talking Book*, *Innervisions*, and *Fullfillingness' First Finale* proved that Wonder was one of the most important singer-songwriter-instrumentalists of the 1970s, then *Songs in the Key of Life* put him in an entirely different league than any of his contemporaries. Even though this album had none of the structural unity of *Innervisions* and is a denser and sometimes less immediately accessible package than *Talking Book*, this 1976 collection was, by far, Stevie Wonder's most exuberant album—his greatest display of keyboard, harmonica, percussion, and vocal performances as well as possibly the best use of guest musicians Wonder ever made. But a package such as this can be a double-edged sword: no subsequent Stevie Wonder album met with such broad critical or commercial success. This is also an album that defies categorization, mixing elements of soul, R&B, jazz, and even a touch of classical music influence.

Songs in the Key of Life opens with "Love's in Need of Love Today." Wonder's lyrics speak of the need for love in the turbulent world of the mid-1970s. It is, however, a timeless soul ballad; Wonder performed the song to great effect on the *America: A Tribute to Heroes* telethon shortly after the September 11, 2001 terrorist attacks. Wonder has turned to the message that love will overcome all evil many times since he began writing his own lyrics in the early 1970s. This anthem-like song of more than seven minutes' duration has a sparser accompaniment than many of the other arrangements on *Songs in the Key of Life*; this places the listener's attention squarely on the lyrics. Musically, "Love's in Need of Love Today" is a soulful, easygoing R&B ballad. Wonder's melody incorporates some interesting points of contrast from phrase to phrase, involving the use of an upward lead in the first antecedent phrase of each stanza, a leap that is contrasted with a more consistently downward stepwise motion in the consequent phrases. The harmony of the oft-repeated chorus includes jazz-oriented added-note chords and some meandering harmonic motion. These features paint the song as somewhat impressionistic, although they can also make it challenging for the casual listener to instantly relate to the song. Stevie Wonder has stated that he was inspired by the 1950s' gospel quartet recordings of Sam Cooke in his writing of "Love's in Need of Love Today" (Myers 2016, 247–248).

The album's short second track, "Have a Talk with God," reinforces the message that love is the answer to the world's ills. The third track, "Village Ghetto Land," is significantly more substantial and fully developed. This piece also helps establish *Songs in the Key of Life* as a widely eclectic collection of Wonder's work as a songwriter, arranger, and performer. Here, Wonder and collaborator Gary Byrd explore late 18th-century European classical court music, aligned with graphic lyrics that describe the harshness of life in the late 20th-century American ghetto. This combination creates an eerie, haunting mood that is as effective in its own way as Wonder's "Living for the City" in documenting ghetto life but using an entirely different musical vocabulary. Wonder's singing is accompanied by synthesized string parts. Because of the artificial tone color of mid-1970s' synthesizers, "Village Ghetto Land" arguably is more effective on the 1995 *Natural Wonder* album, on which the strings of the Tokyo Philharmonic Orchestra accompany Wonder in an orchestration by conductor Henry Panion III.

One of the best-remembered songs on *Songs in the Key of Life* follows "Contusion," an instrumental jazz/rock fusion piece. "Sir Duke" is a tribute to Wonder's musical heroes of the big-band jazz era, including Count Basie, Glenn Miller, Louis "Satchmo" Armstrong, and "the king of all, Sir Duke" Ellington. This song incorporates elements of funk, R&B, reggae, and disco. The main musical reference to big-band jazz is the use of a horn section to supplement Wonder's regular backing band, Wonderlove. When Motown released "Sir Duke" as a single in spring 1977, it hit No. 1 on the R&B and pop charts.

The next track, "I Wish," also topped both the R&B and pop charts. Musically, this song feels like a direct continuum from "Sir Duke," although the funk/disco quotient is ratcheted up a couple of notches. It is a thoroughly danceable song, but the real interest lies in its lyrics. Throughout his lyrics-writing career, Steve Wonder has rarely been overtly and obviously autobiographical. In fact, it could be argued that by retaining the moniker "Stevie Wonder" instead of his given name, Stevland Morris has maintained a healthy distance between his personal and professional lives. The song "I Wish," however, contains much autobiographical insight into not only Wonder but also the young Stevland Morris.

On one level, "I Wish" seems to be a simple paean to the composer's childhood—the years before Morris became Wonder. It is important to remember that Wonder was a child star from the age of 12 onward; therefore, he did not have the opportunity to grow up as a regular teenager. And that is not even considering the differences between growing up unsighted versus growing up sighted. Wonder includes one curious turn of phrase that can raise questions in the mind of the listener. At the start of the song, Wonder sets up the time frame of his reminiscences by singing, "Thinking back to when I was a little nappy-headed boy." At first hearing, the line might be interpreted simply as a reference to Wonder/Morris's childhood. But why does Wonder use the reference "nappy-headed?" Some readers might recall that in the 1990s, the noted African American children's author Carolivia Herron encountered heavy criticism when she used the word "nappy" in the title of her book *Nappy Hair*. The issue around Herron's use was that some considered the word derogatory and a physical stereotype. The term did not appear to generate the same level of consternation in the mid-1970s, when Wonder wrote and recorded "I Wish." Interestingly, it is now used as part of the title of Nappturality, "one of the first, and largest internet forums for Black women with natural hair" since 2002 (Pile 2020). Could Stevie Wonder's use of the term have come from a desire to paint Stevland Morris as an anonymous black youth facing an uncertain future in world in which American blacks had considerable difficulty surviving, let alone getting ahead? Perhaps. Could Wonder's use of the term have come from a personal experience of texture, something that could be relied on if one did not have sight? Perhaps. The point is, no matter what Stevie Wonder's intentions were in using a somewhat racially loaded term, its use can cause the listener to ask questions concerning racism in particular and social conditions in general.

As Wonder sings that he wishes those days of childhood mischief and innocence had not passed so quickly and that they could return, one cannot help but hear the song as an expression of the plight of the child star. The fact that Wonder speaks so little of his childhood in his other work adds to the importance of "I Wish" as a documentary of his pre-fame years. It is simultaneously one of his funkiest and most touching compositions.

The album's next track, "Knocks Me off My Feet," is a gentle moderate-tempo love ballad. Wonder, who wrote the words and music for this song—as well as played all the instruments and provided all the vocal parts—does a nice job of capturing the spirit of the great Motown love songs of the 1960s. In fact, the melodic hooks in the song closely resemble the style of 1960s' Motown. A significant part of the song's success lies in Wonder's text painting. He sets the line, "There's something 'bout your love, that makes me weak and knocks me off my feet" with a deliberate rhythmic stumble.

"Pastime Paradise" explores an entirely different subject and in an entirely different musical style. Wonder's lyrics speak of how some people waste their lives living in the past, dedicated to the "evils of the world," when they should be living for "the future paradise" of a world of peace. He sets these lyrics to an interesting mixture of Latin dance and Spanish classical music styles. The synthesized, classically oriented strings recall "Village Ghetto Land." The text, too, deals with similar issues, especially with a focus on how improving race relations and achieving racial equality can help to bring about world peace. Wonder's somewhat stark minor-key melody is haunting and well supported by the ostinato percussion and synthesized string figures. Although "Pastime Paradise" was not necessarily the best-known or best-remembered song on the album, it reemerged in the form of rapper Coolio's version, "Gangsta's Paradise," which topped the charts in 1995.

One of the highlights of *Songs in the Key of Life*—and one of the songs that achieved significant radio airplay—was Wonder's tribute to his young daughter, Aisha, "Isn't She Lovely." The vocal melody and the instrumental accompaniment are instantly engaging, but one of the highlights of the six-and-a-half-minute song is Wonder's extended harmonic solo. In fact, Wonder exhibits the kind of chorus-to-chorus long-range shaping that characterizes some of the work of the greatest jazz improvisers. Although the lyrics of "Isn't She Lovely" are brief—three short stanzas—they serve an important purpose in relationship to the focus of *Songs in the Key of Life*. By including this song on the album, Wonder expands the range of the spirituality that he finds in love to include love of and love within the family unit, especially when it includes children.

The track that follows "Isn't She Lovely," "Joy inside My Tears," is not nearly as memorable or distinctive as some of the other tracks. By contrast, in the next track, "Black Man," Stevie Wonder sounds like a man who truly stands committed to everything he sings about. The lyrics of Wonder and his cowriter, Gary Byrd, work their way through history and provide a chronicle of human achievement, with the race of the innovators identified. The point is that all of humanity is creative and fully worthy of equal treatment. One of the downsides of the song—perhaps best suggested by its title—is that it is not nearly as gender inclusive as it is racially inclusive; Sacagawea's assistance to Lewis and Clark is the sole example that the songwriters cite of a woman until Harriet Tubman is mentioned in the recording's fade out.

Several tracks on *Songs in the Key of Life* do not represent what some listeners might customarily think of as soul music. Jazz-rock fusion, classical, funk, and lite jazz all have homes on the album. With its gospel music influence, "Ebony Eyes," a tribute to "Miss Black Supreme," the "pretty girl with the ebony eyes," is one of the songs more in keeping with the spirit of traditional soul music. Throughout this massive two-plus album set, however, Wonder sings with a sense of expression that continues his style of soul, a style that went back to his early recordings as the teenaged "Little Stevie Wonder" back in the early 1960s.

"(YOU MAKE ME FEEL LIKE A) NATURAL WOMAN": ARETHA FRANKLIN AND CAROLE KING

Credited to the famous Brill Building songwriting team of Gerry Goffin and Carole King, along with record producer Jerry Wexler (who provided the title and concept for the song), "(You Make Me Feel Like a) Natural Woman" was a hit for Aretha Franklin in 1967. The song was later a centerpiece of King's *Tapestry*, one of the most important coming-of-age albums of the early 1970s that, in many ways, helped define the 1970s' women's movement. The song itself, with its combination of gospel-inspired music and lyrics that celebrated female sexuality and emotional and physical desire, brought together the sacred and the secular to greater extent than virtually any other song of the late 1960s and early 1970s.

The British Invasion of 1964 to 1965 had fundamentally changed the expectations for rock bands, British, American, and otherwise, particularly because the most successful band, the Beatles, had two of the popular music world's most commercially successful songwriters of the day in John Lennon and Paul McCartney. Because the new paradigm was for groups to include one or more songwriters, the dominance of the Brill Building songwriters—the New York-based Tin Pan Alley–like scene of the late 1950s and early 1960s—waned somewhat. When considering the Brill Building songwriters, particularly the songwriting teams, it is important to keep in mind that a high proportion were young, white, Jewish writers who demonstrated an affinity for crafting believable and commercially successful songs for African American singers. They also wrote for everyone from middle-of-the-road pop stylists to rock bands, but the bond between the Brill Building songsmiths and black performers was especially noteworthy. Lyricist Gerry Goffin and composer Carole King's main connections to soul had been in the first several years of the 1960s, when singers such as Earl-Jean (e.g., "I'm Into Something Good"), Little Eva (e.g., "The Loco-Motion" and "Keep Your Hands Off My Baby"), the Cookies (e.g., "Chains"), the Shirelles (e.g., "Will You Love Me Tomorrow"), the Drifters (e.g., "Up on the Roof"), and others had enjoyed success on the R&B and pop charts with Goffin and King songs. As a composer, some of King's work of the late 1960s and early 1970s exhibited stronger ties to the gospel tradition than her early-1960s songs for the artists listed above. This effectively started with "(You Make Me Feel Like a) Natural Woman."

Franklin's recording made it into the Top 10 of the U.S. R&B and pop charts. As *AllMusic* critic John Bush wrote, it was the centerpiece of her commercially successful and critically acclaimed 1968 album, *Lady Soul*. Of Franklin's performance of "(You Make Me Feel Like a) Natural Woman," Bush wrote, "One of the landmark performances in pop music, the song floats serenely through the verses until, swept up by Ralph Burns' stirring string arrangement again and again, Franklin opens up on the choruses with one of the most transcendent vocals of her career"

(Bush n.d.-a). In fact, along with Otis Redding's "Respect" and her own "Think," "(You Make Me Feel Like a) Natural Woman" became part of the trio of songs perhaps most closely associated with Franklin.

As a singer, King demonstrated ties to black gospel and soul music, particularly on the 1968 recording of the Goffin and King song "That Old Sweet Roll (Hi-De-Ho)," by King's band, the City. This song, incidentally, was covered by British blue-eyed soul singer Dusty Springfield in 1969 and was finally made popular by the jazz-rock band Blood, Sweat & Tears in 1970. King's piano playing on her original recording of "That Old Sweet Roll (Hi-De-Ho)" is firmly in the gospel style. And it is this combination of vocal and pianistic ties to African American musical styles that helped define both King's recording of "(You Make Me Feel Like a) Natural Woman" and the entire *Tapestry* album. In fact, King's inclusion of the song that she, Gerry Goffin, and Jerry Wexler wrote for Aretha Franklin played a notable role in broadening the scope of this, the album that for several years was the best-selling album by any female vocalist.

Although that record has since been broken, *Tapestry* at once helped define the women's movement of the early 1970s and the emerging introspective singer-songwriter movement in the popular music of the era. *Tapestry* was an album with lyrics that generally promoted self-worth and empowerment and with compositions, lead vocals, and piano—including numerous piano solos—by King. To top it off, the inner-sleeve photographs show Carole King acting as musical leader of her accompanying—mostly male—musicians, and the famous album cover shows King, the natural woman sitting at home in her jeans with her rather annoyed-looking cat in the foreground.

This brings us to the meat of "(You Make Me Feel Like a) Natural Woman." Aside from the high quality of the performances by Franklin and King, the song itself is significant. The gospel style suggests something transcendent, something sacred. What Gerry Goffin's lyrics and Jerry Wexler's title concept essentially glorify and make sacred, though, is female sexuality and emotional and physical desire. Perhaps just as much as the iconic recordings by Franklin and King, it is this freeing gospel affirmation that made this a culturally significant song from the era that saw the publication of *Our Bodies, Ourselves*, marches by women demanding the end to employment and other gender-based discrimination, and so on. It was a song that resonated perfectly with its time, perhaps more so the Carole King recording; however, even a few years earlier, when Franklin's version became a pop and R&B hit, these sentiments were in the air and found an allied musical statement in the song.

Over the years, "(You Make Me Feel Like a) Natural Woman" has been recorded by several prominent female artists, including Céline Dion, Mary J. Blige, Peggy Lee, and others; however, none have surpassed the success of the Franklin and King performances. The song has also been modified and put into male form by men; however, again, those recordings are not nearly as noteworthy. "(You Make Me Feel Like a) Natural Woman" remained one of the signature songs of both Franklin and King. Franklin's performance of "Natural Woman" at the 2015 Kennedy Center Honors, at which King was one of the honorees, highlighted the tight bond between the song and the singers most closely associated with it by. According to *Billboard* reporter Cathy Applefeld Olson, "In what was clearly a surprise to King, the show closed when Aretha Franklin stepped out to bring down the house with '(You Make Me Feel Like a) Natural Woman.' Perfection" (Olson 2015). *The New Yorker*'s David Remnick spoke with audience members at a subsequent Franklin concert and found that, more than Franklin's highly acclaimed, multiple-Grammy Award-winning recordings and performances of the past, it was the video of Franklin's performance of the song at the Kennedy Center Honors—a video that had "gone viral"—that brought audiences out to hear Franklin in concert late in her career (Remnick 2016). The video of Aretha Franklin's surprise performance, which includes King's reaction, as well as that of Barack and Michelle Obama, can be found at the time of this writing on several YouTube channels (see, for example, https://www.youtube.com/watch?v=XHsnZT7Z2yQ, which includes the introduction of the song by the actress portraying King in a production of *Beautiful: The Carole King Musical*, accessed January 20, 2020).

NOTES

1. Adapted from Perone (2012). "*Live at the Apollo,*" v. 1, 27–31.
2. Adapted from Perone (2018). "Mariah Carey," 62–65.
3. Adapted from Perone (2012). "*What's Going On,*" v. 2, 117–122.
4. Adapted from Perone (2012). "*The Miseducation of Lauryn Hill,*" v. 4, 127–131.
5. Adapted from Perone (2016). "Respect," 197–200.
6. Adapted from Perone (2012). "*Dusty in Memphis,*" v. 1, 225–232.
7. Adapted from Perone (2012). "*Songs in the Key of Life,*" v. 3, 79–88.

CHAPTER 3

Impact on Popular Culture

The impact of soul music on popular culture can be seen in many ways, although perhaps most visibly in films and on television. While the most obvious examples might involve popular hits that find their way into soundtracks and commercials, the impact of the genre on general popular culture can also be seen in such things as the use of well-known ensemble types (e.g., three-piece so-called girl groups), either in parody or to suggest a connection with a particular era, or music designed to sound like the soul music of a particular time period. References such as these can only work effectively if the public is, at the very least, familiar with aspects such as the types of performers and/or music associated with the genre during a particular time. In other words, the music and the performers must have made an impact on popular culture. In this chapter, we will examine some of the ways in which soul music has become integrated into popular entertainment media, as well as several examples of how soul songs directly influenced the creation of other songs that themselves became iconic pieces of popular culture.

Perhaps one of the best examples of using general knowledge of a record company and some of its most iconic major performers is the 1981 stage musical *Dreamgirls*. The musical's connections to the real-life history of Motown Records and, in particular, Diana Ross and the Supremes, are readily apparent. The 2006 film version of *Dreamgirls*, however, makes the connection to a soul-oriented label and soul performers of the 1960s into the mid-1970s even clearer. For example, the Dreams, a three-voice female vocal ensemble in which one of the singers emerges as a star while another descends into obscurity suggests a connection to Diana Ross's ascent to superstardom and Florence Ballard's descent and death. In addition, the songs written by Henry Krieger and Tom Eyen for *Dreamgirls* are clearly modeled on the hits of the Supremes, Ross as a solo artist, and their fellow Motown stars, including Marvin Gaye and the Jackson 5. The "hints" at the real-life musicians who served as models for the characters go well beyond the music. For example, the same style of knit hat worn by Marvin Gaye on the cover of his 1973 *Let's Get It On* album is worn by the film's Jimmy "Thunder" Early while Early is recording a demo of a song of social consciousness (the song itself suggests Gaye's "What's Going On"). Although it would be possible to enjoy the film version of *Dreamgirls* as a music-based fictional film, the fact that artists such as the Supremes, Marvin Gaye, and the Jackson 5 (who are also suggested by the appearance of a young brother-based, early 1970s band in the movie) were well known within popular culture makes the musical much more than just a work of fiction.

As opposed to a somewhat thinly disguised fictionalization based on the story of the Supremes, Diana Ross, and Motown, the use of a three-voice "girl group" in the film version of the musical comedy *Little Shop of Horrors* is meant for humorous effect. However, the group, which functions essentially as a Greek chorus throughout the musical, is modeled in appearance; the arrangement of the three-part texture; and the style of the songs that the musical's songwriters, composer Alan Menken and lyricist Howard Ashman, provided for the trio. The standard of the three-voice, early 1960s' "girl group," was established by the Cookies, the Shirelles, the Supremes, the Ronettes, the Chiffons, and others. The characters who perform as the vocal trio in *Little Shop of Horrors* are transparently identified as Crystal, Ronette, and Chiffon, intentionally referencing three of the real-life early 1960s' groups. The important thing to consider regarding this trio is that the joke works best if one is familiar with the girl-group format and style and with the names of three of the prominent such groups of the early 1960s—in other words, if the style and the groups (e.g., the Crystals, the Chiffons, and the Ronettes) are fully imbedded in popular culture. Incidentally, the former lead singer of the Four Tops, Levi Stubbs, voiced the killer plant in the film version of *Little Shop of Horrors*. As Audrey II, Stubbs sang one of the movie musical's most dramatic numbers, "Mean Green Mother from Outer Space." In this case, part of the joke is that "Mean Green Mother from Outer Space" and Stubbs's singing style in the piece is about as far removed from the romantic hits of the Four Tops as one can imagine; the words "sugar pie, honey bunch" (from the Four Tops' hit "I Can't Help Myself") certainly have no place in Stubbs's feature number in *Little Shop of Horrors*.

Impact on Popular Culture 177

Another musical that illustrates the extent to which soul music has been integrated into general popular culture is *Hairspray*. In the 2007 film version of the show, Queen Latifah portrayed Maybelle "Motormouth" Stubbs, a radio DJ who plays soul and R&B records for the fictional *Corny Collins Show*'s "Negro Day." Latifah performed Aretha Franklin–style vocals on songs such as "Big, Blonde and Beautiful" and "I Know Where I've Been," the latter of which is a particularly strong example of the style of 1960s' soul.

One way the impact of soul on popular culture is seen is through parody. When Ray Charles hosted NBC's *Saturday Night Live* on November 12, 1977, one of the skits involved a fictional group called the Young Caucasians. The group, which consisted of regular *Saturday Night Live* cast members Dan Aykroyd, John Belushi, Jane Curtin, Bill Murray, Laraine Newman, and Gilda Radner, offered Charles their rendition of "What'd I Say." The singers clearly enunciated the lyrics as "What did I say," with the joke being based on the sextet's stereotypical whiteness, to parody the adoption of R&B and soul standards by white singers such as Pat Boone back in the late 1950s, and songs associated with black vocal groups being covered by white groups, such as in the case of the Crew-Cuts' recording of the Chords' "Sh-Boom." But, again, the joke only fully works if the audience is familiar with Ray Charles; his performing style on piano and voice; the premise of the 1950s and early 1960s' covers of soul and R&B by white performers; how the vocal styles and the arrangements of these covers differed from the those of the originals; and, perhaps just as importantly, the central object at the core of the skit, Charles's song "What'd I Say."

The Isley Brothers' 1959 song "Shout" might not have performed as well on the singles charts of the day as one might reasonably assume, but it was a significant seller and became one of the most persistent songs of the era as a result of the original recording, a plethora of covers, its use in films, parodies, and even its rewrite as a theme song for an NFL football team. The call-and-response figures in this song tie it to the Isley Brothers' experience in gospel music; however, it is also simultaneously a party song and a song live bands frequently cover. "Shout" is also one of the two best-remembered such call-and-response songs of its time, the other being Ray Charles's "What'd I Say."

"Shout" reentered popular culture consciousness—if it had ever really left—with its inclusion in the 1978 John Landis film *National Lampoon's Animal House*. In the film, the story of which takes place in the early 1960s, the fictional R&B band Otis Day and the Knights performs "Shout" at a fraternity toga party, arguably one of the funniest scenes in the movie, especially as the dancers get closer and closer to the floor as Day and the Knights diminuendo on the oft-repeated line, "a little bit softer now" and then rise as Day and the Knights crescendo on the similarly repeated line "a little bit louder now." In its 2000 ranking of the 100 funniest movies of the first 100 years of the movie industry, the American Film Institute ranked *National Lampoon's Animal House* at No. 36 (*American Film Institute Website* 2000). Readers without access to the entire film can find the toga party scene on YouTube at the time of this writing (see, for example, https://www.youtube.com/watch?v=MG7KCOO76Wc, accessed January 22, 2020).

In 1987, Scott Kemper recorded a commercial jingle version of "Shout" that quickly became known throughout Western New York as an unofficial fight song of the NFL's Buffalo Bills. The Bills-oriented version of "Shout" was widely played by television and radio stations, as well as at home games whenever the Bills scored a touchdown. The Buffalo Bills' version of "Shout" became especially well-known between 1990 and 1993 when the team won the AFC championship and appeared in four consecutive Super Bowl games. In 1993, however, after Polaroid obtained the rights to the Isley Brothers' song and raised the royalty rate for its use, the Buffalo Bills organization announced that it would no longer use the song. Public outcry in western New York was so strong that the team's owner, Ralph Wilson, relented, and "Shout" continues to be a regular part of the professional football experience in Buffalo. For readers who have not heard the Buffalo Bills' version of "Shout" in the context of television or radio advertisements for games or at a game itself, a recording can be found on several YouTube channels at the time of this writing (see, for example, https://www.youtube.com/watch?v=PHbnQXsyDrE, accessed January 22, 2020).

Other sports franchises use songs that are location-based to fire up their fans. In the case of professional baseball's Philadelphia Phillies, it is "TSOP (The Sound of Philadelphia)," originally recorded by MFSB, the studio musicians who backed up numerous Philadelphia soul singers on their hits. The continuing association of "TSOP" with the Philadelphia Phillies in broader popular culture is suggested by the title of a 2018 *NBC Sports Chicago* article on baseball player Manny Machado's meetings with several teams as a free agent: "'Sweet Home Chicago,' 'New York Groove' or 'TSOP?' Who Gets the Encore After Manny Machado's Free-Agent Tour?" (Duber 2018).

Despite the iconic nature of the toga party scene in *National Lampoon's Animal House* involving the song "Shout," perhaps the best example of the impact of soul music and soul musicians (not to mention Chicago-style electric blues) on popular culture in popular Hollywood movies can be found in another movie associated with many of the same principals as those from *Animal House*: *The Blues Brothers*. Starring John Belushi and Dan Aykroyd, this 1980 John Landis film included appearances and performances by jazz, blues, and soul performers including Cab Calloway, James Brown, John Lee Hooker, Aretha Franklin, and Ray Charles. Perhaps the best sequence that illustrates the connections of these musicians and their work with popular culture is Franklin's performance of her song "Think" in a diner, in her *Blues Brothers* role as a waitress.

There are also cases that might better be characterized as one-off examples of soul music successfully being used in film soundtracks that work well because the music is so firmly etched in popular culture. One of the most memorable examples is the inclusion of Dusty Springfield's blue-eyed soul recording of "Son of a Preacher Man" in Quentin Tarantino's 1994 film *Pulp Fiction*. The song joined other wildly eclectic musical and other popular culture references from the 1950s through the 1980s in the movie. These ranged from lookalikes of 1950s' stars Buddy Holly, Mamie Van Doren, and Ed Sullivan, to the inclusion of Kool & the Gang's 1973 hit "Jungle Boogie" in the soundtrack, and a script reference to the hairstyle of 1980s' new wave group A Flock of Seagulls' lead singer Mike Score.

In addition to the later prominent placement of soul classics in films and television programs, the impact of soul on popular culture can also be seen in brief uses of well-known recordings. Recently, for example, an episode of the Amazon Prime program *The Grand Tour* that aired in December 2019 included a brief excerpt from Sam & Dave's recording "Hold On, I'm Coming" in the soundtrack. Brief, seemingly incidental incorporations of soul classics can play a role in the film or television show's narrative, such as was the case in *The Grand Tour*, but the significance might be lost on some audience members. However, audience members who are familiar with the songs, whether from when they initially were hits or when, several years later, they became well-known as "oldies," can make a connection between the song and the narrative, even if it is fleeting. Incidentally, the three British stars of *The Grand Tour*, Jeremy Clarkson, James May, and Richard Hammond, have made perhaps more than their fair share of references to classic soul music on their Amazon Prime show and the program they hosted previously on the BBC: *Top Gear*. For example, in the February 14, 2019 episode of *The Grand Tour*, Clarkson introduced his commentary on the present state of highway construction in China with the words, "There ain't no mountain high enough, and ain't no valley low enough," a quote from the 1960s Ashford and Simpson–penned song "Ain't No Mountain High Enough," a hit for the duo of Marvin Gaye and Tammi Terrell in 1967 and for Diana Ross in 1970. In recent years, too, Clarkson has compared the exhaust sound on a sportscar he was reviewing to Otis Redding's deep voice.

Some songs were so iconic that they immediately become fodder for parody. One particularly interesting example is James Brown's "Papa's Got a Brand New Bag." The fact that some of the lyrics were difficult to decipher and widely open to interpretation played into a skit by British comedians Peter Cook and Dudley Moore titled variously as "Mama's Got a Brand New Bag" and "Bo Dudley," the latter title being based on the character that Moore plays in the skit. Although the racial references in the Cook and Moore skit do not wear well today, the point of the skit was not to disparage blacks, but to point out that some white listeners just did not understand soul music. It also pointed out the pretentiousness of musicologists and music fans who sift through popular-song lyrics trying to find deeper and perhaps hidden meanings that were never intended by the songwriters, performers, arrangers, and producers. As was the case with the later *Saturday Night Live* skit with Ray Charles, the Cook and Moore's skit only succeeds if the audience member/viewer is familiar with the James Brown hit, suggesting that in both the United States and the United Kingdom, "Papa's Got a Brand New Bag" had become part of general popular culture soon after its release. A studio version of Cook and Moore's "Mama's Got a Brand New Bag"/"Bo Dudley" routine as released on record is available on YouTube at the time of this writing (see, https://www.youtube.com/watch?v=-8UXY6tehLM, accessed January 8, 2020). A live performance of the routine, as performed on the British television program *Not Only But Also*, is also available on YouTube (see, https://www.youtube.com/watch?v=enwpzA_eXsI, accessed February 11, 2020).

The connection between soul music and humor can also be found in the popular—some might say notorious—"Take Me to the River." Al Green and Teenie Hodges cowrote the song back in the early 1970s. Green's label mate Syl Johnson enjoyed an R&B chart hit single with "Take Me to the River," and Green included the song on his 1974 album, *Al Green Explores Your Mind*. Four years later, the new wave rock band Talking Heads included it on their album *More Songs about Buildings and Food* and made it part of their live repertoire. Unfortunately, the song might be best known, however, for being sung, beginning at the end of the 20th century, by the kitschy animatronic mounted fish Big Mouth Billy Bass, a novelty that was popular and widely parodied for several years. Big Mouth Billy Bass was equipped with a motion sensor that caused Billy to break into part of "Take Me to the River" whenever someone got close to it. Big Mouth Billy Bass later returned to the marketplace with versions that sang "Take Me to the River," "Don't Worry, Be Happy," and "I Will Survive," and, approximately 20 years after its first appearance, it can now be interfaced with Amazon's Alexa.

One particular television theme song might be the best example of the extent to which soul and its gospel cousin were firmly fixed in American popular culture in the 1970s and 1980s. Norman Lear's program *The Jeffersons*, a spin-off from his groundbreaking *All in the Family*, ran from 1975 to 1985 and was one of the more popular and longest-running situation comedies of the period. Ja'Nat DuBois wrote and sang the show's theme song, "Movin' On Up" (Fearn-Banks 2006, 434). Interestingly, DuBois's song takes the lyrical theme of being lifted higher, which in gospel songs has a religious connotation and which in some earlier soul songs refers to the effects of love (e.g., the Jackie Wilson hit "(Your Love Keeps Lifting Me) Higher and Higher"), and turns it into a celebration of economic and social-class achievement ("movin' on up to a deluxe apartment in the sky"). Because *The Jeffersons* entered the upper reaches of the television prime time ratings several times and ran for 11 seasons, "Movin' On Up" was firmly established as part of popular culture. The song in its original context at the opening of each episode of *The Jeffersons* can be found on several YouTube channels (see, for example, https://www.youtube.com/watch?v=FHDwRECFL8M, accessed February 11, 2020).

Another television series, *A Different World*, a spin-off from the extremely popular *The Cosby Show*, ran for six seasons from 1987 to 1993. The program used three different versions of its theme song, written by Stu Gardner, Bill Cosby, and Dawnn Lewis. A version by Aretha Franklin replaced Phoebe Snow's original recording in the show's second season. In the final season, however, Boyz II Men provided the theme song. All three versions exhibit strong ties to the soul of the 1960s through early 1990s. Both the Snow and Franklin recordings are the closest to classic 1960s and 1970s soul; however, even though Boyz II Men enjoyed most of their commercial success with hip-hop-influenced ballads, their version exhibits some perhaps unexpectedly strong ties to gospel and classic soul.

Certainly, part of the story of the legacy of soul songs can be found in the cover versions discussed in this volume's chapter "Legacy." But what of songs that inspired later songs that were even more widely known than the original inspirations? We might consider that evidence of the impact of soul on popular culture. Although one could cite numerous examples, let us consider just two that helped to define the Rolling Stones in 1965, the year in which that British rock band really emerged as superstars. As Paul Tryna wrote in his biography of the Rolling Stones' founder Brian Jones, the Mick Jagger and Keith Richards-composed song "The Last Time" "showcased Mick and Keith as snotty young geniuses. Which they were, although not as complete as the single suggested. The song itself owes much to a Staple Singers track Keith had heard back in Chicago [where the band had previously recorded], and the Staple Singers' version [the mid-1950s recording "This May Be the Last Time"] was based on an old gospel tune that they extensively reworked with a new harmonized chorus" (Trynka 2014, 136). Similarly, Tryna traces the distinctive opening four-on-the-floor rhythmic beat of the Rolling Stones' "(I Can't Get No) Satisfaction" to the opening of Martha and the Vandellas' recording of "Nowhere to Run" (Trynka 2014, 146).

Because national television advertising campaigns are so fully focused on sales, it seems reasonable that their use of songs and styles from popular music might be some of the most focused on making an immediate impact with the potential consumer. As a result, musicians, styles, and songs Madison Avenue uses must be part of the general popular culture to best generate sales. Celebrities from the world of soul have appeared in television commercials over the years, including Aretha Franklin in an ad for American Express (see, https://www.ispot.tv/ad/7JCY/american-express-the-journey-never-stops-for-aretha-franklin, accessed January 22, 2020); James Brown in a television ad campaign for McDonald's (see, https://www.youtube.com/watch?v=Yt_RUlHaZt8, accessed January 22, 2020); and an animated Ray Charles in a commercial for California Raisins (https://www.youtube.com/watch?v=U9Pr-L367N8, accessed January 22, 2020). Incidentally, portrayed as a real group, the California Raisins recorded a version of "I Heard It Through the Grapevine" in the mid-1980s (see, https://www.youtube.com/watch?v=UShiwymsX0w, accessed February 3, 2020). Gladys Knight appeared in a commercial for Aunt Jemima pancake syrup (see, https://www.youtube.com/watch?v=B1zmnWUKe50, accessed January 22, 2020), as well as one for Velveeta (see, https://www.youtube.com/watch?v=Ujg35KBv9y4, accessed February 11, 2020). Even a cursory search of YouTube and other internet video sites turns up many other examples, including a Stevie Wonder appearance in a television advertisement for TDK tape (back in the tape-recording era) (see, for example, https://www.youtube.com/watch?v=ra4NHsmtB4U, accessed January 22, 2020); Wonder singing a jingle in a Kodak batteries advertisement (see, for example, https://www.youtube.com/watch?v=XNrqhqCAKxA, accessed

January 22, 2020); Wonder using Kodak batteries in a cassette recorder as he works out what is presumably a new musical composition (see, for example, https://www.youtube.com/watch?v=hblBIC5hrLI, accessed January 22, 2020); and numerous others. This, again, suggests the widespread public recognition of these musicians and their work, in short demonstrating the extent to which they were part of the American popular culture landscape.

The iconic nature of Lionel Richie and Michael Jackson and their music in the popular culture of the 1980s was confirmed by their appearances in television commercials for Pepsi. Commercials that were part of the "Pepsi: The Choice of a New Generation" advertising campaign can be found on YouTube. For example, two of Lionel Richie's mid-1980s Pepsi commercials can be found at https://www.youtube.com/watch?v=zaQKarpx5LM (accessed February 11, 2020). The most famous soul-Pepsi connections, however, can be found in Michael Jackson's endorsements of the soft drink. Jackson and his brothers appeared in an advertisement as part of the "Pepsi: The Choice of a New Generation" in which Pepsi-related lyrics were set to the music of Jackson's "Billie Jean." One posting of this famous commercial on YouTube has had over 90 million views to date (see, https://www.youtube.com/watch?v=po0jY4WvCIc, accessed February 11, 2020).

Unfortunately, at a 1984 commercial shoot for Pepsi, Jackson received second- and third-degree burns when a pyrotechnics display ignited prematurely. Plastic surgery, skin grafts, and reliance on painkillers were the results of the accident. *Us Weekly* posted a video with footage from several takes of the commercial—including the disastrous one—on its YouTube channel (see, https://www.youtube.com/watch?v=BqfJZGUNo5A, accessed February 11, 2020). Because Jackson was so firmly ensconced in popular culture, media coverage of the accident was extensive at the time. Shortly after Jackson's death in 2009, articles appeared in the media about the 1984 accident and the impact it had on Jackson for the next quarter century (see, for example, Goldman 2009). Ultimately, Jackson made additional Pepsi commercials after his recovery. In fact, at the time Jackson's post-accident commercial deal was announced, it was touted by the *Guinness Book of World Records* as "'the biggest commercial sponsorship deal' ever struck between a corporation and a performer" (Taylor 1986).

The importance of Michael Jackson and his music in popular culture was also confirmed by the extensive media coverage of his 2005 trial on child molestation, alcohol, and conspiracy charges. One of the unforgettable images from the media coverage of Jackson's exit from the courthouse was the sight of Jackson fan Fariba Garmani releasing white doves in celebration of Jackson's acquittal on the ten charges that had been brought against him (see, https://www.youtube.com/watch?v=CuctBAv2XoE, for fan reaction to the announcements of the not-guilty verdicts and Garmani's release of one of the doves, accessed February 11, 2020). Garmani's act itself received extensive media coverage (see, example, Covarrubias and Saillant 2005). The iconic nature of the Jackson trial was not limited to American popular culture. Anecdotally, I was in the United Kingdom at the time of the trial, and British television news programs featured actors reenacting the trial, such was the fascination with Jackson's trial overseas.

Fascination with Jackson certainly did not begin and end with his 2005 trial. In 1992, the year before the first child molestation charges against Jackson, ABC presented a miniseries, *The Jacksons: An American Dream*, that dealt with the early life and work of the Jackson 5 and the other members of the family. The 2004 television biopic *Man in the Mirror: The Michael Jackson Story* dealt with Jackson's later life and career. Most recently, the 2019 Dan Reed documentary *Leaving Neverland* focused on the stories of two of Jackson's alleged molestation victims. The allegations put forth in *Leaving Neverland* subsequently were countered by the 2019 Amazon Prime Video production *Michael Jackson: Chasing the Truth*, a documentary that focused on insights from Jackson's immediate circle, which portrayed the musician in a dramatically different light than that suggested in *Leaving Neverland*.

One of the more memorable 21st-century examples of the Madison Avenue/soul connection is the song "My Girl." Smokey Robinson and Ronald White of the Miracles penned and produced "My Girl" for the Temptations. The Temptations included the track on their album *The Temptations Sing Smokey*, and Motown released it as a single, which became one of the group's biggest hits. In 2003 Luckie & Co., an advertising firm, used the song for a television campaign for McKee Foods' Little Debbie Snacks. Luckie & Co. then revived the television ad in 2005 (Lovel 2005). In the commercial, a young boy opens a package of Little Debbie snacks in a classroom and tentatively sings the first line. He is gradually joined by other children, until the entire class is singing "My Girl." At the time of this writing, at least one YouTube channel has a posting of the advertisement (see, for example, https://www.youtube.com/watch?v=PlOyQbjoyZw, accessed January 22, 2020).

Sometimes, the genre itself rather than a specific well-known song has demonstrated soul's impact on popular culture. One example that has appeared throughout 2018 and 2019 is the lonely water cooler commercial for the Coca-Cola Company–owned product vitaminwater. The water cooler sings a hip-hop-based slow-jam soul song of lament hoping that he can become "as fun as vitaminwater." Two female backing vocalists, represented in the commercial by two drawers of the adjacent filing cabinet, accompany the cooler. Interestingly, this example of soul music in the world of television commercials has been published by several YouTube channels, including one with well over 145,000 views that loops the advertisement so that the viewer can hear the song for nearly five minutes (see, for example, https://www.youtube.com/watch?v=SP-7FYS2R1Q, accessed February 11, 2020). The commercial relies on the fact that slow-jam quiet storm soul is associated by the public with lamentations over lost love (in this case, the office workers who no longer congregate around the water cooler). Even the vocal texture of a lead singer accompanied by two backing singers is something of a popular culture stereotype of soul music.

Some soul performers became pop culture icons. and the impact was not always solely through their music. For example, the image of the Supremes in sparkling evening gowns is firmly etched into popular culture. Because of the tremendous popularity of his music videos and his extensive touring in support of his 1980s and 1990s albums, Michael Jackson's stage costumes, including the single sequined glove, is perhaps the strongest example of how a performer's look itself can become an inescapable part of popular culture. The impact of stage costumes can be seen in their inclusion in the collection on display at the Rock and Roll Hall of Fame, which, incidentally, at one time displayed the famous glove. This writer suspects that anyone familiar with Jackson's performance of "Billie Jean" at Motown's televised 25th anniversary celebration in 1983 who saw a single glove anywhere would almost immediately think of Jackson (for the segment of the Motown celebration that contains Jackson's performance, see, https://www.youtube.com/watch?v=45Ph_MXIP1o, accessed February 11, 2020). Incidentally, by the press coverage of the auction of Jackson's white-sequined glove in 2009, when it sold for $350,000, confirmed its iconic nature (see, for example, Michaud 2009). At that time, designer John Kehe published an article in *The Christian Science Monitor* with his account of how the glove had initially come into being by happenstance (Kehe 2009). Such was the iconic nature of this piece of stage costuming that various other stories about the gloves and Jackson appeared online and in print as the auction was announced, approached, and took place.

As given more detail in the chapter "Legacy," the impact of soul music on popular culture can also be found in the numerous jukebox musicals and biopics that have been produced, particularly in the 21st century.

Yes, shows such as *Ain't Too Proud to Beg* and films such as *Cadillac Records* and *Ray* are part of the continuing legacy of soul; however, they only work commercially if they can bring in audiences, and they can only bring in audiences if the artists and their music remain part of popular culture, if not for the entire populace, at least for some sizable segment of the potential audience.

CHAPTER 4

Legacy

The story of the legacy of soul music can be found in several places. Later artists have remade some songs from the past, and the legacy of some recordings have advanced because they have been sampled in the production of new hip-hop-era songs. Films about old soul record labels and biopics about artists of the past have also helped keep the legacy of the music and the musicians alive. In other cases, the fact that some songs of the past played sociologically significant roles has led to their inclusion in film soundtracks, either to establish a time and place or to recapture the sociological role of the songs. Another consideration, with which we will end the chapter, is the question of the extent to which soul as a genre truly ended in the 1980s, as suggested by some writers, and whether subsequent incarnations of soul are just a revisiting of the legacy of the 1950s through the 1980s or truly part of the overall and ongoing evolution of the genre. In studying the legacy of any genre of music, there is necessary overlap with the genre's impact on popular culture. I have attempted to minimize the overlap between this chapter and the chapter "Impact on Popular Culture" and suggest you read the two in tandem to round out the ongoing importance of soul music.

Let us first consider a few of the old soul hits of the past that artists have covered in the intervening years as part of the story of the legacy of the genre. For example, in 1991, BeBe & CeCe Winans recorded "I'll Take You There," a song written by record producer Al Bell under his given name, Alvertis Isbell. Originally released in 1972 by the Staple Singers, "I'll Take You There" is probably the Staple Singers' best-remembered recording. Bell's lyrics speak of a place where there are no worries and where racism does not exist, a hope that rang true in the early 1990s as strongly as it had two decades before. The Winans' R&B chart-topping recording connected directly to the legacy of the Staple Singers' original recording, not only by means of the song itself and the Winans' style but also because it featured a guest appearance by the Staple Singers' Mavis Staples. BeBe & CeCe Winans were not the only artists to keep the legacy of "I'll Take You There" alive in the early 1990s. The group General Public recorded a cover version that made it into the pop Top 40 in 1994, and the hip-hop group Salt-N-Pepa included a sample of "I'll Take You There" in their well-known 1991 hit "Let's Talk About Sex."

Later covers of classic soul songs certainly are not limited to the example of "I'll Take You There." A wide variety of musicians has continued to cover Curtis Mayfield's "People Get Ready," for example, well-recognized for its important role in galvanizing protesters during the civil rights movement in the 1960s. *AllMusic* lists Aretha Franklin, the Chambers Brothers, Al Green, Rod Stewart and Jeff Beck, Dionne Warwick, Glen Campbell, Seal, the Blind Boys of Alabama, Bob Dylan, Petula Clark, and numerous others as having recorded the song (*AllMusic.com* n.d.). That this list includes a racial and genre-based diversity suggests both how the legacy of what started out as a hit song for the Impressions has crossed over various boundaries. This suggests not only that the legacy of the song continues to expand but also the impact and iconic nature that it enjoys in late 20th-century and early 21st-century popular culture.

Some artists from outside the traditional soul realm have paid tribute to the genre, not just by including particular songs in their stage repertoires or recordings; they have recorded entire albums or concerts that focus entirely on soul and helped further the legacy of the genre. Such is the case with Rod Stewart's 2009 album *Soulbook*, as well as three 21st-century albums and a concert film by former Steely Dan and Doobie Brothers member Michael McDonald.

British rock singer Rod Stewart has been associated with rock, blues, and mid-20th-century American pop music. In particular, Stewart's early 21st-century projects focused on the classic American songbook, which includes jazz songs, show tunes, and other Tin Pan Alley songs from the early-to-mid 20th century. Stewart's 2009 album *Soulbook* focused on soul classics, including "It's the Same Old Song," "(Your Love Keeps Lifting Me) Higher and Higher," "The Tracks of My Tears," "Rainy Night in Georgia," "You've Really Got a Hold on Me," and others. Several long-standing soul musicians, as well as some relative newcomers, contributed to Stewart's *Soulbook*, including Stevie Wonder, Mary J. Blige, Jennifer Hudson, and Smokey Robinson. Wonder and Robinson's contributions directly connected Stewart's work with the classic soul of the 1960s and 1970s, and Blige and Hudson's contributions connected songs from that period with the then-currently popular soul singers of the early 21st century.

Although Michael McDonald has enjoyed a lengthy solo career, he was previously associated with both Steely Dan and the Doobie Brothers. Arguably, throughout his career as a singer-songwriter-pianist, McDonald has contributed to the blue-eyed soul subgenre, particularly through his vocal style. McDonald's 2003 album, *Motown*, and his 2004 album, *Motown Two*, furthered the legacy of the classic Motown brand of soul. Between the two albums, McDonald recorded such Motown works as "I Heard It Through the Grapevine," "Signed, Sealed, Delivered I'm Yours," "Ain't Nothing Like the Real Thing," "How Sweet It Is (To Be Loved by You)," "Ain't No Mountain High Enough," "I Was Made to Love Her," "Reach Out, I'll Be There," "The Tracks of My Tears," "What's Going On," and others. McDonald followed these albums up with the 2009 Joe Thomas–directed concert film *A Tribute to Motown*, which included songs from *Motown* and *Motown Two* and guest artists such as Toni Braxton, India.Arie, Take 6, and Billy Preston. Like the Rod Stewart project, McDonald's guest artists connected his work directly to the classic soul and soul performers of the 1960s and 1970s (e.g., Preston), while lending the old songs a more contemporary feel through the contributions of artists such as Braxton, Take 6, and India.Arie.

Similarly, in 2007, the 1990s' Motown hit vocal group Boyz II Men recorded the cover album *Motown: A Journey Through Hitsville USA*. This album included "Just My Imagination (Running Away with Me)," originally a hit for the Temptations; "Ain't Nothing Like the Real Thing"; and "Mercy Mercy Me (The Ecology)," both hits for Marvin Gaye; and "The Tracks of My Tears," originally a hit for Smokey Robinson and the Miracles. In a somewhat unusual move, Boyz II Men also recorded a new version of "End of the Road," a song they had earlier released when they were first on Motown.

I have not dealt extensively with the sampling of earlier soul recordings during the hip-hop age of the 1980s through the present in this chapter, because it has been so prevalent that there is not sufficient room for full study. To put it another way, the example of Salt-N-Pepa mentioned above is just the tip of the iceberg. For example, Coolio's "Gangsta's Paradise" is based on Stevie Wonder's "Pastime Paradise." This is one of the most important adaptations of earlier soul material in that it brought Wonder back to the top of the charts nearly 20 years after he had first recorded the song. Kanye West's sample of the Ray Charles song "I Got a Woman" for West's 2005 track "Gold Digger" is also significant. The prevalence of soul samples in hip-hop is suggested by the fact that at the time of this writing, Apple Music Hip-Hop is marketing a collection of hip-hop recordings that sample earlier soul music from Motown (see, https://music.apple.com/us/playlist/sampled-the-spirit-of-motown/pl.29d92747861c4e708efe663d65413d16, accessed February 11, 2020). Apple Music's collection includes recordings by MC Lyte, Nas, Run-DMC, Jay-Z, Ja Rule, Kanye West, and several others. Suffice it to say that streaming and download services have ample opportunity to release numerous additional such playlists and collections.

The live musical theatre stage and Hollywood films have also helped preserve and further the legacy of soul music. The range of these productions includes biopics, completely fictional productions that focus on the music—or at least the musical styles—of earlier soul music, and at least one somewhat-thinly disguised semifictional show.

One of the better-known productions that brought back the soul styles of the early 1960s through the early 1970s was the 1981 stage musical *Dreamgirls*. The show's connections to the real-life story of Diana Ross, the Supremes, and the history of Motown into the 1970s are readily apparent; however, more so in the 2006 film version of the show. Despite the controversy that arose because of the show's and the film's suggestions that the history of Motown might have been far less rosy than what is popularly assumed, *Dreamgirls* is important as part of the story of the legacy of soul music. Henry Krieger and Tom Eyen provided songs that, although clearly modeled on the styles that ran through Motown soul of the period, sounded original enough that they didn't sound overly derivative. The film version of *Dreamgirls* also moved the legacy of soul music forward through noteworthy vocal performances by Beyoncé and Jennifer Hudson, the latter of whom received an Academy Award for Best Supporting Actress in her movie debut.

In so far as Ray Charles was one of the most iconic figures in American music in the second half of the 20th century, the 2004 Taylor Hackford biopic, *Ray*, is an important part of the legacy of soul. Jamie Foxx starred as Charles in the movie and won the Academy Award for Best Actor. In addition to telling the story of Ray Charles from his birth into his long career, the film features numerous Jamie Foxx performances of Charles's classics.

Similarly, the 2008 Darnell Martin film *Cadillac Records* tells the story of the founding, struggles, and artistic success and significance of Chess Records. The bulk of the musicians portrayed in the film came out of the blues genre and include Willie Dixon, Little Walter, Howlin' Wolf, and Muddy Waters. Rock and roll pioneer Chuck Berry is also among the characters in the movie. The film's main tie to soul is in the person of Etta James, played by Beyoncé. Beyoncé's performance of "At Last" alone was significant in moving the legacy of soul music forward, as the song became something of a signature song for her. Her recording and her live performances of "At Last" also revived interest in Etta James.

Other works devoted to the life and works of musicians associated with the soul genre include *Beautiful: The Carole King Musical*, a 2013 production that toured the United States in 2019 and 2020. King's association with soul includes her early songs, written in collaboration with then-husband Gerry Goffin, for African American soul singers including Little Eva ("Keep Your Hands off My Baby" and "The Loco-Motion"), the Cookies ("Chains" and "Don't Say Nothin' Bad (About My Baby)"), Earl-Jean ("I'm Into Something Good"), the Shirelles ("Will You Love Me Tomorrow"), and Aretha Franklin ("[You Make Me Feel Like] A Natural Woman"). It also includes the soul/gospel-inspired songs that King performed as a singer-songwriter in the 1970s, such as the songs on her iconic album, *Tapestry*. All these hits are included in the production, which also features the Carole King character recounting stories about how the songs came into being.

In a similar vein, the year 2019 was marked by emergence of the musical *Ain't Too Proud to Beg: The Life and Times of The Temptations*. This show, on Broadway at the time of this writing in late 2019, is scheduled for a national tour in 2020. The musical includes all the hits associated with the Temptations throughout their career (e.g., "My Girl," "Ain't Too Proud to Beg," "Cloud Nine," "Just My Imagination [Running Away with Me]," and so on), with a focus on the Temptations' popular hits of the 1960s and early 1970s. The Broadway musical's music director, Kenny Seymour, said of the show, "We have young people, we have seniors, we have all nationalities, people from different countries, and almost immediately when the music starts, they're all clapping and just enjoying themselves in unison" (*International Musician* 2019, 18). This suggests the extent to which the music of the Temptations continues to transcend generational, national, and racial boundaries.

An upcoming biopic about Aretha Franklin, which is set to star Jennifer Hudson will undoubtedly advance the legacy of soul music. Given Hudson's performances in the classic soul style in *Dreamgirls* and in numerous live concert and television appearances, one can reasonably assume that she will be able to capture Franklin's vocal style. A late 2019 report published by NBC News suggested that the first teaser from the film—which is scheduled to be released in late 2020—suggested to critics that Hudson was up to the task (*Variety* 2019).

Several soul classics from the early 1960s were intrinsically tied with the period's struggle for racial equality and civil rights, but perhaps none more so than the Impressions' recording of Curtis Mayfield's "People

Get Ready" and Sam Cooke's 1964 recording of his own composition "A Change Is Gonna Come." Director Spike Lee's 1992 film *Malcolm X* includes Cooke's song in the soundtrack. It is an interesting choice in that "A Change Is Gonna Come" is widely interpreted as an anthem for the civil rights movement, which Malcolm X had rejected in no small part because of its emphasis on racial integration. Although Lee's inclusion of the song can be interpreted as simply a way of musically connecting the events of Malcolm X's life to the sounds of the time—the recording was on the charts the year Malcolm X was assassinated—there is more to the way in which the film uses Sam Cooke's song. "A Change Is Gonna Come" is heard at a critical juncture in the film, and its placement creates implications that enhance the film's dramatic impact.

As *New York Daily News* critic David Hinckley put it in an article about the music of *Malcolm X* that appeared in the *Chicago Tribune*, "The show-stopper comes when Malcolm drives to the Audubon Ballroom the night of his death. Lee puts us in the car with Malcolm, letting us watch as his world closes in and listen as Sam Cooke sings 'A Change Is Gonna Come.' It's not only a brilliant emotional crescendo, it's also a perfect musical choice: a song singularly worthy of the moment" (Hinckley 1992). What the author does not detail—because his article is focused on how the closely guarded song came to be available to Lee—are the deep implications of the song in the context of Lee's narrative.

As mentioned earlier, I hear the song as setting the time period and as providing a musical link to the struggle against discrimination and for racial equality that was at the core of the civil rights movement and Malcolm X's more radical movement. At the same time, the placement of the song, as Malcolm drives to the ballroom, almost looking as though he knows what fate awaits him, suggests that the "change" Cooke sings about also represents a fundamental change in the struggle for racial equality that would come with the assassination of Malcolm X.

I have placed discussion of Spike Lee's inclusion of "A Change Is Gonna Come" in this chapter, as opposed to the chapter "Impact on Popular Culture" because of context. Certainly, the fact that Sam Cooke's song was well known and part of the popular-culture landscape helps "A Change Is Gonna Come" work effectively in the film. However, the film reinforces the original context of the song to such an extent that the its placement helps preserve and advance the legacy of "A Change Is Gonna Come" for later generations than those who might have first experienced it nearly 30 years before.

As Hinckley 1992 details, Allen Klein, who owns the rights to Cooke's "A Change Is Gonna Come," had only given permission for its inclusion in a movie soundtrack twice. As a result, its inclusion in Spike Lee's *Malcolm X* is significant. Not only does the song convey the time, the sentiments of the civil rights movement, and possibly foretell Malcolm X's demise, it is also one of the rare opportunities to hear the song in a television/film context.

When considering the legacy of soul music, it is also important to consider that many of the great songs and albums of the past are available for purchase in physical media, download, or streaming at the time of this writing. Interestingly, through services such as iTunes and physical media (e.g., CDs) vendors such as Amazon, the Isley Brothers' 1975 album *The Heat Is On* is available, ranging from $4.99 to around $6.99. Similarly, Al Green's 1973 album *Let's Stay Together* is available for a relatively low price, and Lauryn Hill's *The Miseducation of Lauryn Hill* can be found for sale as low as $4.49. Although it is a more recent album, John Legend's *Once Again* can be found at prices between approximately $7 and $10. Some of the older, high-demand albums (e.g., Aretha Franklin's *Lady Soul*) are in the $9.99 area in early 2020.

In addition—and this certainly is not unique to the soul genre—numerous studio and live audio and visual recordings of soul stars and near stars of the past and present are available through sources such as YouTube. This is important because YouTube provides access to some of the lesser-known performers and recordings of the past, which, in some case are difficult to obtain except on the original vinyl recordings. What is perhaps most important about websites such as YouTube is that many of the live performances—even of major stars—were either not issued on home video or received minor distribution for home video and, in some of those cases, only many years ago. To cite just one example, at the time of this writing, a live video of Percy Sledge performing "When a Man Loves a Woman" is available on YouTube, a performance that without the internet as a resource might otherwise have been forgotten (see, https://www.youtube.com/watch?v=EYb84BDMbi0, accessed February 11, 2020). Incidentally, this is a particularly interesting performance, because the great Otis Redding introduced Sledge, but more importantly, because it offers an extended version of the song, in contrast to the tighter, shorter form of the famous studio recording released as a single.

The expansion of streaming audio and internet-radio resources of the 21st century have also made soul music readily available in any broadcast radio market, even music that might otherwise have been difficult to obtain or only available through physical media. For example, iHeartRadio's "Classic Soul" playlist includes a wide range of selections from the 1960s and 1970s, including Dobie Gray's "Drift Away," Sam Cooke's "A Change

Is Gonna Come," Aretha Franklin's version of "Respect," the Drifters' "Up on the Roof," and Gladys Knight and the Pips' "Neither One of Us (Wants to Be the First to Say Goodbye)," just to name several examples from near the top of the playlist, as observed in January 2020 (see, https://www.iheart.com/playlist/classic-soul-312064750-T5ae7pKapChP8iJs3Dn2sd/, accessed January 10, 2020). The service's "70s Soul" playlist includes Marvin Gaye's "What's Going On," the Isley Brothers' "That Lady," Aretha Franklin's version of "Bridge over Troubled Water," Diana Ross's recording of "Ain't No Mountain High Enough," and the Spinners' "Could It Be I'm Falling in Love," again, just to name a handful available in January 2020 (see, https://www.iheart.com/playlist/70s-soul-312064750-9VQXGeENQqE5vbeDs7zAXf/, accessed January 10, 2020).

A cursory search of Pandora Radio's site for "soul" reveals channels such as "Philly Soul," "BET Soul," "Neo-Soul Radio," "R&B/Soul Radio," and "70s Classic Soul" (see, https://www.pandora.com/search/soul/all, accessed January 10, 2020). Other streaming audio services, including Amazon Music Unlimited and Apple Music, just to name two, provide a breadth and depth of access to soul music, ranging from across the entire and ongoing life-span of the genre.

The importance of streaming audio, internet radio, and websites such as YouTube—the massive shift in how consumers obtain music—is that soul hits are more readily available than they were even when they were at the top of the charts. Similarly, current hits in the genre are also more easily accessible than the hits of decades ago would have been during their initial run of popularity. This is particularly true of the music available on internet radio sites. As discussed earlier, live performances that were never officially released, television appearances that have not been replayed in years or decades, and obscure studio recordings and album cuts that might never have been previously available except through physical media can now be found on YouTube and similar sites. So, these electronic resources has advanced the legacy of a wide range of soul. Although the preservation of the legacy of the genre is perhaps not as dramatic as is the case with genres such as blues and country music—in which obscure recordings from the 1910s and 1920s that were, in some cases, never reissued can now be accessed on the internet—official videos, videos constructed by fans, and recordings from vinyl releases posted by fans have all broadened and deepened the availability of the range of soul.

Another interesting consideration with regard to the legacy of soul is the varying definitions of exactly what the genre is and the implications of those definitions. Some writer-scholars essentially limit the genre to the 1950s through the 1970s. For example, in his article in the *Grove Dictionary of American Music,* David Brackett wrote, "By the mid-1970s the up-tempo numbers in the sweet style began to be called disco. Ballads formed the most obvious aural connection to soul music of the late 60s and early 70s, but by 1982, even *Billboard* had to concede that Soul was no longer an adequate label for African American popular music in general, and changed the name of the soul chart to Black Music" (Brackett 2013, 609). Similarly, David Ritz, who has written and cowritten several biographies of soul musicians and liner notes for CD reissues of soul albums, wrote in his *Encyclopedia Britannica* article on the genre, "Soul became a permanent part of the grammar of American popular culture. Its underlying virtues—direct emotional delivery, ethnic pride, and respect for its own artistic sources—live on as dynamic and dramatic influences on musicians throughout the world. To varying degrees, the power and personality of the form were absorbed in disco, funk, and hip-hop, styles that owe their existence to soul" (Ritz 1999).

This is not to suggest that soul as a genre ceased to exist by the 1980s and that various aspects of the genre were infused or integrated into what ended up labeled different genres, the disco, funk and hip-hop mentioned by Ritz. The legacy of soul can be felt in all these primarily African American popular music styles from the 1970s through the present. Ritz's assessment, however, seems to suggest that soul exists only within those genres. I argue that part of the legacy of soul, and the part that the Ritz article would have missed because of its end-of-the-century publication date, is that in the neo-soul boom that started in the 1990s and that has continued through the first two decades of the 21st century, has not only found genres such as hip-hop exhibiting the clear influence of earlier soul music but also seen new soul music emerge that integrates the influence of genres such as funk and hip-hop. In other words, in the work of some of the artists of the 1990s through the present detailed in the Must-Hear Music chapter, the style is not as much hip-hop influenced by soul as much as it is new soul that integrates some of the rhythmic, sampling, and production influences of hip-hop. What critics who discuss the apparent death of soul as a genre in the 1980s also fail to account for is the 21st-century emergence of biopics and jukebox musicals that have brought back the music of Ray Charles, the Temptations, Aretha Franklin, Etta James, and others. That stars such as John Legend, Jennifer Hudson, Beyoncé, and Jamie Foxx have included songs from these earlier legendary performers in their own repertoire, as detailed earlier in this chapter, also keeps the spirit of soul alive and thriving. The incorporation of these songs in to the repertoires of performers who are active today suggests that the songs are not simply oldies but are timeless enough to speak to audiences in an entirely different era.

Although the circumstances under which it occurred were tragic, the continuing relevance of soul, and particularly that which is closest to its cousin gospel, as a genre through which complex and intense emotions can be expressed musically was confirmed by a performance of "It's So Hard to Say Goodbye to Yesterday" by Alicia Keys and Boyz II Men at the January 26, 2020, Grammy Awards Ceremony as a tribute to basketball great Kobe Bryant and his daughter, Gianna, who were among nine people who perished in a helicopter crash shortly before the Grammy ceremony took place. The song itself was recorded by G. C. Cameron for the 1975 film *Cooley High*. Although it was a minor hit for Cameron, the Boyz II Men cover that was released in 1991 made a substantial hit of the song; the Boyz II Men single topped the R&B charts and nearly topped the pop charts. Part of the January 26, 2020 performance by Boyz II Men and Grammy host Alicia Keys and its context were covered in a report by *Entertainment Tonight*, which, at the time of this writing, is available on YouTube (see, https://www.youtube.com/watch?v=ad_FGzNnC0U, accessed February 11, 2020).

Bibliography

Abbott, Kingsley, ed. 2001. *Callin' Out around the World: A Motown Reader*. London: Helter Skelter Publishing.
Aletti, Vince. 1976. "Songs in the Key of Life." *Rolling Stone*, December 16. Accessed August 29, 2019. https://www.rollingstone.com/music/music-album-reviews/songs-in-the-key-of-life-186350/.
AllMusic.com. n.d. "The Impressions: 'People Get Ready.'" *AllMusic.com*. Accessed October 30, 2019. https://www.allmusic.com/song/people-get-ready-mt0005674487/also-performed-by.
American Epic. 2016. PBS television series. Directed by Bernard MacMahon. A multipart documentary on the early roots of the music recording industry in the United States.
American Film Institute Website. 2000. "AFI's 100 Years . . . 100 Laughs." *American Film Institute*. Accessed December 18, 2019. https://www.afi.com/afis-100-years-100-laughs/.
Anderson, Kelsey. 2018. "Bills Fans Celebrate 25th Anniversary of the Return of Iconic Shout Song." *WIVB.com*, September 13. Accessed December 18, 2019. https://www.wivb.com/news/bills-fans-celebrate-25th-anniversary-of-the-return-of-iconic-shout-song/.
Ankeny, Jason. n.d.-a. "*Let's Get It On*." *AllMusic*. Accessed July 25, 2019. https://www.allmusic.com/album/lets-get-it-on-mw0000474663.
Ankeny, Jason. n.d.-b. "Mariah Carey." *AllMusic*. Accessed October 14, 2019. https://www.allmusic.com/artist/mariah-carey-mn0000262255/biography.
The Associated Press. 2019. "Lizzo Named *The Associated Press*' Entertainer of the Year." *The Associated Press*, December 27. Accessed December 28, 2019. https://apnews.com/8190c94a40966816eba418c088766a3b.
Bego, Mark. 2012. *Aretha Franklin: The Queen of Soul*, paperback ed. New York: Skyhorse Publishing.

Benadon, Fernando, and Ted Gioia. 2009. "How Hooker Found His Boogie: A Rhythmic Analysis of a Classic Groove." *Popular Music* 28, no. 1 (January): 19–32.

Benjaminson, Peter. 1979. *The Story of Motown*. New York: Grove Press.

Billboard. 2009. "Artists of the Decade." *Billboard*, December 11. Accessed November 18, 2019. https://www.billboard.com/articles/news/266420/artists-of-the-decade.

Billboard. 2011. "The 40 Biggest Duets of All Time." *Billboard*, February 14. Accessed November 4, 2019. https://www.billboard.com/articles/list/473075/the-40-biggest-duets-of-all-time.

Billboard.com. n.d. Accessed December 23, 2019. https://www.billboard.com/. *Billboard* magazine's website contains present-day and historic chart information about soul, R&B, pop, and recordings in other genres.

Biography.com. 2019a. "Etta James." *Biography.com*, July 30. Accessed October 3, 2019. https://www.biography.com/musician/etta-james.

Biography.com. 2019b. "Jackie Wilson." *Biography.com*, July 26. Accessed November 6, 2019. https://www.biography.com/musician/jackie-wilson.

Birchmeier, Jason. n.d. "Hot Buttered Soul." *AllMusic*. Accessed July 31, 2019. https://www.allmusic.com/album/hot-buttered-soul-mw0000651407.

BMI. 1999. "BMI Announces Top 100 Songs of the Century." BMI.com, December 13. Accessed September 9, 2019. www.bmi.com/news/entry/19991214_bmi_announces_top_100_songs_of_the_century.

Bogdanov, Vladimir, John Bush, and Stephen Thomas Erlewine, eds. 2003. *All Music Guide to Soul*. Ann Arbor, MI: Backbeat Books.

Bolton, Michael. 2012. *The Soul of It All: My Music, My Life*. New York: Center Street.

Borja, Jonathan. 2016. "The Jackson 5." In Moskowitz, David, ed. *The 100 Greatest Bands of All Time: A Guide to the Legends Who Rocked the World*, v. 1. Santa Barbara, CA: Greenwood Press, pp. 323–330.

Bowman, Bob. 2008. Liner notes for *Otis Blue—Otis Redding Sings Soul*. CD, Rhino Records RF2 422140.

Brackett, David. 2013. "Soul Music." In Garrett, Charles Hiroshi, ed. *The Grove Dictionary of American Music*, 2nd ed. New York: Oxford University Press, pp. 607–609.

Bradley, Lloyd. 2010. "One of the Stax Label's Greatest Triumphs." BBC online, Accessed August 6, 2019. https://www.bbc.co.uk/music/reviews/zpvh/. A highly favorable review of the Staple Singers' *BeAttitude: Respect Yourself*.

Browne, David, Elias Leight, Brittany Spanos, Mosi Reeves, Richard Gehr, Maura Johnston, Joe Levy, and Will Hermes. 2018. "The 50 Greatest Aretha Franklin Songs." *Rolling Stone* online, August 16. Accessed July 26, 2019. https://www.rollingstone.com/music/music-lists/the-50-greatest-aretha-franklin-songs-110647/day-dreaming-1972-200622/.

Bibliography

Bush, John. n.d.-a. "Aretha Franklin: *Lady Soul*." *AllMusic*. Accessed November 11, 2019. https://www.allmusic.com/album/lady-soul-mw0000194521.

Bush, John. n.d.-b. "Lauryn Hill: *The Miseducation of Lauryn Hill*." *AllMusic*. Accessed August 27, 2019. https://www.allmusic.com/album/the-miseducation-of-lauryn-hill-mw0000034642.

Cantwell, David. 2015. "The Unlikely Story of 'A Change Is Gonna Come.'" *The New Yorker*, March 17. Accessed November 29, 2019. https://www.newyorker.com/culture/culture-desk/the-unlikely-story-of-a-change-is-gonna-come.

Charles, Ray, and David Ritz. 2004. *Brother Ray: Ray Charles' Own Story*, 3rd Da Capo Press ed. Cambridge, MA: Da Capo Press.

Cohodas, Nadine. 2000. *Spinning Blues into Gold: The Chess Brothers and the Legendary Chess Records*. New York: St. Martin's Press.

Coker, Cheo H. 1995. "Brown Sugar." *Rolling Stone*, September 7. Accessed August 28, 2019. https://www.rollingstone.com/music/music-album-reviews/brown-sugar-2-189501/. A review of D'Angelo's album *Brown Sugar*.

Covarrubias, Amanda, and Catherine Saillant. 2005. "A Release of Doves and Emotions." *Los Angeles Times*, June 14. Accessed January 22, 2020. https://www.latimes.com/archives/la-xpm-2005-jun-14-me-scene14-story.html.

Crouch, Ian. 2015. "Percy Sledge, Pop Miracle." *The New Yorker* online, April 17. Accessed July 23, 2019. https://www.newyorker.com/culture/culture-desk/percy-sledge-pop-miracle.

Dahl, Bill. n.d. "Robert Cray: Artist Biography." *AllMusic*. Accessed August 15, 2019. https://www.allmusic.com/artist/robert-cray-mn0000830425/biography.

Dahl, Bill. 2002. Liner notes for *The Essential Drifters*. CD, Atlantic Records R2 76075.

Dobkin, Matt. 2004. *I Never Loved a Man the Way I Loved You: Respect, and the Making of a Soul Music Masterpiece*. New York: St. Martin's Press.

Dolan, Jon. 2018. "Aretha's Greatest Albums: *I Never Loved a Man the Way I Love You* (1967)." *Rolling Stone* online. August 17. Accessed July 26, 2019. https://www.rollingstone.com/music/music-features/aretha-franklin-never-loved-man-way-love-you-712306/.

Douglas, Tony. 2005. *Jackie Wilson: Lonely Teardrops*. New York: Taylor & Francis.

Dozier, Lamont, with Scott B. Bomar. 2019. *How Sweet It Is: A Songwriter's Reflections on Music, Motown and the Mystery of the Muse*. New York: BMG Books.

Dr. Licks. 1989. *Standing in the Shadow of Motown*. Milwaukee, WI: Hal Leonard. A biography and assessment of the work of Motown studio electric bassist James Jamerson. The book includes transcriptions of some of Jamerson's best-known bass lines.

Duber, Vinnie. 2018. "'Sweet Home Chicago,' 'New York Groove' or 'TSOP?' Who Gets the Encore After Manny Machado's Free-Agent Tour?" *NBC Sports Chicago*. December 20. Accessed December 23, 2019. https://www.nbcsports.com/chicago/white-sox/sweet-home-chicago-new-york-groove-or-tsop-who-gets-encore-after-manny-machado-free-agent-tour-mlb-rumors-hot-stove-white-sox-yankees-philadelphia-phillies.

Early, Gerald. 1995. *One Nation under a Groove: Motown and American Culture*. Hopewell, NJ: The Ecco Press.

Edmonds, Ben. 2001. *What's Going On: Marvin Gaye & the Last Days of the Motown Sound*. Edinburgh: Canongate.

Edmonds, Ben. 2002. Liner notes for *What's Going On*. CD, Motown 440 064 022 2.

Ehrlich, David. 2015. "James Bond Movie Theme Songs, Ranked Worst to Best." *Rolling Stone*, November 2. Accessed August 21, 2019. http://www.rollingstone.com/movies/lists/james-bond-movie-theme-songs-ranked-worst-to-best-20151102.

Emerson, Ken. 2006. *Always Magic in the Air: The Bomp and Brilliance of the Brill Building Era*. New York: Penguin Books.

Erickson, Brad. n.d. "'People Get Ready'—The Impressions (1965)." Library of Congress. Accessed August 1, 2019. http://www.loc.gov/static/programs/national-recording-preservation-board/documents/PeopleGetReady.pdf.

Erlewine, Stephen Thomas. n.d.-a. "Bill Withers: *Still Bill*." *AllMusic*. Accessed October 18, 2019. https://www.allmusic.com/album/still-bill-mw0000311926.

Erlewine, Stephen Thomas. n.d.-b. "Whitney Houston: *The Preacher's Wife*." *AllMusic*. Accessed December 17, 2019. https://www.allmusic.com/album/the-preachers-wife-mw0000613508.

Escot, Colin. 2000. Liner notes for *From Elvis in Memphis*. CD, RCA 07863 67932 2.

Everitt, Lauren. 2012. "Whitney Houston and the Art of Melisma." *BBC News Magazine*. February 15. Accessed December 17, 2019. https://www.bbc.com/news/magazine-17039208.

Faulkner, Sam. 2005. "Alicia Keys: Songs in A Minor." *New Musical Express (NME)*. September 12. Accessed November 13, 2019. https://www.nme.com/reviews/album/reviews-nme-5498.

Fearn-Banks, Kathleen. 2006. *The A to Z of African-American Television*. Lanham, MD: Scarecrow Press.

Ferris, Jean. 2014. *America's Musical Landscape*, 7th ed. New York: McGraw-Hill.

Fournier, Rasa. 2007. "Yvonne Elliman: Still Rockin'." *MidWeek*. May 11, Accessed August 27, 2019. http://archives.midweek.com/content/story/theweekend_coverstory/yvonne_elliman_still_rockin/.

Fox, Jon Hartley. 2009. *King of the Queen City: The Story of King Records*. Urbana: University of Illinois Press.

Fricke, David. 2011. "Leiber and Stoller: *Rolling Stone*'s 1990 Interview with the Songwriting Legends." *Rolling Stone*, August 22. Accessed September 9, 2019. www.rollingstone.com/music/news/leiber-stoller-rolling-stones-1990-interview-with-the-songwriting-legends-20110822.

Galloway, A. Scott. 2001. Liner notes for *Petals: The Minnie Riperton Collection*. Two CDs, The Right Stuff 72435-29343-2-4

Garvey, Marianne. 2019. "Mariah Carey's 'All I Want for Christmas Is You' Hits No. 1 for the First Time Ever." *CNN.com*, December 16. Accessed December 16, 2019. https://www.cnn.com/2019/12/16/entertainment/mariah-carey-all-i-want-for-christmas-is-you-trnd/index.html.

Gaye, Frankie, and Fred E. Basten. 2003. *Marvin Gaye, My Brother*. San Francisco, CA: Backbeat Books.

Gaye, Marvin. 1973. Liner notes for *Let's Get It On*. LP, Tamla T 329-V1. Reissued on CD as Motown 440 064 021-2, 2002.

George, Nelson. 1988. *The Death of Rhythm and Blues*. New York: Pantheon Books.

George, Nelson. 2007. *Where Did Out Love Go?: The Rise and Fall of the Motown Sound*. Champaign: University of Illinois Press.

Getlen, Larry. 2014. "Ahead of the 'Pack': How the Shangri-Las Created Punk." *New York Post*, May 17. Accessed December 18, 2019. https://nypost.com/2014/05/17/ahead-of-the-pack-how-the-shangri-las-created-punk/.

Gibney, Alex, director. 2014. *Mr. Dynamite: The Rise of James Brown*. DVD. Santa Monica, CA: Universal Music Enterprises 602547506429. A *HBO Documentary Films* biography of James Brown and his work into the 1970s.

Gillett, Charlie. 1974. *Making Tracks: Atlantic Records and the Growth of a Multi-Billion-Dollar Industry*. New York: E.P. Dutton.

Gillett, Charlie. 1996. *The Sound of the City: The Rise of Rock and Roll*, 2nd ed. New York: Da Capo Press.

Gioia, Ted. 2016. *How to Listen to Jazz*. New York: Basic Books.

Gleiberman, Owen. 2018. "Film Review: *Superfly*." *Variety*. June 12. Accessed September 4, 2019. https://variety.com/2018/film/reviews/superfly-review-trevor-jackson-1202841165/.

Goldman, Russell. 2009. "The Accident that Sparked Jackson's Addiction: Michael Jackson Said Injuries from this 1984 Fire Led to His Drug Addiction." ABC News, July 15. Accessed January 22, 2020. https://abcnews.go.com/Business/MichaelJackson/story?id=8092565&page=1.

Gordon, Robert. 2015. *Respect Yourself: Stax Records and the Soul Explosion*, paperback ed. New York: Bloomsbury.

Gordy, Berry. 1994. *To Be Loved: The Music, the Magic, the Memories of Motown, an Autobiography*. New York: Time Warner Books.

Greenblat, Mike. 2015. "The Tragic Life of Tammi Terrell." *Goldmine*, April 9. Accessed October 23, 2019. https://www.goldminemag.com/articles/tragic-life-tammi-terrell.

Greenfield, Robert. 2011. *The Last Sultan: The Life and Times of Ahmet Ertegun*. New York: Simon & Schuster. A biography of the head of Atlantic Records, one of the major soul labels.

Grimes, William. 2016. "Lonnie Mack, Singer and Guitarist Who Pioneered Blues-Rock, Dies at 74." *The New York Times*, April 22. Accessed October 9, 2019. https://www.nytimes.com/2016/04/23/arts/music/lonnie-mack-singer-and-guitarist-who-pioneered-blues-rockdies-at-74.html.

Guralnick, Peter. 1986. *Sweet Soul Music*. New York: HarperCollins Publishers.

Harrell, Phil. 2018. "'Fight the Power': A Tale of 2 Anthems (With the Same Name)." *National Public Radio*, December 7. Accessed December 20, 2019. https://www.npr.org/2018/12/07/673845242/fight-the-power-american-anthem-public-enemy-isley-brothers. In addition to information about the Isley Brothers' and Public Enemy's songs "Fight the Power" and transcriptions from an interview with Ernie Isley and Chuck D, this webpage contains a link to a recording of the NPR feature on the songs.

Harvey, Josephine. 2019. "It's Only October but It Seems All We Want for Christmas Is Mariah Carey." *Huffington Post*, October 23. Accessed October 23, 2019. https://www.huffpost.com/entry/christmas-mariah-carey-top-500-itunes_n_5dafe681e4b0422422cdd544?ncid=NEWSSTAND0001.

Hildebrand, Lee. 1994. *Stars of Soul and Rhythm & Blues*. New York: Billboard Books.

Hinckley, David. 1992. "How Spike Lee Snagged Sam Cooke's Anthem." *Chicago Tribune*, December 10. Accessed December 11, 2019. https://www.chicagotribune.com/news/ct-xpm-1992-12-10-9204220646-story.html.

Hirshey, Gerri. 1984. *Nowhere to Run: The Story of Soul Music*. New York: Crown Publishers.

Hollywood Walk of Fame Website. 2019. "Jackie Wilson." *Hollywood Walk of Fame*. Accessed November 7, 2019. http://www.walkoffame.com/jackie-wilson.

International Musician. 2019. "Kenny Seymour: Music Director Underscores the Universality of Music." *International Musician*, November, 18–19. A profile of the music director of the musical *Ain't Too Proud to Beg: The Life and Times of the Temptations*.

Irby, Samantha. 2019. "*TIME* Entertainer of the Year—Lizzo." *TIME*, December 11. Accessed December 28, 2019. https://time.com/entertainer-of-the-year-2019-lizzo/.

Ivory, Steven. 2003. Liner notes for *Lionel Richie: The Definitive Collection*. CD. Motown 440 048 140-2.

Jackson, John A. 2004. *A House on Fire: The Rise and Fall of Philadelphia Soul*. New York: Oxford University Press.

Jet. 1986. "Nina Simone Reveals: 'Mississippi Goddam' Song 'Hurt My Career.'" *Jet*. March 24: 54–55. Also available online. Accessed July 11, 2020. https://books.google.com/books?id=C7EDAAAAMBAJ&source=gbs_all_issues_r&cad=1.

Katzif, Mike. 2007. "How American Idol Uses (and Abuses) Melisma." *National Public Radio*. January 11. Accessed October 14, 2019. https://www.npr.org/templates/story/story.php?storyId=6791133.

Kehe, John. 2009. "Michael Jackson's Famous Glove: Where It All Started." *The Christian Science Monitor*, June 26. Accessed December 23, 2019. https://www.csmonitor.com/USA/2009/0626/p02s19-usgn.html.

Kellman, Andy. n.d.-a. "Alicia Keys: Here." *AllMusic*. Accessed November 13, 2019. https://www.allmusic.com/album/here-mw0002987407

Kellman, Andy. n.d.-b. "Kahlid: Free Spirit." *AllMusic*. Accessed October 4, 2019. https://www.allmusic.com/album/free-spirit-mw0003260242.

Kemp, Mark. 2009. "From Elvis in Memphis." *Rolling Stone* online, August 5. Accessed August 2, 2019. https://www.rollingstone.com/music/music-album-reviews/from-elvis-in-memphis-250301/.

The Kennedy Center Website. n.d. "Ray Charles, Biography." The Kennedy Center. Accessed December 13, 2019. https://www.kennedy-center.org/artist/A3706.

Knight, Gladys. 1997. *Between Each Line of Pain and Glory: My Life Story*. New York: Hyperion.

Kornhaber, Spencer. 2015. "How 'When a Man Loves a Woman' Captured the Terror of Love." *The Atlantic*. April 14. Accessed December 10, 2019. https://www.theatlantic.com/entertainment/archive/2015/04/when-a-man-loves-a-woman-and-the-terror-of-true-love/390522/.

Kot, Greg. 2011. "Valerie Simpson on Nick Ashford: 'I'm Not Used to Him Not Being Here Yet.'" *Chicago Tribune*, November 17. Accessed October 21, 2019. https://www.chicagotribune.com/entertainment/ct-xpm-2011-11-17-ct-ent-1117-valerie-simpson-20111117-story.html.

Kot, Greg. 2014. *I'll Take You There: Mavis Staples, the Staple Singers, and the March up Freedom's Highway*. New York: Scribner.

Kreps, Daniel. 2015. "'Stand By Me' Singer Ben E. King Dead at 76." *Rolling Stone*. May 1. Accessed December 6, 2019. https://www.rollingstone.com/music/music-news/stand-by-me-singer-ben-e-king-dead-at-76-79694/.

Lang, Cady. 2018. "Mariah Carey's New Year's Eve Tea Disaster Is the Hottest Meme of 2018 So Far." *Time*, January 2. Accessed October 14, 2019. https://time.com/5084034/mariah-carey-hot-tea-meme-nye-2018/.

Leeds, Alan. 2004. Liner notes for *Live at the Apollo*. CD, Polydor B0001715-02.

Lovel, Jim. 2005. "More of 'My Girl' for Little Debbie." *Adweek*. August 16. Accessed December 10, 2019. https://www.adweek.com/brand-marketing/more-my-girl-little-debbie-81102/.

MacMahon, Bernard, director. 2015. *American Epic*. PBS television series.

Marchese, Joe. 2016. Liner notes for *Land of 1000 Dances: The Complete Atlantic Singles, Vol. 1*. CD, Atlantic Records/Real Gone Music RGM-0487.

Mason, Stewart. n.d. "Sister Rosetta Tharpe: Complete Recorded Works, Vol. 2 (1942–1944)." *AllMusic.com*. Accessed December 12, 2019. https://

www.allmusic.com/album/complete-recorded-works-vol-2-1942-1944-mw0000178723.

Mayfield, Todd. 2017. *Traveling Soul: The Life of Curtis Mayfield*. Chicago, IL: Chicago Review Press.

McBride, James. 2016. *Kill 'Em and Leave: Searching for James Brown and the American Soul*. New York: Spiegel & Grau.

McDonough, Jimmy. 2017. *Soul Survivor: A Biography of Al Green*. New York: Da Capo Press.

Medley, Bill, and Mike Marino. 2014. *The Time of My Life: A Righteous Brother's Memoir*. Boston, MA: Da Capo Press.

Michaels, Sean. 2009. "Etta James: I'm Gonna Whup Beyoncé's Ass." *The Guardian*, February 6. Accessed September 11, 2019. https://www.theguardian.com/music/2009/feb/06/beyonce-etta-james-barack-obama?fb=native.

Michaud, Chris. 2009. "Michael Jackson's Glove Sells for $350,000 at Auction." *Reuters*, November 22. Accessed December 23, 2019. https://www.reuters.com/article/us-jackson-glove/michael-jacksons-glove-sells-for-350000-at-auction-idUSTRE5AL02A20091123.

Moore, Sam, and Dave Marsh. 1997. *Sam and Dave: An Oral History*. New York: Avon Books.

Myers, Marc. 2016. *Anatomy of a Song: The Oral History of 45 Iconic Hits that Changed Rock, R&B, and Pop*. New York: Grove Press.

Myers, Marc. 2018. "The Story Behind 'Ain't No Mountain High Enough.'" *The Wall Street Journal*. January 29. Accessed October 23, 2019. https://www.wsj.com/articles/the-story-behind-aint-no-mountain-high-enough-1517235736.

Myrie, Russell. 2008. *Don't Rhyme for the Sake of Riddlin': The Authorised Story of Public Enemy*. Edinburgh: Cannongate.

National Recording Preservation Board of the Library of Congress. n.d. "Complete National Recording Registry Listing." Accessed November 8, 2019. https://www.loc.gov/programs/national-recording-preservation-board/recording-registry/complete-national-recording-registry-listing/.

Neal, Mark Anthony. 1999. *What the Music Said: Black Popular Music and Black Public Culture*. New York: Routledge.

The New York Times News Service. 1987. "'Quiet Storm' Radio Format Weathers Well with 'Beautiful Black.'" *Chicago Tribune*. March 5. Accessed December 4, 2019. https://www.chicagotribune.com/news/ct-xpm-1987-03-05-8701180072-story.html.

Olson, Cathy Applefeld. 2015. "Carole King, George Lucas & More Feted at 2015 Kennedy Center Honors." *Billboard*. December 7. Accessed November 11, 2019. https://www.billboard.com/articles/news/6786000/kennedy-center-honors-2015-carole-king-george-lucas.

Orosa, Rosalinda L. 2014. "Mariah's Influence on Today's Artists." *The Philippine Star*. September 14. Accessed October 14, 2019. http://www.philstar

.com/entertainment/2014/09/14/1368802/mariahs-influence-todays-artists.

O'Shea, Mick. 2012. *Amy Winehouse: A Losing Game*. London: Plexus.

Pareles, Jon. 2016. "John Legend: Love Songs That Bow to Dark Shadows." *The New York Times*. November 30. Accessed November 22, 2019. https://www.nytimes.com/2016/11/30/arts/music/john-legend-darkness-and-light-review.html.

Pegg, Nicholas. 2016. *The Complete David Bowie*. London: Titan Books.

Perone, James E. 2006a. *The Sound of Stevie Wonder: His Words and Music*. Santa Barbara, CA: Praeger Publishers.

Perone, James E. 2006b. *The Words and Music of Carole King*. Santa Barbara, CA: Praeger Publishers.

Perone, James E. 2008. *The Words and Music of Prince*. Santa Barbara, CA: Praeger Publishers.

Perone, James E. 2012. *The Album: A Guide to Pop Music's Most Provocative, Influential, and Important Creations*. Santa Barbara, CA: Praeger Publishers.

Perone, James E. 2016. *Smash Hits: The 100 Songs That Defined America*. Santa Barbara, CA: Greenwood Press.

Perone, James E. 2018. *Listen to Pop!: Exploring a Musical Genre*. Santa Barbara, CA: Greenwood Press.

Perone, James E. 2019. *Listen to the Blues!: Exploring a Musical Genre*. Santa Barbara, CA: Greenwood Press.

Perone, James E. 2020. *Listen to Movie Musicals!: Exploring a Musical Genre*. Santa Barbara, CA: Greenwood Press.

Pile, Tatiana. 2020. "3 Natural Hair Bloggers Reminisce About the Early Days of the Movement." *Huffington Post*. February 3. Accessed February 3, 2020. https://www.huffpost.com/entry/natural-hair-internet-pioneers-curly-nikki-nappturality-brosiaaa_n_5e2b2a19c5b6779e9c322c44.

Posner, Gerald. 2002. *Motown: Music, Money, Sex, and Power*. New York: Random House.

Quinn, Eithne. 2012. "'Tryin' to Get Over': *Super Fly*, Black Politics, and Post-Civil Rights Film Enterprise." *Cinema Journal* 49, no. 2, (Winter): 86–105.

The Recording Academy. n.d. "Grammy Hall of Fame List." Accessed December 14, 2019. https://www.grammy.com/grammys/awards/hall-of-fame.

Remnick, David. 2016. "Soul Survivor: The Revival and Hidden Treasure of Aretha Franklin." *The New Yorker*. March 28. Accessed November 11, 2019. https://www.newyorker.com/magazine/2016/04/04/aretha-franklins-american-soul.

Ritz, David. 1999. "Soul Music." *Encyclopedia Britannica* online. Accessed January 21, 2020. https://www.britannica.com/art/soul-music.

Ritz, David. 2002. "Remembering Miracles." Liner notes to *Smokey Robinson & the Miracles: Ooo Baby Baby: The Anthology*. Two CDs, Motown 440 064 481-2.

Ritz, David. 2003. *Divided Soul: The Life of Marvin Gaye*, reprint ed. Cambridge, MA: Da Capo Press.

Ritz, David. 2014. *Respect: The Life of Aretha Franklin*. New York: Little, Brown and Company.

Roberts, Randall. 2015. "Appreciation: Percy Sledge's 'When a Man Loves a Woman,' a Great American Ballad." *Los Angeles Times* online. April 14. Accessed December 2, 2019. https://www.latimes.com/entertainment/music/posts/la-et-ms-percy-sledge-when-a-man-loves-a-woman-great-american-ballad-20150414-story.html.

Robertson, Robbie, Jim Guerinot, Sebastian Robertson, and Jared Levine. 2013. *Legends, Icons & Rebels: Music That Changed the World*. Plattsburgh, NY: Tundra Books. This book, aimed at teen readers, profiles several soul legends and their contributions. The volume also includes two CDs.

The Rock and Roll Hall of Fame. 1988. "The Supremes." Accessed October 21, 2019. https://www.rockhall.com/inductees/supremes.

The Rock and Roll Hall of Fame. 2015. "Bill Withers." Accessed October 18, 2019. https://www.rockhall.com/inductees/bill-withers.

The Rock and Roll Hall of Fame. 2018. "Nina Simone." Accessed November 8, 2019. https://www.rockhall.com/nominee/nina-simone.

Rolling Stone. 2011. "500 Greatest Songs of All Time." *Rolling Stone*. April 7. Accessed November 29, 2019. www.rollingstone.com/music/lists/the-500-greatest-songs-of-all-time-20110407.

Rolling Stone. 2012. "500 Greatest Albums of All Time." *Rolling Stone*. May 31. Accessed December 18, 2019. www.rollingstone.com/music/lists/500-greatest-albums-of-all-time-20120531.

Romanowski, Patricia, and Holly George-Warren, eds. 1995. *New Rolling Stone Encyclopedia of Rock and Roll*. New York: Fireside.

Rosen, Jodie. 2010. "Wake Up!" *Rolling Stone*. September 20. Accessed November 22, 2019. https://www.rollingstone.com/music/music-album-reviews/wake-up-185174/.

Ross, Graeme. 2017. "Otis Redding Playlist: 'Stompers' and Heartbreakers from the King of Soul." *The Independent*. December 8. Accessed November 15, 2019. https://www.independent.co.uk/arts-entertainment/music/otis-redding-playlist-stax-soul-a8096616.html.

Scaggs, Austin. 2009. "King of Blue-Eyed Soul: Rod Stewart Covers the R&B Greats." *Rolling Stone*. November 12. Accessed December 10, 2019. https://www.rollingstone.com/music/music-news/king-of-blue-eyed-soul-rod-stewart-covers-the-rb-greats-76557/.

Shaw, Arnold. 1986. *Honkers and Shouters: The Golden Years of Rhythm and Blues*, paperback ed. New York: Macmillan.

Sigerson, Davitt. 1987. "Michael Jackson: Bad." *Rolling Stone*. October 22. Accessed August 29, 2019. https://www.rollingstone.com/music/music-album-reviews/bad-251305/.

Smith, Mychal Denzel. 2018. "Curtis Mayfield: Super Fly." *Pitchfork*, June 17. Accessed August 30, 2019. https://pitchfork.com/reviews/albums/curtis-mayfield-super-fly/.

Som, Nicholas. 2019. "Soul Shelter." *Preservation* 71, no. 3 (Summer): 9. A brief report on preservation efforts on Nina Simone's childhood home.

Songfacts.com. n.d. "'When a Man Loves a Woman' by Percy Sledge." *Songfacts.com*. Accessed December 10, 2019. https://www.songfacts.com/facts/percy-sledge/when-a-man-loves-a-woman.

Songwriters Hall of Fame. 2012. "'Stand by Me.'" Songhall.com. Accessed September 9, 2019. https://www.songhall.org/awards/winner/stand_by_me.

Sullivan, Caroline. 2006. "John Legend, Once Again." *The Guardian*. October 20. Accessed December 2, 2019. https://www.theguardian.com/music/2006/oct/20/popandrock.urban.

Taylor, Clarke. 1986. "Michael Jackson Signs up with Pepsi." *Los Angeles Times*, May 7. Accessed January 18, 2020. https://www.latimes.com/archives/la-xpm-1986-05-07-ca-3866-story.html.

Thorn, Tracey. 2016. "From Adele to Mariah Carey: Why We Love Big Voices." *The Telegraph*. February 21. Accessed October 14, 2019. http://www.telegraph.co.uk/music/what-to-listen-to/from-shirley-bassey-to-adele-why-we-love-big-voices/.

Thornburg, Rebecca. 2018. "Buffalo 'Shout' Song Unites Generations of Passionate Bills Fans." *WKBW.com*, August 29. Accessed December 18, 2019. https://www.wkbw.com/news/buffalo-shout-song-unites-generations-of-passionate-bills-fans.

Tillet, Salamishah. 2010. "Freedom Then, Freedom Now!" Liner notes to John Legend: *Wake Up!* CD, Columbia Records 88697 37082 2.

Touré. 2018. "The Andantes: The Girl Group Left Behind." *AARP The Magazine*. November 28. Accessed November 15, 2019. https://www.aarp.org/entertainment/music/info-2018/motown-girl-group-the-andantes.html.

Trust, Gary. 2016. "Ask *Billboard*: Is 'I Will Always Love You' the Most Enduring Hit of the Rock Era?" *Billboard*. October 4. Accessed August 29, 2019. https://www.billboard.com/articles/columns/chart-beat/7533218/ask-billboard-is-i-will-always-love-you-the-most-enduring-hit-of. A follow-up to the author's original 2012 article in the wake of the song's 2016 reemergence on the country charts.

Trynka, Paul. 2014. *Brian Jones: The Making of the Rolling Stones*. New York: Plume.

Unterberger, Richie. n.d. "Nina Simone: Broadway—Blues—Ballads." *AllMusic*. Accessed November 8, 2019. https://www.allmusic.com/album/broadway-blues-ballads-mw0000103984.

USA Today. 2006. "MTV at 25: Moments of Sex, Drugs, and Rock and Roll." *USA Today*. July 28. Accessed November 4, 2019. https://usatoday30.usatoday.com/life/television/news/2006-07-27-mtv-cover_x.htm.

Variety. 2019. "Jennifer Hudson Commands 'Respect' as Aretha Franklin in First Teaser." *CNBC.com*. December 23. Accessed December 23, 2019. https://www.nbcnews.com/news/nbcblk/jennifer-hudson-commands-respect-aretha-franklin-first-teaser-n1106276.

The Vocal Group Hall of Fame. n.d. "Inductees." Accessed January 20, 2020. http://vocalgroup.org/inductees/.

Wald, Gayle. 2007. *Shout, Sister, Shout!: The Untold Story of Rock-and-Roll Trailblazer Sister Rosetta Tharpe*. Boston, MA: Beacon Press.

Ward, Thomas. n.d. "'Dr. Feelgood.'" *AllMusic*. Accessed July 29, 2019. https://www.allmusic.com/song/dr-feelgood-love-is-a-serious-business-mt0004001631.

Warner, Jay. 1998. "The Supremes." The Vocal Group Hall of Fame. Accessed October 21, 2019. http://vocalgroup.org/inductees/the-supremes/.

Werner, Craig. 2004. *Higher Ground: Stevie Wonder, Aretha Franklin, Curtis Mayfield, and the Rise of Fall of American Soul*. New York: Crown Publishers.

Werner, Craig. 2006. *A Change Is Gonna Come: Music, Race & the Soul of America*. Ann Arbor: University of Michigan Press.

White, Adam, and Barney Ales. 2016. *Motown: The Sound of Young America*. New York: Thames & Hudson.

Wilner, Paul. 1977. "Isley Brothers: A Family Affair." *The New York Times*, May 13. Accessed December 26, 2019. https://www.nytimes.com/1977/03/13/archives/westchester-weekly-isley-brothers-a-family-affair.html.

Wilson, Mary, with Marc Bego. 2019. *Supreme Glamour*. New York: Thames & Hudson.

Wolf, Daniel. 1995. *You Send Me: The Life and Times of Sam Cooke*. New York: William Morrow & Co.

Wright, Vickie, Louvain Demps, Marlene Barrow-Tate, and Jackie Hicks. 2007. *Motown from the Background: The Authorized Biography of the Andantes*. East Sussex, UK: Bank House Books.

Zappa, Frank, with Peter Occhiogrosso. 1989. *The Real Frank Zappa Book*. New York: Poseidon Press.

Index

"ABC," 93
Abramson, Herb, 12. *See also* Atlantic Records
Adderley, Cannonball, 5, 76
Adele, 6, 28, 39, 84, 85
Adler, Lou, 122
Aguilera, Christiana, 40
"Ain't No Mountain High Enough," 15–17, 24, 179–180, 189, 194
"Ain't No Sunshine," 8, 161–162, 164
"Ain't Nothing Like the Real Thing," 15, 24, 189
"(Ain't That) Good News," 48–49, 50, 52
Ain't That Good News (Sam Cooke album), 48–52
"Ain't Too Proud to Beg," 153, 154
Ain't Too Proud to Beg: The Life and Times of the Temptations, 155, 186, 191
"Air on the G String," 141
Al Green Explores Your Mind (Al Green album), 75, 180
"All I Could Do Was Cry," 96
"All I Want for Christmas Is You," 41–42
"All Night Long (All Night)," 46, 47
All That Jazz, 57

All the Way (Etta James album), 98
"All the Way Down," 97–98
"Alone at Last," 160
Alpert, Herb, 122
"Alright," 53
"Amen," 87
America: A Tribute to Heroes, 168
American Idol, 40–41
American Teen (Khalid album), 10
"And When I Die," 27
The Andantes, 7
Angelou, Maya, 99
The Animals, 138
"Another Saturday Night," 50, 52
Anthony, Ray, 19, 97
Applebaum, Stan, 58
Archer, Luther, 55
Archer, Rodney, 55
"Are You Sure," 149
Armstrong, Louis "Satchmo," 52, 169
A$AP Rocky, 101
Ashford, Nickolas, 15–17, 179–180
Ashman, Howard, 176
"At Last," 19–20, 96–97, 139, 190–191
At Last! (Etta James album), 96
Atkins, Cholly, 11
Atlantic Records, 4, 6, 11, 12, 22, 44, 75–76, 114, 135, 144

Austin Powers in Goldmember, 18, 19
Aykroyd, Dan, 45, 133, 136, 177, 179

"Baby, Baby, Baby," 61
"Baby Boy," 18
Baby Huey & the Babysitters, 109
"Baby Love," 151
"Baby Workout," 159
Babyface, 30–31, 84
Bach, Johann Sebastian, 141
Bacharach, Burt, 76, 145
Back in Memphis (Elvis Presley album), 117–119
"Back in My Arms Again," 151
"Back Stabbers," 12
"Back to Black," 26, 27
Back to Black (Amy Winehouse album), 27
"Backlash Blues," 137
The Backstreet Boys, 30
"Bad," 95
Bad (Michael Jackson album), 95
"Bad Girl," 130
Bahler, Tom, 94
Baker, Anita, 132
"Ball of Confusion (That's What the World Is Today)," 154
Ballard, Florence, 150, 175. See also The Supremes
Ballard, Hank, and the Midnighters, 3, 96
"Ballerina Girl," 46
Banks, Homer, 148, 149, 150
The Bar-Kays, 6–7, 76
Barrow, Marlene, 7. See also The Andantes
Barry, John, 150
Basie, William "Count," 169
Bass, Fontella, 11
Bassey, Shirley, 28
Battiste, Harold, 51

Be Altitude: Respect Yourself (Staple Singers album), 147–150
"Beat It," 94–95
The Beatles, 25, 28, 43, 44, 89, 117, 131, 143, 150, 172
"Beautiful," 81
Beautiful: The Carole King Musical, 174, 191
"Beauty Is Only Skin Deep," 153, 154
Beck, Jeff, 188
The Bee Gees, 26
Bell, Al, 13, 147, 148, 187
Bell, Thom, 12
Bell, William, 122
Belushi, John, 45, 133, 136, 177, 179
Benson, George, 57, 84, 163, 164
Benson, Obie, 69
Berlin, Irving, 52
Berns, Bert, 120–121
Berry, Chuck, 11, 117, 190
The Best Little Whorehouse in Texas, 5, 84
"Best Thing That Ever Happened to Me," 104, 105
Beyoncé, 9–10, 18–20, 39, 40, 84, 97, 190–191. See also Destiny's Child
"Big, Blonde and Beautiful," 177
The Big Chill, 143
The Big Three, 44, 117
"Billie Jean," 94, 95, 183, 185
"Bills, Bills, Bills," 18
Birdsong, Cindy, 150. See also The Supremes
"Black Man," 171
Blakey, Art, 5
Blige, Mary J., 25, 174, 188
The Blind Boys of Alabama, 188
"Blood on the Leaves," 140
Blood, Sweat & Tears, 26, 27, 173
Bloom, Bobby, 150
"Blowin' in the Wind," 69, 164, 166–167
Blue Note Records, 5

The Blues Brothers, 64, 133, 179
The Bodyguard, 5, 84
Bolton, Michael, 6, 20–21, 25
"Boogie Chillen," 157
Booker T. & the M.G.'s, 6, 11–12, 74
Boone, Pat, 177
Bowie, David, 12, 20–21, 23
Boyz II Men, 29–32, 40, 155, 181, 189, 196
Braxton, Toni, 24, 189
"Breakfast in Bed," 145
"Brick House," 46, 48
Bricusse, Leslie, 137
"Bridge over Troubled Water," 16, 162–163
Briefcase Full of Blues (Blues Brothers album), 133
Brigati, Eddie, 22. *See also* The Rascals
Brill Building songwriters, 57, 172
"Bring It on Home to Me," 62
"Bring the Boys Home," 88
Bristol, Johnny, 17
Broadway—Blues—Ballads (Nina Simone album), 138
Brown, Georgia, 129
Brown, James, 9, 25–26, 32–39, 115, 130, 179, 180, 182
Brown, Roy, 2–3
Brown, Ruth, 12
Brown Sugar (D'Angelo album), 52–56, 80
"Brown Sugar," 53
Browne, Jackson, 8
Brunswick Records, 160, 161
Bryant, Eldridge "Al," 153. *See also* The Temptations
Bryant, Gianna, 31–32, 196
Bryant, Kobe, 31–32, 196
Buddah Records, 105
Buffalo Bills, 89, 178
Burch, Elder J.E., 1–2
Burke, Solomon, 119, 120–121
Burleigh, Henry Thacker, 1

Burns, Ralph, 172
Butler, Jerry, 121
"By the Light of the Silvery Moon," 160
"By the Time I Get to Phoenix," 6, 13, 75, 77–78
Byrd, Gary, 168, 171

Cadillac Records, 10, 19, 20, 97, 186, 190–191
"Caged Bird," 99
Calloway, Cab, 179
Cameron, G. C., 32
Campbell, Glen, 6, 78, 88, 188
"Can I Touch You . . . There?," 25
"Can't Take My Eyes off of You," 83
Captain & Tennille, 131
Carey, Mariah, 31, 39–42, 47, 84, 85
Carmichael, Hoagy, 49, 58, 103, 159
Carnes, Kim, 46–47
Carter, A. P., 5
Cavaliere, Felix, 22. *See also* The Rascals
"Chains," 172
Chalmers, Charles, 6, 73, 74, 77
The Chambers Brothers, 188
"A Change Is Gonna Come," 51, 52, 62, 63, 64, 120, 191–194
Charles, Ray, 4–5, 12, 18, 28, 42–45, 46–47, 48, 50, 60, 103, 117, 140, 156, 177, 179, 182
Chazelle, Damien, 110
Checker, Chubby, 36
Chenier, Clifton, 44–45
Chess, Leonard, 10, 97. *See also* Chess Records
Chess, Phil, 10, 97. *See also* Chess Records
Chess Records, 10, 11, 19, 129
The Chiffons, 27, 176
Chivian, Babe, 120–121
The Chords, 177
The City. *See* King, Carole
Clark, Petula, 144, 188

Clarkson, Geoffrey, 52
Clarkson, Harry, 52
Clarkson, Jeremy, 17, 179–180
Clarkson, Kelly, 40
Cleveland, Al, 69, 131
"Cloud Nine," 154
The Coasters, 12
Cochran, Eddie, 117
Cole, Nat King, 52
Columbia Records, 41, 61
"Come Get to This," 67
"Come See About Me," 151
The Commodores, 8, 45–48
Commodores, 46
Condon, Bill, 19
"Contusion," 169
Cook, Peter, 180
Cooke, Sam, 4, 48–52, 62, 101, 119, 120, 121, 122, 133, 156, 168, 191–194
The Cookies, 25, 26, 27, 29, 145, 172, 176, 191
Cooley High, 196
Coolio, 170–171, 189
Cosby, Bill, 181
Cosby, Henry, 131, 164, 165
"Could It Be I'm Falling in Love," 194
Covay, Don, 114, 149
Cox, Jimmy, 140
Cray, Robert, 4
"Crazy in Love," 18
Creatore, Luigi. *See* Hugo & Luigi
Creed, Linda, 12, 84
Creedence Clearwater Revival, 105, 138–139
The Crew-Cuts, 177
Crewe, Bob, 83
Criminal Minds, 97
Cropper, Steve, 25, 115, 120, 122, 135, 136. *See also* Booker T. & the M.G.'s
"Cruisin'," 55
Crutcher, Bettye, 148

"Cry," 6, 21
The Cryin' Shames, 57
The Crystals, 25
Curtin, Jane, 45, 177
Cuz I Love You (Lizzo album), 10

"Dancing in the Streets," 152
D'Angelo, 52–56, 80
Dangerous (Michael Jackson album), 95–96
Dangerously in Love (Beyoncé album), 18
Darkness and Light (John Legend album), 110
The Dave Clark Five, 143
David, Hal, 76, 145
Davis, Billy, 130
Davis, Mac, 118
Day, Bobby, 93
Daydream (Mariah Carey album), 40
The Dells, 11
Demps, Louvain, 7. *See also* The Andantes
Denver, John, 88
Destiny's Child, 18
Diana Ross & the Supremes: Number 1's, 152
The Diary of Alicia Keys (Alicia Keys album), 98, 100
Dick Clark's New Year's Rockin' Eve with Ryan Seacrest, 41
"Didn't It Rain," 156
A Different World, 181
Dion, Céline, 84, 174
"Distant Lover," 67–68
Dixon, Willie, 11, 190
"Do It to Me," 47
"Do Right Woman—Do Right Man," 62
"(Do the) Mashed Potatoes," 36
Do the Right Thing, 90
"Doggin' Around," 159
"Don't Let Me Be Misunderstood," 137, 138

"Don't Let Me Lose This Dream," 61
"Don't Stop 'til You Get Enough," 93–94
"Don't Worry, Be Happy," 181
"Doo Wop (That Thing)," 79, 80–81
The Doobie Brothers, 24, 91
Dorsey, Thomas A., 2, 117, 156
The Dorsey Brothers, 52
Dowd, Tom, 144
"Down by the Riverside," 156
"Down in the Valley," 120–121
Dozier, Lamont, 151–152
"Dr. Feelgood (Love Is a Serious Business)," 61–62
Dreamgirls, 10–11, 19, 175–176, 190
"Drift Away," 193
The Drifters, 56–59, 130, 172, 194
"Drown in My Own Tears," 60–61
"Drunk in Love," 18–19
DuBois, Ja'Nat, 181
Dunbar, Paul Laurence, 99
Dusty in Memphis (Dusty Springfield album), 143–147
Dylan, Bob, 46–47, 69, 88, 127, 164, 166–167, 188

Earl-Jean, 145, 172, 191
"Easy," 46, 47
Easy Mo Bee, 100
Eberle, Ray, 19, 97
"Ebony Eyes," 171
"Eddie, You Should Know Better," 113
"The Edge of a Dream," 127
Edmonds, Kenneth Brian. *See* Babyface
Edwards, Dennis, 153, 154. *See also* The Temptations
Eli and the Thirteenth Confession (Laura Nyro album), 27
"Eli's Coming," 27
Elliman, Yvonne, 26

Ellington, Edward Kennedy "Duke," 169
The Emancipation of Mimi (Mariah Carey album), 40
"End of the Road," 29–30, 189
"Endless Love," 46
Epic Records, 93
Epworth, Paul, 28
Ertegün, Ahmet, 12, 56. *See also* Atlantic Records
The Esquires, 141
Etta James (Etta James album), 97–98
The Everly Brothers, 43, 133
Evers, Medgar, 136
"Every Beat of My Heart," 104
"Every Ghetto, Every City," 82
"Every Time He Comes Around," 128
"Everything Is Everything," 82–83, 107
"Everything's Alright," 26
"Ex-Factor," 80
"Exhale (Shoop Shoop)," 84
Eyen, Tom, 175–176, 190

Fair, Yvonne, 38
The Falcons, 116
"Falling in Love," 51
FAME Studios, 59–60, 74
The Famous Flames. *See* Brown, James
"Fantasy," 40
Father of the Bride II, 19–20, 97
"Feeling Good," 137
Feeling Good: The Very Best of Nina Simone (Nina Simone album), 136–141
The 5th Dimension, 8, 27
"Fight the Power," 89–90, 92
"Final Hour," 81
Fisk University Jubilee Singers, 1
Fitzgerald, Ella, 28, 138
The Five Crowns, 56

Floyd, Eddie, 135
"Flyin' High (In the Friendly Sky)," 70, 71
Fogerty, John, 122. *See also* Creedence Clearwater Revival
"For Better or Worse," 114, 115
"For Once in My Life," 164
"For the Love of You," 91
"Forgive Them Father," 82
Fosse, Bob, 57
The Four Seasons, 29
The Four Tops, 7, 29
Foxx, Jamie, 43, 190
Frank (Amy Winehouse album), 27
Frank, Anne, 100
Franklin, Aretha, 2, 3, 12, 27, 28, 39, 50, 59–65, 84, 88, 97, 99–100, 123–126, 135, 145–146, 171–174, 179, 181, 188, 191, 194
Franklin, Carolyn, 3, 60, 61, 62–63, 124
Franklin, Erma, 3, 60, 124
Franklin, Melvin, 153. *See also* The Temptations
"Freddie's Dead," 112, 113
Free Spirit (Khalid album), 10
Freed, Alan, 3
"Freedom for the Stallion," 24
Friedman, Gary William, 147
From Elvis in Memphis (Elvis Presley album), 117–119
The Fugees, 79, 81
Fulfillingness' First Finale (Stevie Wonder album), 109, 167
The Funk Brothers, 7
"Funky Broadway," 114, 116
Fuqua, Harvey, 17

Gamble, Kenny, 12–13, 93
"Gangsta's Paradise," 170–171, 189
Gardner, Stu, 181
Garmani, Fariba, 184
Garrett, Lee, 166
Gaudio, Bob, 83
Gay, Marvin, Sr., 68

Gaye, Anna Gordy, 68, 70, 71
Gaye, Frankie, 69, 70
Gaye, Marvin, 7, 15–16, 46, 53, 65–72, 91–92, 98, 105, 108, 109, 112, 167, 176, 194
General Public, 188
"Gentle on My Mind," 118
George, Langston. *See* Knight, Gladys, and the Pips
"Georgia on My Mind," 43
Gerry and the Pacemakers, 28, 44
Gershwin, George, 139
"Get a Job," 130
Get Lifted (John Legend album), 107–108
Gilley, Mickey, 103
"The Girl Is Mine," 94
Girl on Fire (Alicia Keys album), 98–99, 101
"Girlfriend," 99
"Give Him a Big Kiss," 25
"Give Me Your Love," 113
The Glenn Miller Orchestra, 19, 97
Glover, Henry, 60
"God Is Love," 71
Goffin, Gerry, 26, 27, 36, 57, 144, 145, 146, 171–172, 173, 191
"Going to a Go-Go," 132
"Gold Digger," 43
Golde, Franne, 46
"Golden Years," 23
"Goldfinger," 28
Golding, Larry, 110
Gonder, Lucas "Fats," 33
"Good as Hell," 10
"Good Lovin'," 22
"Good Rocking Tonight," 2–3
"Good Times," 49–50, 52, 62
"Goodnight Baby," 135
Gordon, Mack, 97
Gordy, Gwen, 67
Gordy, Berry, Jr., 7, 11, 17, 68, 69, 129, 130, 151, 158. *See also* Motown Records
Gordy Records. *See* Motown Records

"The Gospel," 101–102
Gospel Train (Sister Rosetta Tharpe album), 2
"Got a Job," 130
Got to Be There (Michael Jackson album), 93
The Grand Tour, 17, 136, 179
Grande, Ariana, 40
"Grandma's Hands," 161
Grant, Earl, 103
Gray, Dobie, 193
The Greatest, 84
Greatest Hits (Al Green album), 73–75
"Greatest Love of All," 81, 84
Green, Al, 8, 53, 54–55, 73–75, 88, 91, 106–107, 108, 123, 180, 188
Greene, Sandra, 67
"Groovin'," 22
Guest, William. *See* Knight, Gladys, and the Pips

Hackford, Taylor, 42, 190
Hairspray, 10–11, 177
Hairston, Jester, 87
Haley, Bill, & His Comets, 43
Hall & Oates, 6, 12, 20, 23, 30, 133
Hall, Daryl, 23, 46–47. *See also* Hall & Oates
Hall, René, 49, 50, 66–67
Hall, Rick, 60
"Hallelujah, I Love Her So," 4–5, 42
Hampton, Riley, 97
Hancock, Herbie, 5
"The Happening," 151
"Hard Times," 109
Hardaway, Lula Mae, 165, 166
"Harlem Nocturne," 100
"Harlem's Nocturne," 100
Harris, R. H., 133
Harris, Wynonie, 2
Harrison, George, 83. *See also* The Beatles
Hatfield, Bobby, 21. *See also* The Righteous Brothers

Hathaway, Donny, 28, 109
"Have a Talk with God," 168
Hawkins, Screamin' Jay, 138–139
Hayes, Isaac, 5–6, 13, 54, 63, 75–79, 100, 135
"Heart and Soul," 49, 58, 103, 159
"The Heat Is On," 90–91
The Heat Is On (Isley Brothers album), 88–92, 193
"Heat Wave," 152
"Hello" (Adele song), 28–29
"Hello" (Lionel Richie song), 46
"Help the Poor," 4
Hendrix, Jimi, 9
Here (Alicia Keys album), 98–99, 101–102
Herman's Hermits, 122
HI Records, 6, 73–74
"Hi-De-Ho (That Old Sweet Roll)." *See* "That Old Sweet Roll (Hi-De-Ho)"
Hicks, Jackie, 7. *See also* The Andantes
The High Priestess of Soul (Nina Simone album), 140
"Higher," 55
"Higher Ground," 166
Hill, Lauryn, 9, 53, 79–83, 99, 107
HIStory; Past, Present and Future, Book I (Michael Jackson album), 95–96
Hodges, Maron "Teenie," 73–74, 75, 180
"Hold On! I'm Comin'," 133–135
Holiday, Billie, 140
Holland, Brian, 151–152
Holland, Eddie, Jr., 151, 154
Holly, Buddy, 117
"Holy War," 102
"Home (When Shadows Fall)," 52
"Honey Love," 56
Hooker, John Lee, 11, 157, 179
Hooven, Joe, 52
"Hope You Feel Better Love," 91

Hot Buttered Soul (Isaac Hayes album), 75–79, 101
Hot on the Tracks (Commodores album), 46
Houston, Cissy, 8, 60, 84, 106
Houston, Whitney, 5, 39, 81, 83–86
"How Sweet It Is (to Be Loved by You)," 24, 189
Howlin' Wolf, 190
Hudson, Jennifer, 9–10, 19, 25, 84, 85, 188, 190, 191
Huff, Leon, 12–13, 93
Hughes, Langston, 137
Hugo & Luigi, 50
"Human Nature," 94
Hurley, John, 145
"Hyperbolicsyllabicsesquedalymistic," 75, 77

"I Am Woman," 125
"I Been 'Buked and I Been Scorned," 9
"I Can Never Go Home Anymore," 26
"I Can See Clearly Now," 149
"I Can't Get Next to You," 74, 154
"I Can't Help Myself," 176
"I Count the Tears," 56
"I Don't Know," 39
"I Don't Know How to Love Him," 26
"I Don't Mind," 115
"I Don't Want to Hear It Anymore," 146
"I Feel the Earth Move," 27
"I Found a Love," 116
"I Found You," 38
"I Got a Woman," 4–5, 42–43, 48–49, 103, 117, 189
"I Got You (I Feel Good)," 35–39
"I Hear a Symphony," 151
"I Heard It through the Grapevine," 24, 104, 105, 107, 189
"I Just Called to Say I Love You," 128
"I Just Can't Stop Loving You," 95
"I Know Better," 110
"I Know Where I've Been," 177
"I Loves You, Porgy," 137, 139
"I Never Loved a Man (The Way I Love You)," 60, 61
I Never Loved a Man the Way I Love You (Aretha Franklin album), 59–63
"I Put a Spell on You," 137
"I Second That Emotion," 131
"I Thank You," 133, 134, 135
"I Used to Love Him," 81–82
"I Want It That Way," 30
"I Want a Tall Skinny Papa," 156
"I Want You Back," 93
"I Was Made to Love Her," 24, 29, 164, 165–166, 167, 189
"I (Who Have Nothing)," 59
"I Will Always Love You," 5, 84
"I Will Survive," 181
"I Wish," 169–170
"I'd Rather Go Blind," 97
"If I Can't Have You,"
"If I Should Die Tonight," 67
"If I Was Your Woman/Walk on By," 100
"If I Were Your Woman," 104
"I'll Be There," 93
"I'll Go Crazy," 33, 35
"I'll Hold You in My Heart," 118
I'll Make Love to You," 30
"I'll Take You There," 147–149, 187–188
"I'm Going Back Home," 137, 140
"I'm Gonna Cry (Cry Baby)," 114–115
"I'm Gonna Make You Love Me," 151
"I'm Into Something Good," 172
"I'm Just Another Soldier," 150
"I'm Moving On," 118

"I'm Still in Love with You," 73
"Imagine," 98, 127
The Impressions, 86–88, 191
"In the Ghetto," 118
"In the Midnight Hour," 114, 115–116
India.Arie, 24, 189
Ingram, James, 24, 46–47
Ingram, Luther, 147
"Inner City Blues (Make Me Wanna Holler)," 72
Innervisions (Stevie Wonder album), 109, 127, 167–168
"Intro," 79
"Irreplaceable," 18
Isbell, Alvertis. *See* Bell, Al
Isley, Ernie, 90. *See also* The Isley Brothers
The Isley Brothers, 3, 25, 88–92, 177, 194
"Isn't She Lovely," 171
"It Must Be Jesus," 42–43, 48–49, 103
"It Tears Me Up," 143
"It's a Man's Man's Man's World," 38
"It's So Hard to Say Goodbye to Yesterday," 31–32, 196
"It's So Nice (To See Old Friends)," 127
"It's the Same Old Song," 24–25, 188
"It's Too Late," 27
"I've Been Loving You Too Long," 121, 123
"I've Got to Use My Imagination," 104

Ja Rule, 190
The Jackson 5, 3, 92–96, 176
Jackson 5 Christmas Album (Jackson 5 album), 93
Jackson, Al, 73–74, 120, 121
Jackson, Gary, 160

Jackson, Jackie, 92. *See also* The Jackson 5
Jackson, Janet, 92
Jackson, Jermaine, 93. *See also* The Jackson 5
Jackson, LaToya, 92
Jackson, Mahalia, 2, 9
Jackson, Marlon, 93. *See also* The Jackson 5
Jackson, Michael, 45, 46–47, 92–96, 166, 183–184, 185. *See also* The Jackson 5
Jackson, Raymond, 148, 149, 150
Jackson, Tito, 93. *See also* The Jackson 5
The Jacksons. *See* The Jackson 5
The Jacksons: An American Dream, 184
Jagger, Mick, 122, 182. *See also* The Rolling Stones
Jamerson, James, 7. *See also* The Funk Brothers
James, Etta, 11, 19, 20, 96–98, 139, 190–191
James, Mark, 119
James, Rick, 89
Jan & Dean, 133
Jarreau, Al, 46–47
Jay and the Americans, 57
Jay-Z, 18–19, 190
Jean, Wyclef, 79. *See also* The Fugees
The Jeffersons, 181
Jenkins, Johnny, and the Pinetoppers, 124
Jesus Christ Superstar, 26
Joel, Billy, 46–47
Johnson, Syl, 75, 180
Jones, Booker T., 149, 161. *See also* Booker T. & the M.G.'s
Jones, Marshall, 149
Jones, Quincy, 24, 95
"Jonz in My Bonz," 53–54
Jordan, Louis, 49
Josea, Joe, 122

218 Index

"Joy Inside My Tears," 171
"Jungle Boogie," 179
"Junkie Chase," 112
"Just a Little Lovin'," 145
Just as I Am (Bill Withers album), 161–162
"Just My Imagination (Running Away with Me)," 154–155, 189
"Just to Be Close to You," 46
"Just to Keep You Satisfied," 68
"Just the Two of Us," 161, 163–164
J.V.B. Records, 59

"Kashmir," 148
"Keep Getting' It On," 67
"Keep on Pushing," 87
"Keep the Faith," 96
"Keep Your Hands Off My Baby," 172
Kehe, John, 185
Kemper, Scott, 178
Kendricks, Eddie, 153, 155. *See also* The Temptations
Kennedy, John F., 150
Kennedy, Robert F., 150
Kenner, Chris, 116
Keys, Alicia, 9, 31–32, 84, 98–102, 196
Khalid, 10
King, B. B., 4, 119, 122
King, Ben E., 56–58, 102–104, 130, 163. *See also* The Drifters
King, Bob, 42, 48–49, 103
King, Carole, 16, 26–27, 36, 57, 81, 125, 144, 145, 146, 162–163, 171–174, 191
King Curtis, 60, 61, 62–63
King, Maurice, 11
King, Pee Wee, 50
King Records, 3, 32
King, Rev. Dr. Martin Luther, 9, 87–88, 127, 150
The Kinks, 28, 143
Klein, Allen, 192–193

Knight, Bubba. *See* Knight, Gladys, and the Pips
Knight, Gladys, 4, 8, 104, 182. *See also* Knight, Gladys, and the Pips
Knight, Gladys, and the Pips, 11, 100, 104–107, 194
"Knocks Me off My Feet," 170
Knowles-Carter, Beyoncé. *See* Beyoncé
Kool & the Gang, 179
Krieger, Henry, 175–176, 190

La La Land, 110
LaBelle, Patti, 12
"Lady," 55
Lady Soul (Aretha Franklin album), 172, 193
Lambert, Dennis, 46
The Lana Sisters, 144
"Land of 1000 Dances," 22, 114, 116
Land of 1000 Dances: The Complete Atlantic Singles, Vol. 1 (Wilson Pickett album), 114–116
Landis, John, 177–178
"The Last Time," 182
Late Registration (Kanye West album), 43
Lauper, Cyndi, 46–47
"Lay Lady Lay," 127
"Leader of the Pack," 25
"Lean on Me," 16, 161, 162–163, 164
Lear, Norman, 181
Leaving Neverland, 184
Led Zepplin, 148
Lee, Peggy, 174
Lee, Spike, 51, 90, 192
Legend, John, 9–10, 107–110
Leiber, Jerry, 57, 58, 102, 103
Lennon, John, 98, 103, 127, 164, 172. *See also* The Beatles
Leoncavallo, Ruggero, 131–132
Let's Get It On (Marvin Gaye album), 65–68, 176

"Let's Get It On," 66, 67
"Let's Stay Together," 8, 54–55, 73, 106
Let's Stay Together (Al Green album), 193
"Let's Talk About Sex," 188
Lewis, C. J., 58
Lewis, Calvin, 141
Lewis, Dawnn, 181
Lewis, Huey, 46–47
Lewis, Jerry Lee, 44
Lewis, Rudy, 57. *See also* The Drifters
Lightfoot, Gordon, 8
Lil Nas X, 5
"Listen to the Music," 91
"Little Child Runnin' Wild," 111–112
Little Eva, 26, 36, 145, 172, 191
Little Milton, 11
Little Richard, 117
Little Shop of Horrors, 11, 176
Little Walter, 190
"The Little White Cloud That Cried," 21
"Live and Let Die," 28
Live at the Apollo (James Brown album), 32–35
Live It Up (Isley Brothers album), 89
"Living for the City," 166, 169
Lizzo, 10
Lloyd Webber, Andrew, 26
"Loan Me a Dime," 24
"Location," 10
"The Loco-Motion," 36, 172
Loes, Harry Dixon, 42
Loesser, Frank, 103
Loggins, Kenny, 47
"Lonely Teardrops," 130, 159, 161
"The Lonesome Road," 156
"Lord, Stand by Me," 102
"Lost Ones," 79–80
"Lost Someone," 34–35
Love, Darlene, 84
"Love Child," 69, 151

"Love Is a Wonderful Thing," 25
"Love Is Here and Now You're Gone," 151
"Love Me Tender," 143
"Love Overboard," 106
"Love Takes Time," 39
"Love Will Conquer All," 46
"The Love You Save," 93
"Love's in Need of Love Today," 168
"Lovin' You," 126, 128
"Lowdown," 24

MacDonald, Ralph, 163
Mack, Lonnie, 20, 22–23
Madonna, 45, 94
Major Lance, 36
Majors, Farrah Fawcett, 106
Majors, Lee, 106
"Make Me Say It Again Girl," 91–92
Malcolm X, 51, 192–193
"Man in the Mirror," 95
Man in the Mirror: The Michael Jackson Story, 184
Mancha, Don Juan, 115
Mann, Barry, 21, 57, 145
Mardin, Arif, 13, 144
Mariah Carey (Mariah Carey album), 39
Marley, Bob, 88
Mars, Bruno, 101
Martha and the Vandellas, 7, 25, 29, 152, 182
Martin, Darnell, 19, 190
Martin, Joseph, 120–121
The Marvelettes, 58
"Mashed Potatoes Time," 36
"Mashed Potatoes U.S.A.," 36
Masser, Michael, 84
Mathis, Johnny, 23
Maxwell, 101
Mayfield, Curtis, 8, 53, 86–88, 106, 109, 111–114, 138, 188, 191–192. *See also* The Impressions
Mayfield, Percy, 118

MC Lyte, 190
McCartney, Paul, 28, 128, 164, 172. *See also* The Beatles
McCary, Michael, 29. *See also* Boyz II Men
McClary, Thomas, 46. *See also* The Commodores
McDonald, Michael, 15, 24–25, 189. *See also* The Doobie Brothers; Steely Dan
McPhatter, Clyde, 56, 118, 158. *See also* The Drifters
"Me and Mrs. Jones," 12
"Me and Those Dreamin' Eyes of Mine," 54
"Mean Green Mother from Outer Space," 176
Medley, Bill, 21. *See also* The Righteous Brothers
Meeropol, Abel, 140
"Meet Me at Mary's Place," 49
The Memphis Horns, 119, 121
Menken, Alan, 176
"Mercy, Mercy, Mercy," 5
"Mercy Mercy Me (The Ecology)," 71, 72, 189
MFSB, 12–13, 112
Michael Jackson: Chasing the Truth, 184
Michel, Pras, 79. *See also* The Fugees
"Midnight at the Oasis," 127
Midnight Magic (Commodores album), 46
"Midnight Train to Georgia," 8, 104, 105–106
The Midnighters. *See* Ballard, Hank, and the Midnighters
Miller, Glenn, 169. *See also* The Glenn Miller Orchestra
Millinder, Lucky, 156
Mills, Blake, 110
The Mills Brothers, 52
Minaj, Nicki, 101
"Mind Games," 127

Minor, Raynard, 160
The Miracles. *See* Robinson, Smokey, and the Miracles
The Miseducation of Lauryn Hill (Lauryn Hill album), 9, 53, 79–83, 99, 107, 193
"Mississippi Goddam," 136, 137, 138
Mitchell, Joni, 8
Mitchell, Willie, 73–74
Modern Sounds in Country and Western Music (Ray Charles album), 50
Moman, Chips, 62, 117–118
"Money Honey," 56, 59
"The Monkey Time," 36
Moore, Dudley, 180
Moore, Johnny, 57. *See also* The Drifters
Moore, Sam, 133, 136. *See also* Sam & Dave
Moore, Warren "Pete," 129. *See also* Robinson, Smokey, and the Miracles
More Songs about Buildings and Food (Talking Heads album), 75, 180
Morgan, Lee, 5
Morris, Aisha, 171
Morris, Nathan, 29. *See also* Boyz II Men
Morris, Wanya, 29. *See also* Boyz II Men
Morton, Shadow, 27
Motown (Michael McDonald album), 15, 24, 189
Motown: A Journey Through Hitsville USA (Boyz II Men album), 31, 189
Motown Records, 7, 11, 31, 58, 68–69, 93, 104–105, 129, 151–152, 153, 164, 167, 190
Motown Two (Michael McDonald album), 24, 189

"Movin' On Up," 181
Moy, Sylvia, 164, 165
Muddy Waters, 190
Muhammad, Ali Shaheed, 53
Muldaur, Maria, 127
Murray, Bill, 45, 177
Muscle Shoals Sound Studio, 74
"Mustang Sally," 22, 114, 116
"My Baby Just Cares for Me," 137
"My Cherie Amour," 164
"My Empty Arms," 160
"My Girl," 121, 132, 153, 154, 184
"My Heart Keeps Singing," 2
"My Jesus Is All the World to Me," 43
"My Love," 46
My Time (Boz Scaggs album), 24

"Name the Missing Word," 148
Nas, 190
Nash, Johnny, 149
Nathan, Syd, 32
National Lampoon's Animal House, 89, 177–178
Natural High (Commodores album), 46
Natural Wonder (Stevie Wonder album), 169
"Neither One of Us (Wants to Be the First to Say Goodbye)," 104, 105, 194
Nelson, Willie, 46–47
"Never Can Say Goodbye," 93
Newley, Anthony, 137
Newman, Laraine, 45, 177
Newman, Randy, 146
Nicholas, J. D., 46. *See also* The Commodores
"Night Train," 35
"Nightshift," 46, 48
19 (Adele album), 28
"No Easy Way Down," 146
"No One," 102

"No Thing on Me (Cocaine Song)," 113
"Nobody Knows You When You're Down and Out," 137, 139–140
Nolo, Tom, 33
Northern Exposure, 19–20, 97
"Not Even the King," 101
"Nothing Even Matters," 82
"Nowhere to Run," 182
NSYNC, 30
Nyro, Laura, 27, 57
Nyx, James, 71

Oates, John, 23. *See also* Hall & Oates
Obama, Barack, 20
Obama, Michelle, 20
Off the Wall (Michael Jackson album), 93–94
The O'Jays, 12
"Old Town Road," 5
Oldham, Will, 110
"Ole Man Trouble," 119–120
"On and On," 104, 106
"On Broadway," 56, 57, 164
Once Again (John Legend album), 108, 193
"One Sweet Day," 31, 40
"One Woman," 75, 77–78
"Ooo Baby Baby," 132
Orange, Walter "Clyde," 46. *See also* The Commodores
Orbison, Roy, 43, 44
"Ordinary People," 107–108
The Originals, 68
Otis Blue/Otis Redding Sings Soul (Otis Redding album), 4, 119–123
"Our Lives," 128
Out of Sight (James Brown album), 38

Page, Gene, 67
Pagliacci, 131–132
Panion, Henry, III, 169

"Papa Was a Rolling Stone," 155
"Papa's Got a Brand New Bag," 34, 35–39, 180
Parker, Charlie, 77
Parton, Dolly, 5, 84
"Pastime Paradise," 170–171, 189
Pate, Johnny, 112
Patterson, Lover, 58
Patton, Edward. *See* Knight, Gladys, and the Pips
Paul, Billy, 12
Payne, Freda, 88
"Peace in the Valley," 2, 117, 156
"Peace Train," 88
Penn, Dan, 62
"Penny Love," 46
"People Get Ready," 86–88, 113, 138, 188
"People Got to Be Free," 22
Percy Sledge: The Ultimate Collection (Percy Sledge album), 143
Peretti, Hugo. *See* Hugo & Luigi
Perfect Angel (Minnie Riperton album), 126–129
"Perfect Duet," 18
Perry, Steve, 46–47
Philadelphia International Records, 12
Philadelphia Phillies, 178
"Piano & I," 99
Pickett, Wilson, 12, 22, 114–116, 149
Pinkney, Bill, 56
The Pips. *See* Knight, Gladys, and the Pips
"A Place Nobody Can Find," 135
"Please Mr. Postman," 58
"Please, Please, Please," 35, 38
"Please Stay (Once You Go Away)," 66–67
Pomus, Doc, 57, 58
Porgy and Bess, 139
Porter, David, 13, 63, 135
Poyser, James, 109
Prater, Dave, 133, 135. *See also* Sam & Dave

The Preacher's Wife: Original Soundtrack Album, 85
Presley, Elvis, 2–3, 43, 44, 117–119, 159
Preston, Billy, 24, 189
Price, Vincent, 94
Prince, 8–9, 98, 167
Prince Royce, 103
Procol Harum, 141
"Proud Mary," 122
"Psychedelic Shack," 154
Public Enemy, 90
Pulp Fiction, 179
"Purple Rain," 9, 98
Purple Rain (film), 98
"Pusherman," 112
"P.Y.T. (Pretty Young Thing)," 94

Queen Latifah, 10, 11, 177
A Quiet Storm (Smokey Robinson album), 132

Radner, Gilda, 45, 177
The Raelettes, 44
Rain Man, 19, 97
"Rainy Night in Georgia," 24–25, 188
The Rascals, 20, 22
Ravel, Maurice, 78
Rawls, Lou, 4, 12
Ray, 42, 44, 156, 186, 190
Ray, Johnnie, 6, 20–21
"Reach Out, I'll Be There," 24, 189
"Reasons," 126
Redding, Otis, 7, 11–12, 25, 50, 60, 119–126, 133, 135, 173, 180
Reddy, Helen, 125
Reed, Dan, 184
Reed, Jimmy, 11
"Reet Petite (The Finest Girl You'd Ever Want to Meet)," 158–159
Reeves, Martha, 151, 152. *See also* Martha and the Vandellas
"Rehab," 27–28
Reiner, Rob, 103

"Remember (Walking in the Sand)," 25, 26, 27
"Respect," 60, 64, 123–126, 173, 194
"Respect Yourself," 147–148
Rhino Records, 119, 122–123, 142
Rhodes, Donna, 6, 73, 74
Rhodes, Sandra, 6, 73, 74, 77
Rhymes & Reasons (Carole King album), 127
Rice, Mack, 116, 148
Rice, Tim, 26
Richard, Renald, 43, 103
Richards, Keith, 122, 182. *See also* The Rolling Stones
Richie, Lionel, 8, 45–48, 95, 183. *See also* The Commodores
"The Riddle Song," 52
"Right On," 71–72
The Righteous Brothers, 6, 20, 21–22, 30, 133, 136
Rihanna, 40
Riperton, Minnie, 39, 126–129
Riser, Paul, 17
The Roar of the Greasepaint—The Smell of the Crowd, 137
Robinson, Fenton, 24
Robinson, Smokey, 13, 25, 55, 75, 108, 121, 132, 153, 154, 184, 188. *See also* Robinson, Smokey, and the Miracles
Robinson, Smokey, and the Miracles, 7, 129–133
"Rock Me Baby," 4, 122
"Rockin' Robin," 93
Rogers, Bobby, 129, 153. *See also* Robinson, Smokey, and the Miracles
Rogers, Claudette, 129–130. *See also* Robinson, Smokey, and the Miracles
Rogers, Emerson "Sonny," 129. *See also* Robinson, Smokey, and the Miracles
Rogers, Kenny, 46–47
"Roll with Me Henry," 96

"Rolling in the Deep," 28–29
The Rolling Stones, 50, 119, 122, 143, 182
"Rome (Wasn't Built in a Day)," 50
The Ronettes, 176
The Roots, 108, 109
Ross, Diana, 15–17, 46–47, 150, 175–176, 194. *See also* The Supremes
Ross, Fred, 68
Ross, Madeline, 68
Rotary Connection, 127
Rudolph, Richard, 13, 126, 128
Ruffin, David, 153, 154. *See also* The Temptations
Run-DMC, 190

Saadiq, Raphael, 55
Sacagawea, 171
Salt-N-Pepa, 188
Salter, William, 163
Sam & Dave, 11, 12, 21, 30, 60, 63, 124, 133–136
"Santa Claus Is Coming to Town," 93
Santana, Carlos, 9, 80
"Satisfaction," 122, 182
"Saturday Night Fish Fry," 49
Saturday Night Live, 45, 133, 177
"Save the Children," 70–71
"Save the Country," 27
"Save Me," 62–63
"Save Room," 108
"Save the Last Dance for Me," 56–57, 58, 59
"Saving All My Love for You," 84
"Say It Loud—I'm Black and I'm Proud," 9, 38
"Say My Name," 18
"Say You, Say Me," 46
Scaggs, Boz, 6, 20–21, 24
Schofield, Willie, 116
Scott, Tom, 95
Scott-Heron, Gil, 9
"The Scratch," 33

Seal, 103, 188
Seals, Dan, 50
The Searchers, 28, 44, 58
"Seeing You This Way," 127
Sembello, Michael, 126, 128. *See also* Wonderlove
"Sensuality," 91
Seymour, Kenny, 191
"Sh-Boom," 177
"Sha La La (Make Me Happy)," 73
"Shake," 121
"Shake It Off," 40
The Shangri-Las, 25–26, 27
Shapiro, Herb, 147
Sharp, Dee Dee, 36
"She's Gone," 23, 30
"She's Out of My Life," 94
Sheeran, Ed, 18
"Shine," 108–109
The Shirelles, 25, 26, 172, 191
"S***, Damn, Mother***ker," 54
"Shop Around," 130–131, 132, 133
"Shout," 88–89, 177–178
Shuman, Mort, 57, 58
"The Sidewinder," 5
Sign o' the Times (Prince album), 167
"Signed, Sealed, Delivered I'm Yours," 24, 164, 165, 166, 167, 189
The Silhouettes, 130
Silk Degrees (Boz Scaggs album), 24
"Silly Love Songs," 128
Silver, Horace, 5
Simon and Garfunkel, 16, 133, 163
Simon, Paul, 46–47, 162–163. *See also* Simon and Garfunkel
Simone, Nina, 9, 23–24, 99–100, 109, 136–141
Simpson, Valerie, 15–17, 179–180
Sinatra, Frank, 138
Sinatra, Nancy, 28
"Sir Duke," 169
"Sittin' in the Sun," 52

"(Sittin' on the) Dock of the Bay," 25, 119–120, 123
"634-5789 (Soulsville, U.S.A.)," 114
"Sixty Minute Man," 3
"Skyfall," 28–29
Sledge, Percy, 25, 141–143, 193
"Slippery When Wet," 46
Sly and the Family Stone, 89
Smith, Bessie, 139–140
Smith, Carl William, 149, 160
"Smooth," 54–55
Snow, Phoebe, 50, 181
"So Much Love," 145
"Some Kind of Wonderful," 56, 57
"Someday," 39
"Someday We'll Be Together," 151
"Someone Like You," 28–29
"Son of a Preacher Man," 145–146, 179
Songs in A Minor (Alicia Keys album), 98, 99–100
Songs in the Key of Life (Stevie Wonder album), 109, 167–171
"Soul and Inspiration," 21
"Soul Man," 63, 124, 133, 134–135, 136
Soul Records, 105
"Soul Serenade," 61
Soul Speak (Michael McDonald album), 24
The Soul Stirrers, 48, 133
Soul Train, 13
Soulbook (Rod Stewart album), 24–25, 188–189
The Southern Tones, 42–43, 48–49
"Spanish Harlem," 59
Spector, Phil, 13, 21
The Spinners, 194
Springfield, Dusty, 6, 26, 28, 88, 143–147, 172, 179
The Springfields, 144
Springsteen, Bruce, 46–47
"Stand By Me," 58, 59, 102–104, 130, 163

Stand By Me, 103
The Staple Singers, 3, 40, 147–150, 182, 187
Staples, Cleotha, 148. *See also* The Staple Singers
Staples, Mavis, 2, 148, 188. *See also* The Staple Singers
Staples, Roebuck "Pops," 3, 4, 120, 147, 148, 149–150. *See also* The Staple Singers
Staples, Yvonne, 148. *See also* The Staple Singers
Starr, Edwin, 69
Station to Station (David Bowie album), 23
Stax Records, 6, 7, 11–12, 73, 74, 75–76, 117, 119, 135
Steely Dan, 24
Stevens, Cat, 88
Stevenson, Mickey, 152
Stevenson, Rudy, 140
Stevenson, William, 149
Stewart, Jim, 134–135
Stewart, Rod, 24–25, 88, 188–189
"Still," 46
Still Bill (Bill Withers album), 162–163
Stockman, Shawn, 29. *See also* Boyz II Men
Stoller, Mike, 57, 58, 102, 103
Stone, Angela, 54
"Stoned Love," 151
"Stoned Soul Picnic," 27
"Stop! In the Name of Love," 151–152
Stover, Elgie, 68, 70, 71
"Strange Fruit," 137, 140
"Strange Things Happening Every Day," 157
"Stranger in My Own Home Town," 118
Strong, Barrett, 69, 74
Stubbs, Levi, 11, 176. *See also* The Four Tops

"Stuck on You," 46
The Stylistics, 12
Sun Records, 117
Sun Valley Serenade, 97
"Sunny," 164
Super Fly (Curtis Mayfield soundtrack album), 111–114
"Superfly," 113–114
"Supernatural Thing," 59
"Superstar," 81
"Superstition," 166
The Supremes, 7, 11, 15, 17, 25, 29, 69, 150–152, 175–176, 185
"Suspicious Minds," 117, 118, 119
The Swampers, 6, 59–60
"Sweet Home," 134
The Sweet Inspirations, 144
"(Sweet Sweet Baby) Since You've Been Gone," 64
"Sweets for My Sweet," 58

"Take a Little Trip," 127
"Take Me to the River," 74–75, 180–181
"Take Me to the Water," 137, 138
"Take My Hand, Precious Lord," 2, 117, 156
Take 6, 24, 189
"Take Time to Know Her," 143
Talking Book (Stevie Wonder album), 127, 167–168
Talking Heads, 75, 180
Tamla Records. *See* Motown Records
Tampa Red, 2, 156
Tapestry (Carole King album), 27, 80, 125, 127, 172, 173
Tarantino, Quentin, 179
Tarplin, Marv, 130. *See also* Robinson, Smokey, and the Miracles
Taylor, James, 8, 57
"Tears Always Win," 101
"The Tears of a Clown," 131–132, 133

Ted Mack's Amateur Hour, 104
"Tell Him," 83
Temperton, Rod, 24
The Temptations, 7, 11, 15, 17, 74, 119, 121, 151, 153–155, 191
"Tennessee Waltz," 50–51
Terrell, Tammi, 7, 15–16
Tharpe, Sister Rosetta, 2, 156–158
"That Lady," 194
"That Old Sweet Roll (Hi-De-Ho)," 26, 147, 173
"That's All," 156
"There Goes My Baby," 56–58, 59
"There'll Be No Second Time," 52
"Think" (Aretha Franklin and Ted White song), 63–65, 173, 179
"Think" (Curtis Mayfield instrumental composition), 113
"Think" (James Brown song), 33–34, 35
This Is It (film), 96
This Is It (Michael Jackson album), 96
"This Little Girl of Mine," 4–5, 42
"This Little Light of Mine," 42
"This Magic Moment," 56–57, 58
"This May Be the Last Time," 182
"This Old Town (People in This Town)," 149
"This Train," 87
"This World," 147
Thomas, Joe, 24, 189
Thompson, Ahmir "?uestlove," 109. *See also* The Roots
The Three Degrees, 12–13
Three Dog Night, 27
"Three Times a Lady," 46
"Thriller," 94
Thriller (Michael Jackson album), 94–95
Through the Storm (Aretha Franklin album), 64
Tindley, Charles Albert, 102
Tiomkin, Dimitri, 23

"Tired of Being Alone," 73
"To Be Young, Gifted and Black," 137
"To Zion," 80, 82
Tokyo Philharmonic Orchestra, 169
Toussaint, Allen, 24
Townsend, Ed, 66–67
"The Tracks of My Tears," 24–25, 130, 131, 132, 133, 188, 189
Treadwell, George, 58
A Tribute to Motown (Michael McDonald concert film), 24, 189
"Trouble in Mind," 156–156
"Truly," 46
"Truth Hurts," 10
"Try Me," 33, 130
"TSOP (The Sound of Philadelphia)," 12–13, 112, 178
Tubman, Harriet, 171
Turner, Big Joe, 12
Turner, Ike, 50, 122
Turner, Tina, 46–47, 50, 122
25 (Adele album), 28
21 (Adele album), 28
"Twist and Shout," 89

"Unchained Melody," 21
"Under the Boardwalk," 56, 57, 59
The Undisputed Truth, 17
Universal Music Group (UMG), 31
"Up on the Roof," 56, 57, 59, 172, 194
"Uptight (Everything's Alright)," 164–165, 166, 167
Uptight (Stevie Wonder album), 165

Valli, Frankie, 83
Van DePitte, David, 66–67, 69
Van Halen, Eddie, 95
Van Steeden, Peter, 52
Vandross, Luther, 132
The Ventures, 52
"Village Ghetto Land," 83, 168–169, 170

Index **227**

Vincent, Gene, 117
The Violinaires, 114
"Vision of Love," 39
The Voice, 102
Voices (Hall & Oates album), 23
Volt Records, 11–12, 73, 119

Waiting to Exhale, 84
Wake Up! (John Legend album), 108–109
"Walk on By," 75, 76–77
"The Wallflower." *See* "Roll with Me Henry"
"Wanna Be Startin' Somethin'," 94
"War," 69
Ward, Billy and his Dominoes, 3, 56, 158
"Warm and Tender Love," 143
Warren, Harry, 97
Warwick, Dionne, 46–47, 61, 84, 100, 145, 188
Washington, Ned, 23
Washington, Grover, Jr., 163–164
"Water Runs Dry," 30
"Watermelon Man," 5
"Way over There," 130
"Way over Yonder," 27
"The Way We Were/Try to Remember," 104
"The Way You Do the Things You Do," 153
"We Are the World," 46–47, 48, 95
"We Gotta Have Peace," 88
"We the People," 149
Weatherly, Jim, 105–106
Webb, Jimmy, 6, 77
"Wedding Bell Blues," 27
Weil, Cynthia, 57, 145
Weiss, Mary, 25–26. *See also* The Shangri-Las
West, Bob, 116
West, Kanye, 43, 107, 140, 189, 190
West Side Story, 95

Wexler, Jerry, 13, 27, 59–60, 142, 144, 171–172. *See also* Atlantic Records
"What'd I Say," 18, 43–45, 117, 177
"What's Going On," 24, 69–70, 71, 72, 88, 98, 176, 189, 194
What's Going On (Marvin Gaye album), 68–72, 112, 167
"What's Happening, Brother," 70, 71
"When a Man Loves a Woman," 25, 141–143, 193
"When It Hurts So Bad," 81
"When Something Is Wrong with My Baby," 60, 135
"When We Get By," 55
"Where Did Our Love Go," 151
White, Clifton, 52
White, Maurice, 103
White, Ronald, 121, 129, 132, 154, 184. *See also* Robinson, Smokey, and the Miracles
White, Ted, 60, 61–62, 64
"A Whiter Shade of Pale," 141
Whitfield, Norman, 13, 69, 74, 154, 155
Whitney (Whitney Houston album), 84
Whitney Houston (Whitney Houston album), 84
"Who," 150
The Who, 28, 143
"Who Do You Think You Are (Jesus Christ the Superstar)?," 149–150
"Wholy Holy," 72
"Why," 23
Wiggins, Dwayne "D. Wigg," 100
"Wild Is the Wind," 23–24, 137
Wilkins, Ronnie, 145
"Will You Be There," 95
"Will You Love Me Tomorrow," 172
will.i.am, 107
Williams, Hank, Sr., 5
Williams, Otis, 153. *See also* The Temptations

Williams, Paul, 153, 155. *See also* The Temptations
Wilson, Jackie, 46, 55, 130, 133, 158–161
Wilson, Mary, 150. *See also* The Supremes
Wilson, Ralph, 178
Winans, BeBe, 187–188
Winans, CeCe, 187–188
"The Windmills of Your Mind," 147
Winehouse, Amy, 6, 26, 27, 39
Winelight (Grover Washington Jr. album), 163–164
Withers, Bill, 8, 16, 109, 123, 161–164
"Without Love," 118
"A Woman, a Lover, a Friend," 159
Wonder, Stevie, 7, 10, 25, 46–47, 69, 83, 95, 108–109, 126, 127, 128, 131, 164–171, 182–183, 188
"Wonderful World," 122
Wonderlove, 126
"Work Song," 76
"Work with Me, Annie," 3, 96
Wright, Andrew, 141
Wright, Syreeta, 166

"Yah Mo B There," 24
The Yardbirds, 143
Yeezus (Kanye West album), 140

"You Are," 46
"You Better Know It," 159
"You Can't Hurry Love," 151
"You Don't Know Like I Know," 133, 134–135
"You Don't Know What You Mean to Me," 133, 134, 135
"You Don't Miss Your Water," 122
"You Give Good Love," 84
"You Keep Me Hangin' On," 151
"(You Make Me Feel Like) A Natural Woman," 27, 64, 146, 171–174
"You Only Live Twice," 28
"You Sure Love to Ball," 68
"You're All I Need to Get By," 15
"Young Americans," 24
Young Americans (David Bowie album), 23
"(Your Love Keeps Lifting Me) Higher and Higher," 24–25, 55, 159–160, 161, 188
"Your Precious Love," 15
"You've Got a Friend," 16, 162–163
"You've Lost that Lovin' Feeling," 21–22, 23, 136
"You've Really Got a Hold on Me," 24–25, 131, 132, 133, 143, 188

Zawinul, Joe, 5

About the Author

JAMES E. PERONE, a native of Columbus, Ohio, earned degrees in music education, clarinet performance, and music theory from Capital University and the State University of New York at Buffalo. Jim is currently a professor emeritus of music at the University of Mount Union in Alliance, Ohio. He has been active as an author since the early 1990s. After researching and writing several music theory–related reference volumes and bio-bibliographies of American composers ranging from Howard Hanson and Louis Moreau Gottschalk to Paul Simon and Carole King, he focused his research and critical analysis more squarely on popular music. Jim's previous publications include *Paul Simon: A Bio-Bibliography* (Greenwood 2000); *Songs of the Vietnam Conflict* (Greenwood 2001); *Music of the Counterculture Era* (Greenwood 2004); *The Words and Music of Carole King* (Praeger 2006); *Mods, Rockers, and the Music of the British Invasion* (Praeger 2008); *The Words and Music of Elvis Costello* (Praeger 2015); *Smash Hits: The 100 Songs That Defined America* (Greenwood 2015); *The Words and Music of James Taylor* (Praeger 2017); *Listen to New Wave Rock!* (Greenwood 2018); and *Listen to the Blues!* (Greenwood 2019). Jim serves as the editor of Greenwood's "Exploring Musical Genres" series and previously served as the editor of Praeger's "The Praeger Singer-Songwriter Collection."

www.ingramcontent.com/pod-product-compliance
Lightning Source LLC
Chambersburg PA
CBHW060949230426
43665CB00015B/2124